S0-AAF-703

SOCIAL MEMORY

NEW PERSPECTIVES ON THE PAST

General Editor
R. I. Moore

Advisory Editors
Gerald Aylmer
Tanya Luhrmann
David Turley
Patrick Wormald

PUBLISHED

IN PREPARATION

* now out of print

SOCIAL MEMORY

James Fentress
and
Chris Wickham

BLACKWELL
Oxford UK & Cambridge USA

Copyright © James Fentress and Chris Wickham 1992

The right of James Fentress and Chris Wickham to be identified as authors of this work has been asserted in accordance with the Copyright, Designs and Patents Act 1988.

First published 1992
Reprinted 1994

Blackwell Publishers
108 Cowley Road
Oxford OX4 1JF
UK

238 Main Street
Cambridge, Massachusetts 02142
USA

All rights reserved. Except for the quotation of short passages for the purposes of criticism and review, no part of this publication may be reproduced, stored in a retrieval system, or transmitted, in any form or by any means, electronic, mechanical, photocopying, recording or otherwise, without the prior permission of the publisher.

Except in the United States of America, this book is sold subject to the condition that it shall not, by way of trade or otherwise, be lent, re-sold, hired out, or otherwise circulated without the publisher's prior consent in any form of binding or cover other than that in which it is published and without a similar condition including this condition being imposed on the subsequent purchaser.

British Library Cataloguing in Publication Data
A CIP catalogue record for this book is available from the British Library.

Library of Congress Cataloging-in-Publication Data
Fentress, James.
Social memory / James Fentress and Chris Wickham.
p.   cm. – (New perspectives on the past)
Includes bibliographical references and index.
ISBN 0–631–16618–1 – ISBN 0–631–16619–X (pbk.)
1. Memory–Social aspects.   I. Wickham, Chris, 1950– .
II. Title.   III. Series: New perspectives on the past (Basil
Blackwell Publisher)
BF378.S65F46 1992
302′.12-dc20   91–27041
                                 CIP

Typeset in 10/12 Plantin by Graphicraft Typesetters Ltd, Hong Kong.
Printed in Great Britain by Athenaeum Press Ltd, Newcastle upon Tyne.
This book is printed on acid-free paper.

Contents

To L. and L.

Editor's Preface

Ignorance has many forms, and all of them are dangerous. In the nineteenth and twentieth centuries our chief effort has been to free ourselves from tradition and superstition in large questions, and from the error in small ones upon which they rest, by redefining the fields of knowledge and evolving in each the distinctive method appropriate for its cultivation. The achievement has been incalculable, but not without cost. As each new subject has developed a specialist vocabulary to permit rapid and precise reference to its own common and rapidly growing stock of ideas and discoveries, and come to require a greater depth of expertise from its specialists, scholars have been cut off by their own erudition not only from mankind at large, but from the findings of workers in other fields, and even in other parts of their own. Isolation diminishes not only the usefulness but the soundness of their labours when energies are exclusively devoted to eliminating the small blemishes so embarrassingly obvious to the fellow-professional on the next patch, instead of avoiding others that may loom much larger from, as it were, a more distant vantage point. Marc Bloch observed a contradiction in the attitudes of many historians: 'when it is a question of ascertaining whether or not some human act has really taken place, they cannot be too painstaking. If they proceed to the reasons for that act, they are content with the merest appearance, ordinarily founded upon one of those maxims of common-place psychology which are neither more nor less true than their opposites.' When historians peep across the fence they see their neighbours, in literature, perhaps, or sociology, just as complacent in relying on historical platitudes which are naive, simplistic, or obsolete.

New Perspectives on the Past represents not a reaction against specialization, which would be a romantic absurdity, but an attempt to come to terms with it. The authors, of course, are specialists, and their thought and conclusions rest on the foundation of distinguished professional research in different periods and fields. Here they will free themselves, as far as it is possible, from the restraints of subject, region and period within which they ordinarily and necessarily work, to discuss problems simply as problems, and not as 'history' or 'politics' or 'economics'. They will write for specialists, because we are all specialists now, and for laymen, because we are all laymen.

For students of society, past or present, memory is everything, both tools and material, both the means and the goal of their labour. But even individual memory is not simply personal: the memories which constitute our identity and provide the context for every thought and action are not only our own, but are learned, borrowed, and inherited – in part, and part of, a common stock, constructed, sustained, and transmitted by the families, communities, and cultures to which we belong. No human group is constituted, no code of conduct promulgated, no thought given form, no action committed, no knowledge communicated, without its intervention; history itself is both a product and a source of social memory.

It would be comforting to think of memory as a simple record, as historians thought of records in those far-off days when they were allowed to believe that truth lay buried in the archives, a sleeping princess awaiting their awakening kiss – as fragments of preserved reality, sometimes more and sometimes less complete, but reflecting, as far as they went, a true image of what used to be. Of course, it is nothing of the kind: it is an artefact and a trickster, and an active trickster at that, not merely a relic of the past, but the past shaped and adapted to the uses of the present – and of the present then as well as the present now. To try to define the role of social memory in shaping both the past and our understanding of it is like trying to model a figure with mercury, or paint a self-portrait in a studio lined on every surface with mirrors. Fentress and Wickham, anthropologist and historian, provide for this intimidating but inescapable task guidance which is both powerful in its logic and immensely rich in its material. Their account of what people have done with their memories, and how, and why, in a remarkable variety of circumstances, is as absorbing in its own right as it is illuminating and suggestive for anybody whose business it is to struggle for an understanding of social action.

R. I. Moore

Foreword

We have called this book *Social Memory* to counterpose its subject to that of the memory of individuals. Yet it is individuals who actually do the remembering; what is social about it? The essential answer is that much memory is attached to membership of social groups of one kind or another. Indeed, Maurice Halbwachs, the first theorist of what he called 'collective' memory, argued that all memory is structured by group identities: that one remembers one's childhood as part of a family, one's neighbourhood as part of a local community, one's working life as part of a factory or office community and/or a political party or trade union, and so on – that these memories are essentially group memories, and that the memory of the individual exists only in so far as she or he is the probably unique product of a particular intersection of groups (Halbwachs 1925; 1950 [trans. 1980]). Halbwachs was part of Emile Durkheim's school, and, like many of Durkheim's followers, put what might seem excessive emphasis on the collective nature of social consciousness, relatively neglecting the question of how individual consciousnesses might relate to those of the collectivities those individuals actually made up. The result was a concept of collective consciousness curiously disconnected from the actual thought processes of any particular person. Thus, an important problem facing anyone who wants to follow Halbwachs in this field is how to elaborate a conception of memory which, while doing full justice to the collective side of one's conscious life, does not render the individual a sort of automaton, passively obeying the interiorized collective will. It is for this reason (as well as to avoid the image of a Jungian collective unconscious) that we shall normally use the term 'social memory' rather than 'collective memory', despite the greater recognizability of the latter phrase.

How does one make individual memory 'social', then? Essentially by talking about it. The sorts of memories one shares with others are those which are relevant to them, in the context of a social group of a particular kind, whether structured and lasting (a family; a factory workforce; a village) or informal and possibly temporary (a group of friends who go to the same pub; a dinner-party). Halbwachs was certainly right to say that social groups construct their own images of the world by establishing an agreed version of the past, and to emphasize that these versions are established by communication, not by private remembrance. Indeed, one's private memories, and even the cognitive process of remembering, contain much that is social in origin, as we shall see.

Memory is a complex process, not a simple mental act; even the words we use to describe the act (*recognize, remember, recall, recount, commemorate*, and so on) show that 'memory' can include anything from a highly private and spontaneous, possibly wordless, mental sensation to a formalized public ceremony. In the first chapter we shall try to say something about memory in general. Nevertheless, the bulk of this book will inevitably be concerned with the more public and social side of memory, rather than with the inexplicable sensations of *déjà vu*: that is to say, with 'commemoration', which we shall define, for the purpose of this book, as the *action* of speaking or writing about memories, as well as the formal re-enaction of the past that we usually mean when we use the word. Within this social perspective, there is an important distinction between memory as action and memory as representation; remembering/ commemorating considered as a type of behaviour, and memory, considered cognitively, as a network of ideas, the latter being the subject matter of chapter 1. A second, related distinction is that between the particular genres and narrative styles of commemoration, which we shall look at in chapter 2, and the contexts in which conversations about the past can have a particular meaning for a particular group, which is the focus of chapter 3. The two sides of this opposition will, however, be joined again in chapters 4 and 5, where we shall explore their linkage in two specific areas, medieval Western Europe and modern Sicily. The counterposition between genre and identity can be considered, in some respects, as one between form and content. But both this distinction and that between action and representation are, to some extent, rhetorical devices; the field is a potentially endless one, made up of innumerable sets of oppositions in inextricable relationships with each other, and any form of order imposed on it is nothing better than a necessary distortion. In our case, the necessity of order is further sharpened by a need to keep our book relatively short and simple, to fit into a series aimed in part at the general reader.

Memory is infinite; all consciousness is mediated through it. Even your immediate perception of the present instant, as you are reading this book, is given all its meaning by memories. Our principal concern here, however, is with thought that explicitly refers to past events and past experience (whether real or imaginary); for recalled past experience and shared images of the historical past are kinds of memories that have particular importance for the constitution of social groups in the present. This is, in fact, the aspect of memory that first got each of us interested in the subject. It is an area that has been much discussed in the last fifteen years, too, thanks above all to the great expansion in the study of oral history that began in the 1970s; as well as, to a lesser extent, to the steady development in the ethnohistorical analysis of oral traditions (that is to say, commemorations of events too far in the past for immediate experience), above all the analyses of sub-Saharan Africa associated with Jan Vansina and his followers and critics. (See, for general accounts of oral history, Joutard 1983; Passerini 1988; Thompson 1988; for oral traditions, Henige 1974; Vansina 1985; Tonkin 1991.)

We shall have something to say about both of these fields in what follows (below, pp. 75ff., 89ff.); but it is important to stress at the outset that an analysis of oral history as such is not our project. Oral history and the study of oral tradition have many purposes, but a major one has always been the reconstruction (or, for the more sophisticated, construction) of the past through oral sources, whether directly or after careful treatment and analysis. (See Passerini 1988; 1–66, 105–53, and Tonkin 1991, the general discussions closest to our own positions.) Much argument about oral sources has, therefore, at least until very recently, simply been about whether they are 'true' or not. In a book about memory, however, the issue of whether or not a given memory is true is interesting only in so far as it sheds light on how memory itself works. We shall be discussing how the past is (or has been) talked about, and about its meaning for the people who talk (or have in the past talked) about it. The social meaning of memory, like its internal structure and its mode of transmission, is little affected by its truth; all that matters is that it be believed, at least at some level – for one should not neglect folk-tales, which are commemorations of the past as well, although they are often not even told as strictly believable.

Social memory is, in fact, often selective, distorted, and inaccurate. None the less, it is important to recognize that it is not necessarily any of these; it can be extremely exact, when people have found it socially relevant from that day to this to remember and recount an event in the way it was originally experienced. The debate about whether it is inherently accurate or not is thus sterile; and it will remain so as long as memory is treated as a 'mental faculty' whose workings can be described in isolation from social context. It is for this reason that we shall not write about accuracy in social memory simply to salvage its reputation from its critics; we prefer to argue that the possibility of such accuracy shows that what distorts memory is not some inherent defect in the process of mental recall, but rather a series of external constraints, usually imposed by society – the constraints are the issue here, not the accuracy. Indeed, the transmission of 'true' information is only one of the many social functions that memory can, in different circumstances, perform. Similar arguments apply to the distinction between 'oral history' and 'oral tradition' itself, for we would maintain that it is relatively unimportant, for an understanding of the meaning the past has for people, whether they experienced it directly or had it recounted to them, or, indeed, read about it in a book. We shall defend these positions in more detail in the course of what follows, when the arguments become relevant; here, they are simply set out to avoid misunderstandings.

This book is the product of a collaboration between two authors, an anthropologist (James Fentress) and a historian (Chris Wickham), with different, if convergent, expertises and interests – and literary styles. We were separately responsible for the drafting of, respectively, chapters 1, 2 and 5, and chapters 3 and 4; but we each substantially revised each other's drafts, and added and subtracted sections; the book as a whole should be regarded as our joint responsibility. We are indebted to Leslie Brubaker and Lisa Fentress, to Elizabeth Tonkin, and to Bob Moore and Patrick Wormald, for systematic encouragement and for detailed critiques of the whole book; to Ceridwen Lloyd-Morgan (especially), Susan Levenstein, Montserrat Cabré, Ian Wood, Jean Dunbabin, and Anthony Faulkes for their critical commentaries on parts of the text; to Sue Bowen, who saved us *in extremis*; and to Dick Holt and Donna Kerner, as well as to virtually everybody else we have talked to over the last couple of years, for bibliographical references, ideas, and discussion.

Rome and Birmingham

1
Remembering

'The horror of that moment,' the King went on, 'I shall never, *never* forget!'

'You will, though,' the Queen said, 'if you don't make a memorandum of it.'

Lewis Carroll,
Through the Looking-Glass

On things inside our heads

Memory is a vast subject, and a complete treatment would range from psychology to philosophy, from neurology to modern history, and from zoology to Proust's *petite madeleine*. More modestly, this book is limited to two tasks. The first is to show something of how memory functions. The second is to look critically at the way historians and social scientists have regarded memory and used it as a tool of research, and to suggest a number of ways in which a better appreciation of the character of their material would yield more convincing results.

By now, branches of history based directly on memory – principally oral history and ethnohistory, but other areas as well – have become established disciplines. They have spawned studies, manuals, specialized periodicals, university faculties with programmes of research, rival schools, and, inevitably, a sometimes acrimonious debate about techniques, and about the value of the eventual products as 'history'. There seems to be no lack of literature on the subject. Yet the debate is often singularly barren, consisting sometimes of little more than self-justification.

What is disappointing is that, for all the presumptive radicalism in the oral historian's claim to rewrite history from the 'bottom up', the debates themselves often remain confined to traditional historiographical issues and perspectives – the relevance of the experience of the common people to history, the historical significance of the view from the bottom up, or the degree of influence that elite culture can exercise over popular culture. There is nothing wrong with these questions; but they are general social historical questions. What usually is missing is any awareness of the special nature of memory as a source. What defines oral history, and sets it apart from other branches of history, is, after all, its reliance on memory rather than texts. Yet oral historians seem reluctant to emphasize this, seemingly preferring to treat memory as a set of documents that happen to be in people's heads rather than in the Public Record Office.

One reason for this reluctance to place memory itself in the centre of the debate may be that oral historians wish to claim a parity of dignity for their sources and subject matter with those of traditional historians (see below, p. 90). Oral historians wish, in short, to be taken seriously. This desire for legitimacy may also help explain the obsession with methodology that characterizes many oral historians and oral history projects. A certain concern with organization is, of course, understandable in a branch of history that relies so much on teamwork, yet all this emphasis on method may obscure the fact that we are not sure what we are after. What is memory? Do we hunt it with a questionnaire, or are we supposed to use a butterfly net?

There is, in other words, a danger of reification. In the enthusiasm to collect 'memory', and to assemble archives of oral testimony, we may quietly be conferring on our subject a thing-like character without ever stopping to ask whether this is justified. Of course, it might be argued that this reification is to be welcomed. Is not the first step in any scientific discourse that of defining its object? To treat memory objectively, it is, then, necessary to define it in an object-like way. This might all be true; still, the entire argument turns on the question of whether memory does, in fact, possess such an object-like character in the first place. If it does not, it may turn out that the 'object' of our enquiries is merely the object of our own imaginations.

The predilection of oral historians to speak of memory in terms of 'records' and 'spoken documents' shows the extent to which reification has already spread. It is a way of speaking about memory that both objectifies it and turns it into a text. In fact, the two claims are both part of the same general paradigm, which we might call the 'textual model' of memory. As we shall see, this model has been, and still is, extremely influential. Nor is this at all surprising, for the model is itself an expression of a general predisposition of modern, literate culture to define knowledge in propositional terms: that is, to define knowledge in terms of statements expressed in language, or as propositions in some logical or scientific notation.[1] Characteristically, we tend to divide knowledge into three broad categories: propositional knowledge, or knowledge *about* things; sensory and experiential knowledge, or knowledge directly *of* things; and skill knowledge, or knowledge *how* to do physical things – such as ride a bicycle (cf. the discussion in Rorty 1980, ch. 3). Of these three types, it is usually only the first that is treated as knowledge in its fullest sense. We shall look at the historical background of this conception of knowledge later in this chapter; here it is only necessary to draw attention to one consequence of this conception: it turns knowledge itself into a sort of 'object' – a something inside our heads.

Mary Warnock puts this very well:

> The [philosophical] orthodoxy has been that knowledge is not a state of mind.... When ... I say that I know something, that is not a report on an inner experience. To say that I know is to lay a claim to the truth of what I assert. [It follows that k]nowledge is more like a piece of property of which we may claim ownership (rightly or wrongly) than it is like a sensation which we experience and attempt to describe. (1987: 39)

The crucial distinction here is that between knowledge and sensation. Knowledge may temporarily 'belong' to us; but it does not constitute a vital part of our being ourselves in the way that sensation does. Knowledge can be added to and subtracted from us without our being changed in any physical way. Having a piece of knowledge in our head is thus very much like having it on a slip of paper in our pocket. Of course, the first bit of knowledge is mental, while the second is physical, and this is a difference that is by no means negligible. Yet the point is that the analogy holds: having knowledge in our heads is, in its mental way, the same thing as having it in our pockets.

The advantage of this doctrine is that it separates the knower from what he or she knows. This establishes the possibility that knowledge can be objectively true. The truth or falsity of what we assert exists independently of ourselves. Nothing is true (or false) just because we happen to assert it; if the assertion is true, then it is true anywhere,

---

[1] The classic statement of this conception of knowledge is Austin 1946. Warnock 1987 and Needham 1981 effectively demonstrate the epistemological roots of the whole discussion of the psychology of memory.

regardless of who asserts it, or where and in what form it is asserted. Thus, the doctrine helps distinguish the objective truth of an assertion, which is not dependent on persons, from the interpretation of the meaning of the assertion, which is an expression of a person's subjective judgement.

The disadvantage of such a doctrine becomes apparent, however, the moment that we try to use it as the basis for a model of memory. Unlike knowing, remembering seems self-evidently a state of mind. Remembering is an experience, or an activity performed by mind. This not only contrasts remembering to knowing, but, in a more radical way, threatens to disjoint the two totally. It seems possible, for example, that we 'know' things (have them in our minds) without necessarily being able to remember them. Knowing something and remembering it are independent of each other. Is the opposite also possible? Can we 'remember' things without 'knowing' them? If we think of 'knowing' as primarily referring to knowing facts that are objectively true, then it is indeed possible, for much of what we remember is in the form of remembered emotions, feelings, and fantasies, or remembered sensory images. These are all things which we may remember without 'knowing' them objectively.

Often, of course, we do remember information as something detached from us; in these cases, the truth of the information has nothing to do with the shape and location of the container which holds it. I discover, for example, an interesting fact which I wish to preserve. What do I do with it? I can write it down, type it into the computer, or fax it by satellite to someone on the other side of the globe. Alternatively, I can decide just to remember it. In so far as the information remains identical, why should its location or form matter? Why should we even imagine that information in our memories is in any respect different from information inside computers?[2]

Yet this is only one part of memory, for much of what we remember refers to us personally, and, therefore, cannot really be anywhere but inside our heads. If I tell a friend my personal memories, they still remain my memories; regardless of who knows them, they still refer to

---

[2] As some readers will have recognized, this is what John Searle calls the 'strong AI' (artificial intelligence) argument, which is, briefly, that as long as the results are the same, we have no business assuming that it makes the slightest difference whether the 'thought process' takes place in a machine or in someone's head. It seems obvious that AI arguments in a general way depend on the separation of knowledge from states of consciousness. We shall see later that this is simply a corollary of the separation of word and object by Descartes and the seventeenth-century empiricists. On AI, see Hofstadter in Hofstadter and Dennett 1982. For criticism, see Searle 1987 and Penrose 1989.

me and describe my own experience. Thus, unlike objective knowledge, which belongs to us only in a contingent and temporary way, personal memories are indissolubly ours; they form a part of us. This is a wider aspect of memory, a part that human beings share with animals. We may distinguish ourselves from a frog in the matter of being able to hold objective facts inside our heads; we can hardly do so in being able to remember. We thus remember knowledge, but we also remember sensation. Memory, in fact, pervades every aspect of our mental lives, from the most abstract and cognitive to the most physical and unconscious. Memory is always at work in our minds; reading this book, looking for a friend, thinking about the news, are all, in part, exercises in memory (Casey 1987: ix; Warnock 1987: 1; Gregory 1984, ch. 9).

In this way, our doctrine of objective knowledge leads us to regard memory as naturally divided into two segments. There is an objective part which serves as a container of facts, most of which might be housed in a variety of other locations. There is a subjective part, which includes information and feelings that are an integral part of us, and which thus are properly located only within us. The first part of memory is comparatively passive; it simply holds knowledge. The second part is more active; it experiences and recalls to consciousness. In this way, a distinction between objective fact and subjective interpretation is posited in the structure of memory itself.

The textual model is one expression of this conception of memory. A text is a physical record; it contains information about the past, some of which is possibly accurate. Treating memory as, in certain instances, analogous to a text captures the sense in which memory, too, is a container of possibly objective information. Using such a container as a source implies developing a method for taking the facts out of the container. In so far as the container is like a text, this means subjecting it to a form of textual analysis. Historians have developed such a methodology. By analysing an oral text, and correlating it with other, written documents and other pieces of information, they can, often with reasonable certainty, 'restore' the text to its 'original' version, and situate this version in its social context, establishing the particular perspective on the past that the 'oral document' takes.

As a convenience, this analogy is often defensible. If we ask someone on the street for directions, we usually treat the response as objective information, not troubling ourselves over the fact that it is just his or her subjective memory. When we try to remember the whereabouts of a misplaced object, we often seem to subject our minds to a sifting and correlating process something like textual criticism. It is sometimes also convenient to forget that, behind the texts of ancient and medieval historians, there often stands little more than the memories of contemporaries, especially if we are reading these texts primarily for their factual content. Only when these earlier historians assert – as they often do – something which we regard as totally impossible, is it then useful to remember that their basis, after all, is 'just subjective memory'.

For all its convenience, however, the textual model is only an analogy. It is not necessary to argue that memory really is organized like texts in the mind. The analogy has its weak points. In the mind, memory is just thought. Texts, by contrast, are physical objects; and one text is separate from the next. If we were not able to separate texts from each other, we would hardly be able to analyse them critically. We can separate memories only mentally, however. In fact, a condition of knowing anything at all through our memory is that memory remains connected. Remembering often entails travelling back along a chain of memories; if the chain were to be shattered, and all the links held separately, we should no longer be able to remember at all. In this sense, a historian studying a text is in no way analogous to a person trying to remember. A text is separated from the historian and completed in itself; it can send its 'messages' to the historian, but it cannot receive them back. A memory is not separated from consciousness in this way; nor is it closed off; between memory and consciousness, therefore, the traffic is always two-way.

It is possible, of course, to construct a theory to support the analogy. The theory would try to show that there exists a part of memory in which exact replicas of past events are stored. We shall examine this theory later in the chapter. Yet even if the theory itself were completely convincing, it would still be difficult to see in what sense these replicas remain objective inside our heads. There is no reason, for example, to suppose that these replicas are any less rooted in the neurochemistry of the brain, or any less bound up with bodily feelings, than are subjective opinions. Nor is there a reason to suppose that memory itself undergoes a change at the point in which it becomes objective. 'Objectively' true is an attribute that can qualify only the information itself; it does not influence the way we know it. In terms of the experience of remembering, there is nothing to distinguish the remembering of true facts from the remembering of nonsense.

The textual model of memory seems ultimately to rest on a confusion. What makes memory usable as a source at all is the fact that we can articulate it. What makes 'objective' memory seem more objective than the memory of feelings and personal experience is simply the fact that we can articulate and communicate the former in words more easily than we can the latter. 'Objective' memory is simply the better vehicle for the conveyance of information; it is the aspect of our memory most easily available to others. This distinction has nothing to do with the structure of memory, however, it is, rather, a social fact. Thus, what emerges at the point of articulation is not the objective part of memory, but its social aspect.

Historians have recently become more willing to confront conceptual issues – the evolution of 'mentalities' or models of 'paradigm change' provides classic instances. Implicit in this is an acceptance of Durkheim's doctrine that collectively held ideas are 'social facts', and, as such, are the result of social and historical forces. Our argument is that memory, too, is a social fact. Admittedly, it is a rather special sort of social fact, for memory is only social in part. Certain of our memories seem indeed to be more private and personal than others. Yet this distinction between personal memory and social memory is, at best, a relative one. Typically, our memories are mixed, possessing both a personal and a social aspect. There seems little reason, therefore, to suppose that memory itself is divided into two compartments – one personal and the other social. Still less is there reason to suppose that one part of our memories is objective while the other is subjective.

In and of itself, then, memory is simply subjective. At the same time, however, memory is structured by language, by teaching and observing, by collectively held ideas, and by experiences shared with others. This makes memory social as well. Any attempt to use memory as a historical source in a sensitive way must confront the subjective, yet social, character of memory from the outset. This is not to say that memory cannot also bear objective information. Historians have always regarded memoirs, first-hand accounts, and eyewitness testimony as excellent historical sources, and this is entirely proper, not to say unavoidable. Yet there exists another possibility; one that is more general, more in tune with the special character of memory, and, perhaps, of special interest to social historians. When we remember, we represent ourselves to ourselves and to those around us. To the extent that our 'nature' – that which we truly are – can be revealed in articulation, we are what we remember. If this is the case, then a study of the way we remember – the way we present ourselves in our memories, the way we define our personal and collective identities through our memories, the way we order and structure our ideas in our memories, and the way we transmit these memories to others – is a study of the way we are.

Social facts evolve and change over time. If this is true of memory, than memory must have its own history. For those who regard memory as simply one of the natural parts of our cognitive apparatus, this suggestion may seem bizarre. In fact, our ways of remembering turn out

to have a long history behind them. The rest of this chapter is an explo-
ration of ways of remembering, in order to show that some of the ways
that seem most natural and spontaneous to us have not always seemed so
at other times and to other people. One of the best means of seeing the
role of memory *for* history is to look at memory *in* history.

Memory of history or 'history' of memory?

In Western society, the history of memory is one of its steady devaluation as a source of knowledge – a devaluation which proceeds in step
with the evolution, and increasing dominance, of the textual paradigm
of knowledge. This devaluation has its own history, some of which is of
very recent vintage. As Edward Casey has pointed out, from the late
nineteenth century until the 1930s, mnemonists ('memory men') were
a regular feature of variety shows and music-hall entertainment. This
same period saw a flowering of tracts and other publicity media,
expounding systems for 'a more powerful memory in just ten days' (1987:
6). Today, the popularity of this literature has decreased. The spread of
more abstract and active paradigms of intelligence has produced a self-
help literature which, instead of promising a stronger memory, promises
to sharpen one's 'competitive edge', by 'aggressive business strategies',
or sometimes simply teaches one how to say 'no'.[3]

Memory has retreated for us more and more into the personal. It is a
source of private, not social, knowledge. It was not always so. A charter
of 1174, granted to the inhabitants of Tonnerre in Burgundy by Guy,
count of Nevers, begins by observing: 'The use of letters was discovered
and invented for the preservation of the memory of things. Whatever we
want to retain and learn by heart we have made out in writing. In this
way, things that we are unable to hold in our weak and fragile memories, are conserved by writing, and by the means of letters which last
forever' (in Le Goff 1988: 140). The observation was a commonplace;
little more, in fact, than a scribal formula. Yet this makes it all the more
significant, for the scribe was making here an assumption which, as
blindingly obvious as it may have seemed to him, may strike us as

---

[3] One should, perhaps, not speak here of the devaluation of memory as such, but rather,
more specifically, of the devaluation of rote memory as a teaching method. The criticism
of rote memory in teaching had already, as we shall see, been made by Rabelais. It was
made again, very forcibly, near the end of the last century, by William James in his *Talks
to Teachers*. From this point onwards, a critique of rote memorization always formed part
of enlightened pedagogy. See Meyers 1968.

unusual: the set of legal and social customs, rights, and duties by which a community lives were normally held in that community's collective memory. As important as it was, writing was still envisioned as an adjunct to memory.

It would be far more difficult to hold this assumption today. To begin with, the set of legal and social information necessary for the smooth running of our society – laws, contracts, scientific and technical skills, mathematical formulae, sports facts, grammatical rules, etiquette, etc., etc. – is simply too vast and complex to be held, even collectively, in memory alone. We need other means. Single individuals try to memorize some of the information that has a direct bearing upon the tiny portion of the social globe that they occupy. Much of this information, however, is characteristically 'off-loaded' into notebooks and agendas. The capacity of writing to freeze information once and for all makes a written note a more convenient way of preserving the memory of detailed and specific information such as addresses and telephone numbers, bank balances and dentist's appointments. This is a pattern that holds on a large scale as well. Information can be held in books and in computers; as long as this information is available when and where it is needed, no one is going to go to the trouble of memorizing it.

Legal documents, for example, are written to be preserved and consulted. The manner in which they are thought out by legal experts, and finally expressed in writing, reflects the capacity of a written text to hold detailed information; to define, in a precise manner, contingencies and eventualities; to make cross-references to other legal documents; and, finally, to preserve this information indefinitely. This level of precision is impossible where contracts and agreements are supported only by living memory. Thus, writing not only freezes memory, but freezes memory in textual forms which evolve in ways quite unlike those of oral memory. The form and syntax of a legal document, whether from the twelfth century or the twentieth, reflect the form and syntax of other written documents. They are typically embedded in a complex of other texts. They refer to these texts; they draw support from them. It is this sense of texts 'talking' to texts that explains why the syntax of a legal document bears so little resemblance to the syntax of either speech or thought.

Thus, the Burgundian scribe's assumption that legal rights and obligations were normally stored in collective memory does not require us to suppose that twelfth-century peasants went around with the texts of documents in their collective heads. The form in which social knowledge is held in collective memory is always very different from the form in which it appears in, say, a law code. This is an important point. The written word is not the mirror of our thoughts. At very best, textual records represent collective consciousness only in an indirect way. In part, this has to do with spontaneity: nothing that we write is ever as scattered and disordered as our thought processes. Yet this is only a small part of the problem, for it is hardly to be supposed that the writers of medieval charters ever intended to produce 'stream of consciousness' literature. The written word not only fails to mirror our thought processes; it rarely even tries.

Not all literate users of language have always been aware of this difference. Medieval Icelandic lawspeakers, for example, were supposed to commit their entire law code to memory (Dennis et al. 1980: 187–8). In the same vein, the twelfth-century scribe's assumption that the words of a charter are simply a written transcription of an agreement that might have been made orally reflects a social context in which oral agreements were not only common, but still regularly accepted in courts of law (Goody 1986: 127ff., 151–9; cf. also Clanchy 1979). In such cases, the writing out of a legal decision or charter would, indeed, appear as, in part at least, a support for oral memory. For us, by contrast, the text is no longer a support for memory, but its replacement.

If written knowledge can substitute for community memory, it is possible that the knowledge of what that community is and was, and what its rights, duties, and traditions are, might be located somewhere other than in the community itself. To groups emerging from pre-literacy, this might seem a frightening and alienating possibility, and this probably helps account for Plato's well-known antipathy towards writing (cf. *Phaedrus*, 275a; the theme is also brought up, *inter alia*, in both the *Theatatus* and the *Republic*). Xenophon records Socrates as reproaching a young noble who possessed a copy of the Homeric poems with words to the effect, 'Just having the book doesn't make you an epic poet' (cited in Cavallo 1988: 29). We may take this as implying that Socrates rejected any form of 'knowing' Homer that did not include an ability to recite him, rejecting, in other words, any sort of distinction between knowing the poems and knowing *about* them (cf. below, p. 44).

Literacy influences the form in which knowledge is articulated. Once knowledge is textualized, it tends to evolve in a characteristically textual way – a way that has little connection with the way knowledge evolves purely in thought and speech. For cultures like our own, long accustomed to this textualization, it may seem difficult to imagine that other cultures might regard knowledge as articulated in a different form. Significantly, all three of these examples – twelfth-century Burgundy, medieval Iceland, ancient Greece – were societies emerging into literacy. The assumptions of these societies still reflected an oral social context, where it was hard to imagine knowledge as existing anywhere else but in people's heads. Consequently, it was hard for people of these societies to imagine how knowledge could be preserved in any way except by living memory. This influenced their conception of memory itself. Oral societies usually accord a greater respect to living memory than, characteristically, does our own.

The rise and fall of artificial memory

The varied techniques by which self-help literature seeks to improve and strengthen memory, are, as Paolo Rossi points out, merely 'intellectual fossils'. They derive ultimately from the far more complex and elaborate mnemonic systems developed in the ancient world and developed and repeatedly re-elaborated from the Middle Ages until the seventeenth century (1988a: 212). From the 'memory theatre' of Giulio Camillo in the early sixteenth century to Leibnitz's project for a universal language which would categorize all knowledge, and from which an encyclopaedic mnemonic reference system could be constructed, the notion of reducing knowledge to a memorizable form continued to obsess European scholars. It will help us to examine briefly what some of these techniques were.

Memory was classed as a branch of rhetoric in the ancient world (Curtius 1967: 68; Yates 1978: 20ff.). The mnemonic techniques of classical Rome were thus developed in reference to oratory. Typically, rhetoric was employed in law suits. A Roman lawyer used the classical technique of the 'artificial memory' as a way of fixing in memory the points of an argument he wished to place before the court. 'Artificial memory' was the memory of 'places and things'. Orators were trained to fix in their memories some stretch of extended, real space – such as a row of shops. This would serve as a mental space in which to hold a series of invented mnemonic images. These images mapped out points that the orator wished to make. As the orator spoke, he would imaginatively proceed along his remembered promenade, noticing the images that he had previously placed there. This allowed him not only to remember all the points he wished to make in his speech, but also to remember them in their proper order.

The images themselves were, necessarily, visual images, although the connections between the remembered images and the points the orator wished to remember were not necessarily visual. They were composite, fixing connections by arbitrary combinations of semantic, visual, and auditory images. Thus, to give one example, an orator who needed to remember that the prosecutor was accusing his client of poisoning someone to obtain an inheritance was advised to remember an older man lying in bed with the defendant kneeling beside him with a goblet (poison) and clay tablets (will). These are simple visual signs. The prosecutor, however, also claimed that the deed had witnesses (Latin: *testis*). To remember this detail, the orator was advised to place on the fourth finger of the defendant's image a set of ram's testicles (from Cicero, *Ad Herennium*, III. xx. 33, cited in Yates 1978: 27).

In principle, rhetoric was the art of speaking effectively; in practice, the term was extended to writing as well. In this way, rhetorical practices from the ancient world – mnemotechnics included -- survived through the Middle Ages. The rediscovery of Plato in the Renaissance added an epistemological dimension to this technique of remembering images. Giulio Camillo argued that the images chosen for his memory theatre were like the statues of ancient Egypt, whose makers, he believed, could bring them to such a state of perfection that they came 'to be inhabited by an angelic spirit: for such perfection could not be without a soul' (Yates 1978: 159; see also 142ff.). The images synthesized a spiritual entity, not an oration. In this way, a memory theatre could be used as an independent source of knowledge. If the images of the memory theatre were truly and perfectly proportioned, they would capture the 'soul' of what was to be remembered, and permit new discoveries through its contemplation.

The roots of this conception lie in Renaissance Neoplatonism. Yet, as Frances Yates remarks, there is more here at stake than abstract philosophical theory. For, the memory theatres of the sixteenth century are manifestations of a different way of envisioning memory, or, perhaps, even a different way of thinking about thinking, than we tend to have today (Yates 1978: 140; for background, cf. Yates 1964). There is an emphasis on the visual character of knowledge. With this visual emphasis comes an emphasis on space: one perceives the details of the images in memory by mentally walking round them, just as if they were statues in a gallery. The resulting paradigm is less abstract than is a textual paradigm of knowledge. Moreover, as in Plato, knowledge is associated with the retention in memory of the images in their entirety: it is a knowledge directly of something, rather than indirectly as facts that can be stated about it.

To us, the elaborate techniques that such systems employ seem strange. They are unlike the simple and arbitrary mnemonic aids, such as rhymes and pat phrases, that we sometimes use, especially in the human and natural sciences, to help fix important bits of scientific terminology in the memory (especially prior to exams). The images chosen to decorate the various memory theatres of the sixteenth century were neither simple nor arbitrary. They were carefully constructed visual images. Thus, they were not mere 'reminders', constructed as a convenient means to retrieve semantic knowledge stored in the memory; instead, they were designed to embody and depict the knowledge they represented. They were 'maps' – things designed to represent other things.

The weakness of memory theatres was that they were cumbersome (Viano 1988). Descartes wanted a simpler method. Would it not be much more efficient, he asked himself, to use, as the mnemonic clues, not images, but causes? Since one cause might be responsible for a large number of individual effects, remembering causes would reduce the bulk of what needed to be memorized (cf. *Regulae ad directionem ingenii*, III, IV, VIII, cited in Viano 1988: 254ff.). This idea led him to another. Descartes observed that the images in memory theatre were complex; they contained too much information. They failed to separate the facts about what was being remembered from fantasies. This overdetermination of the memory image was, of course, from the perspective of Giulio Camillo, one of its chief virtues: the images in the memory theatre were chosen as objects of mental contemplation; their surplus of symbolic meaning was what qualified them as sources of knowledge. For Descartes, this was a disadvantage. He insisted on simplicity and transparency as the cardinal virtues of any mnemonic system.

Descartes' criticisms were echoed by similar considerations on the parts of Francis Bacon, Hobbes, and others; and this new view on memory was later reflected in Leibnitz's art of combination. (For Bacon, see Rossi 1988a: 223–4, 236–7; for Hobbes, see Warnock 1987, ch. 2; for Leibnitz, see Rossi 1988a: 233–7; Viano 1988: 266–9.) By now, however, the whole perspective was changing. Instead of a search for the perfectly proportioned image containing the 'soul' of the knowledge to be remembered, the emphasis was on the discovery of the right logical category. The memory of this system of logical categories and scientific causes would exempt the individual from the necessity of remembering everything in detail. Knowledge, in other words, was becoming separate from the individual knower. As this happened, a semantic model of memory gradually replaced a visual model. This meant that the dominant mode of mnemonic connection became logical, a chain of connections and causes articulated in syntactic 'space', rather than in a visual representation of space.

This new emphasis on the linguistic components of knowledge – semantics and logic – was in line with the evolution of philosophical and scientific thought. Thought was separated from the physical world, and science was free to develop in the direction of mathematical formalism. The trend was also reflected in empiricist philosophy, as a nominalist conception of knowledge supplanted an older realism. Knowing something implied knowing about it – its name and its position in a schema of classification and description. Knowing plants, wrote the botanist Tournefort in 1694, is the same thing as knowing the names to be assigned to them (Rossi 1988a: 231). The problem of memorizing the world, characteristic of the sixteenth century, evolved into the problem of classifying it scientifically.

The scientific and philosophic developments of the seventeenth century were associated with a facility in using the properties of language for the construction of increasingly abstract systems of classification and meta-reference. This development was accompanied by a technological change that was hardly less important than the development of writing itself – the spread of printing. By the time of Linnaeus (1707–78), for example, it was common to see graphs and charts on the printed page. The visual representation of knowledge, first in written texts, later in printed books with diagrams and illustrations, had begun to lay bare the formal, syntactical, and logical structure of knowledge itself. As this occurred, knowledge itself grew more sophisticated (Febvre and Martin 1958).

The epistemological devaluation of memory as a source of knowledge reflected this pattern of changes. As knowledge came to be increasingly characterized as consisting of statements about reality rather than images of reality held in the mind, the justification for elaborate techniques of visual memory disappeared. The separation of knowing from the visual imagination implied the separation of mind from matter; the knower from the knowledge. Knowledge henceforth resided in texts, and needed to be ordered in an explicitly textual fashion. Rabelais' description of the disorder of the library of St Victor in Paris was an early satire on the confusion of the older method of ordering knowledge (*Gargantua et Pantagruel*, II. vii).

During this period, there arose a more active conception of intellect itself. Intellect, or 'judgement', appeared as a sort of mental power that invested inert matter with life. The text-like knowledge housed in the memory was passive, but the powerful mind was active. Memory could seem a relatively sluggish aspect of an otherwise active intellect. Montaigne could remark that 'an excellent memory is often conjoined with the weakest intellects.'[4]

In words worthy of Saki, Montaigne sang the praises of forgetfulness. Forgetting, he observed, is creative. If I always remembered everything,

---

[4] *Essais*, I. ix: 'Il se voit par experience plustost au rebours que les memoires excellentes se joignent volontiers aux jugemens debiles.'

I would never need to invent; there would be no need for me to demonstrate my cleverness through successfully hiding my ignorance. What is more, if I remember a witty observation, it is advantageous to forget who first said it. In this case, it will appear to me as if it were my own, and this is helpful to me, for, as it is often to be observed, one understands one's own ideas better than those of anyone else. The mind was thus an active force, and, ironically, it was rendered all the more powerful by its incorrigible forgetfulness.

The written word was fecund, yet it was inactive. The knowledge in books was a knowledge of the past; the knowledge that the active mind strove for was knowledge of the future. Libraries, wrote Montaigne, were places of collective forgetfulness; their value lay in the chances they provided for serendipity, the happy discovery of unsuspected pieces of forgotten knowledge (*Essais*, II. ix).

Words and things

Montaigne's comments were prescient, prefiguring the paradoxes later associated with the Cartesian conception of mind. Implicit in this conception is an idea of memory as primarily a storage system or repository of knowledge. As such, memory is passive; it simply houses information. But this is not the only sense in which we think of our memories. When we say, 'I remember', or 'I'm trying to remember', or 'the memory just came to me', we are using the notion of memory in a more active sense. It is in this sense that remembering seems to be a mental experience, and one, moreover, under some degree of conscious control. In this way, memory appears not merely as a mechanism that copies information and stores it in our heads, but also as the experience of retrieving that information and combining it to form new thoughts.

Many of the classic difficulties in philosophical or psychological treatments of memory arise in the attempt to reconcile these two aspects. The source of many of these difficulties lies in the preliminary assumption that memory is, in the first instance, a storage system. This assumption suggests a model of how memory as a whole works. We can either visualize this model, in the classical way, as the intellect inspecting texts and images engraved or hung on the walls of memory, or we can see it, in the more modern sense, as a *homunculus* at the control board, accessing bits of information from memory's data bank. As it stands, of course, the model is merely an analogy. The difficulty arises in the attempt to translate this analogy into a more convincing description (for the *homunculus*, cf. Dennett 1979, part II).

We might put this problem in a slightly different way. We can take the question, 'How does memory serve as a source of knowledge?' in two senses. On the one hand, we can take it as simply a question about how memory copies and stores information; on the other, we can take it as a question about how memory, first, copies and stores information, and *then* uses that information to form new ideas. In either case, however, the assumption remains that memory is, in the first instance, a copy and store mechanism. This assumption is not, however, necessary; nor, as we shall see, do we have any real ground for asserting it at all. Thus, we can take the question of how memory helps us know as simply asking what constitutes the *experience* of memory. This can be our starting-point.

Our own notion of memory has, as we have seen, a historical dimension. We saw in the previous section that this notion of memory descends, to a large extent, from Descartes, Leibnitz, and the seventeenth-century empiricists. The new notion that began to emerge at this time reflected the need of science to free itself from the visual conception of knowledge implicit in the memory theatre of Giulio Camillo. As a path to scientific knowledge, such a conception now appeared to be both cumbersome to use and inherently deceptive. There arose an increasing understanding of, and dependence upon, the potential of language and scientific notation for synthesis and abstraction. A notion of textual memory as that part of memory that is inherently objective and rational, as against sensory and personal memory as that part of memory that is inherently subjective and non-rational, was one of the results of this process in which the relationship between language and the world it describes was radically rethought.

This implies that not only our notion of memory as a mental category, but even our own personal experience of memory, has probably been influenced by this process of rethinking. It follows that one way of uncovering the experience of memory is to ask whether an experience of memory different from our own is possible, and, if so, what would it be like. We have already suggested that a different experience is, in fact, possible. We can now look for ways to describe this difference.

Earlier in the chapter, we cited a Burgundian scribe who observed that 'The use of letters was discovered and invented for the preservation of the memory of things.' This is surely a *non sequitur*. What writing preserves is not the memory of *things*, but that of *words*.

A sliding from words to the things they represent is common enough, and, in this particular example, probably easy to explain. No doubt, what the scribe meant to emphasize was that the charter itself preserved a concrete set of rights and obligations. In neglecting to mention that this preservation only came about through the medium of preserved words, the scribe was merely making the same assumption that underlies much of our own conversation. We listen for the message; we pass directly and unconsciously from the words to the 'things' that these words mean. Yet a distinction between the 'memory of words' and the 'memory of things' exists, and we might begin by asking how this distinction manifests itself.

All societies, even the most primitive, possess ways and techniques of preserving their 'memory of things': the variety is extraordinary. They support geographical memory by mapping out the sky in the figures of the zodiac, thus helping shepherds count the seasons and mariners steer their course. They organize the landscape for the Australian Aboriginals (Oppenheim 1964: 370ff.; Munn 1973). They conserve social information as well: the tattoos of Malaysian tribes record genealogies, kinship, and clan affiliations in etchings on the body (Delano Smith 1987).

We can call these information-bearing representations, functioning as *aides-mémoire*, 'maps' for short. The capacity for the making of these maps in support of social memory is archaic and spread throughout the world (Leroi-Gourhan 1965: 212–32). As Robinson and Petchenik remark, 'Anything that can be spatially conceived, can be mapped – and probably has been' (in Harley and Woodward 1987: 4). It makes little difference, moreover, whether such a map represents a space which is real or imaginary: maps of the underworld are no less maps than are representations of our own back garden. Similarly, it makes little difference whether the map itself is a real, constructed representation or an imaginary one. The signs of the zodiac provide a map of the skies; and it is unnecessary to specify whether this map is actually drawn or only 'seen' in the stars. Thus, a 'map', in the sense that we are using the term, is a visual concept, a constructed or projected image, referring to and bearing information about something outside itself. It is a concept that supports the 'memory of things'.

In terms of the 'copy and store' conception of memory, it does not really matter whether we regard these mnemonic maps as an example of the 'memory of words' or the 'memory of things'. In terms of the experience of memory, however, it does make a considerable difference. If we regard such mnemonic maps as conceptualized information, we might regard the memory of such maps as analogous to the memory of texts. We might even regard the making of such mnemonic maps as a primitive form of 'writing', or writing, as it were, *avant la lettre*.

Regarding the memory of maps as analogous to the 'memory of words' would, however, disregard those ways in which it is also akin to the 'memory of things'. A mnemonic map is a visual image, and as we saw, the visual expression of knowledge is more complex than the semantic. It is also more difficult to communicate. Thus, a map, collectively held in the memory of a group, may also be regarded as being similar to the images of the memory theatre. In this case, the map would be a conceptualized image, but not a primitive text.

In reality, the question of whether mnemonic maps are texts or images is one that cannot be given an *a priori* answer. It can be answered only in reference to the map-making cultures themselves. We are, of course, quite accustomed to seeing graphs and charts. We interpret these as the visual representations of knowledge that might, in principle, be represented in other forms. For us, therefore, a mnemonic map would be just an extension of our 'memory of words'. This is not, however, to say that all cultures who make such maps regard them as representations of their semantic or logical knowledge. In fact, in most of the examples cited above, members of the culture would probably have difficulty in conceiving of their maps as other than direct representation. The map would embody the 'thing' it represented.

In this context, it is significant that maps supporting the 'memory of things' considerably antedate the texts that support the 'memory of words'. Edmund Leach makes this point when he comments that 'the making and reading of two-dimensional maps is almost universal among mankind, whereas the reading and writing of linear scripts is a special accomplishment, associated with a high level of social and technical sophistication' (1976: 51). Writing is associated with semantically organized knowledge which can be transmitted in spoken or written language. A text conserves the 'memory of things' through the medium of words. A map may represent this textual memory; it may also be a simple representation without the mediation of language.

How did this conception of language as a medium of preservation first arise? The Burgundian scribe's initial comment was that 'the use of letters was discovered and invented for the preservation of the memory of things'. Interestingly enough, this may be literally true. The perception that writing, in fact, preserved the 'memory of words' arose after the invention of writing, not before. Scholars believe that the Sumerian ideogram, pressed into clay, evolved from a direct, 'thing-to-thing' system of representation (Schmandt-Besserat 1978). Thus, the idea that it was language that served as the basis of writing seems not, at least at first, to have occurred to the ancient Sumerians.

How did a system of mnemonic aids, which preserved the 'memory of things' by representing these 'things' on clay tablets, evolve into writing – a means of representing 'things' through signs that stood for 'words'? According to the French Assyriologist Jean Bottéro, the notion of language as an autonomous descriptive medium, independent of the context of speaking, arose slowly in the ancient Near East as cuneiform

was developed and perfected (1987: 89–113). Moreover, the intuition
that it was language that was taking over the job of describing from
direct representation did not arise through the intuition that individual
ideograms stood for 'words', not 'things'. In fact, throughout their long
history, cuneiform ideograms continued to be regarded as representations of 'things' rather than 'words'. They could be vocalized in either
the Sumerian or the Akkadian language. They also served as the basis of
divination, and this required that they be understood as visual signs
embodying the 'things' they represented in all their aspects (Bottéro
1987: 133–70; also 1974).

It is more likely that the intuition that writing represented language
arose from the realization that clusters of ideograms did not represent
reality directly, but rather through their relations to each other – not, in
other words, through relations of material things, but through relations
of syntax. Thus, it would be one thing to construct a set of *aides-mémoire*
in which every image is a map representing a thing, but quite another to
use these maps to state a proposition. When this happens, the maps will
come to be ordered in a sequence that is syntactically determined;
ordered, in other words, as 'language'. As this was noticed, the difference between 'words' and 'things' could no longer be ignored. Language
itself was becoming visible in text. If this reconstruction is correct,
however, it follows that people had to wait for a means of displaying
language visually before they could clearly perceive the difference
between 'word' and 'thing' (Bottéro 1987: 128–30).

The argument of Bottéro is speculative. None the less, it is in line
with what anthropologists have frequently observed. In preliterate
societies, language is not separated from the context of speaking; at best,
it is only weakly perceived as existing independently (Goody 1977). In
these societies, the semantic message is not separated from the context
in which the message is delivered; the promise is not distinguished
from the act of promising. A blessing or curse is an act, and the words
used in this act are simply part of the total performance.

In a curious way, the behaviour of the Babylonian scribes resembles
our own. We are so accustomed to using words to support our 'memory
of things' that we do not always notice that they are there. We fail to
remember that we are using a medium at all. Implicitly, cuneiform
represented a system of supporting the 'memory of things' through the
medium of words from the outset. It simply took Near Eastern scribes a
long time to 'see' this. In both cases, there is a tendency to overlook the
distinction between 'words' and 'things'.

There is a difference between the two examples as well. We are so
accustomed to using texts that we tend to see them everywhere. A

picture, a way of dressing, and a decorating style are all interpreted 'semiotically' as making a 'statement' about something. The Near Eastern scribes did not see texts wherever they looked. They did not, at first, even recognize their texts as texts. Their world was one of 'things'; the signs that they made were simply 'things' that stood for other 'things'.

Literate cultures thus tend to semanticize 'things' into meanings, while non-literate cultures tend to reify 'words' into things. The experience is different, but, curiously, the final effect is the same. What this suggests is that, first, our experience of the opposition of 'words' to 'things' is, to a certain extent, determined by our culture. This does not mean that we do not experience it subjectively as well; but it does imply that our subjective experience does not define the structure of memory itself. In memory itself, the frontier between 'word' and 'thing', or 'semantic' and 'sensory', is neither where our culture might experience it nor where a preliterate culture might experience it. This suggests, finally, that, in terms of memory itself, such a frontier need not be assumed to exist at all.

Memory and cognitive psychology

Changes in our epistemological paradigm reflect changes in the way in which we think – especially the way in which we think about thinking. Epistemology thus translates itself into psychology. We have seen that a textual conception of memory fits into a broader, historical context, and that this conception has a number of paradoxes associated with it. These difficulties have not gone unperceived, and we should look at some of the ways that cognitive psychologists and empiricist philosophers have attempted to cope with these problems.

The easiest, and probably the most common, solution is to divide memory into two or more sorts. The kind of memory which can hold objective knowledge constitutes one part; other kinds of memory constitute other parts. Thus, according to Endel Tulving, a psychologist at the University of Toronto and a leading authority on memory, our memories are divided into at least two 'systems' – a 'semantic memory system' and an 'episodic memory system'. These two systems are said to underlie two different forms of consciousness. Semantic memory underlies 'knowing consciousness', while episodic memory underlies 'self-knowing consciousness'. Thus, semantic memory governs our knowledge of events independent of our own personal experience of ourselves, while episodic memory underlies our subjctive sense of identity (Tulving 1983; for an extended discussion, see Gardner 1985).

As the terms themselves imply, the distinction between 'semantic memory' and 'episodic memory' reflects an epistemological distinction between rationally organized memory – that is, memory ordered as a network of concepts – and non-rationally organized experience – that is, remembered personal experience, sequenced temporally, or, as the theory has it, 'episodically'. In itself, it is not an objection to the theory to point this out. Tulving can claim that these epistemological categories are also universal psychological categories of mind. Yet are they really so universal? Is the distinction between the semantic and the episodic observable in all cultures? The short answer is 'no' – only in cultures with a conception of semantically organized knowledge akin to our own. In non-literate cultures, Tulving's distinctions would probably be unintelligible. The theory is also difficult to apply to literate cultures with visually orientated conceptions of knowledge, such as the sixteenth-century examples discussed above. The theory would render a work such as Loyola's *Spiritual Exercises* incomprehensible, for here true knowledge is underpinned by vividness of the sensory experience in personal meditation.

Tulving's own choice of terms is frequently revealing. According to him, semantic memory remembers through 'symbols', while episodic memory remembers through recalling 'experience'. 'Symbol' is being used here in the sense of a 'logical symbol', i.e., a sign that has a semantic equivalent. This is not its only possible meaning, however. Even today, a conception of the symbolic that contrasts it with sensory experience is a narrow one, for such a conception would seem to preclude the use of 'symbol' in regard to the visual arts. Around 1400, the Florentine humanist, Coluccio Salutati, gave quite a different account of the visual image: 'Since one enters into understanding and knowledge of spiritual things through the medium of sensible things [...], so long as we apprehend the picture as something made by a man's hand, not something itself divine, [we may still see in it] a similitude of divine providence, direction, and order' (in Baxandall 1971: 60–1).

These words imply a theory of knowledge that is antithetical to the semantic paradigm; they sum up an entire range of medieval and Renaissance thought on visual images and their relation to the real world. The fact that even today the idea of a meaningful visual image is perfectly understandable to most people seems to suggest that the rationalistic theory of memory fails to do justice not only to the memories of earlier periods in our history, but also to our own intuitions.[5]

---

[5] We cite Tulving's theory only as an example, for there is no space here for a general discussion of psychological theories of memory. Our criticism of Tulving comes down to two points. First, he has made no attempt to validate his results cross-culturally. This is a criticism that could be applied to cognitivists generally. Second, his separation of semantic

Memory and the empiricist philosophers

Any theory of knowledge must, at some point or another, confront our notion of how our minds work, if only, finally, to conclude that there is no necessary relation between the two at all. Empiricist philosophers since the seventeenth century have perceived this very clearly. They saw that their conception of objective knowledge would have to be associated with an explanation of how it is that we can remember objectively. Their preferred notion of memory was that of retained sensory images. This description, however, posed an immediate problem. As Hobbes saw, in order to show how memory preserves true sensory information, we first have to show how, in our minds, we can distinguish true retained perception from mere 'fancy'. We have, in other words, to suppose the existence of some mental property that allows us to distinguish true memory from mere imagination. Hume argued that this property was the superior vividness and life-like character of true memory (*Treatise of Human Nature*, 1739, I.i.3). This was a line that many empiricists adopted. In this way, philosophers from Hobbes and Hume to Russell have argued for the existence of some property in mental experience – a specific quality in true memories, a sign infallibly attached to them – that allows us, purely on the basis of our experience of them, to separate truth from fiction (Warnock 1987: 15–22, with citations).

The argument that there is some sign attached to true memories that allows us to recognize that they are true assumes that we do, in fact, always distinguish truth from fancy. It is by no means certain, however, that we always do. In an account of his earliest memory, Goethe describes how, shortly after the birth of his sibling, he, tempted by friends of his own age, threw the family china into the street below. As an event, the incident is not problematic – merely an outburst of jealousy, we might presume. As a memory, however, it is more ambiguous, for, as Goethe wrote in his autobiography, he did not know whether the memory of the incident was a real memory, or whether it was merely the memory of the incident as he had reconstructed it in his childish imagination after hearing the story repeated by his parents (Wollheim 1980).

---

from sensory produces a conception of memory which is counter-intuitive. This is a more complex objection, for although cognitive psychologists usually distinguish between semantic and episodic systems in memory, not all do so in as uncompromising a manner as does Tulving. Thus, Baddeley, one of the major modern theorists of the discipline, speaks of a 'synaesthesia' in memory, referring to the way that memory at one level evokes that at another. He explicitly doubts the practical usefulness of Tulving's distinction (Baddeley 1976: 317–18; 1990). See also Mishkin and Appenzeller 1987, and Neisser 1981.

Goethe's experience makes the empiricist claim seem doubtful. The image was undoubtedly vivid enough to Goethe, yet this did not reassure him that what he clearly remembered was not his own imaginings. His experience, moreover, is not uncommon; many people find their childhood memories ambiguous in just this way. It is easy to mistake a memory for the 'real thing' when the memory is vivid enough, for we often fail to recognize that what we remember are only memories, not preserved sense data. This ambiguity can be disconcerting, for it undermines any easy faith that we have in our ability always to distinguish true memories from imagination, from our experience of the memories alone.

The empiricists' dilemma is rooted in their conception of memory as retained sense data. This conception can probably be traced ultimately to Aristotle's problematic account of perception in *De Anima*,[6] yet the empiricists developed this conception within the confines of a Cartesian notion of mind that would have been entirely foreign to Aristotle. The empiricists needed to show how the image of, say, a strawberry, perceived by mind and stored in memory, could be identical to the strawberry in reality, without that image itself being, in any sense, made up of 'strawberry'. Only if this image could be both true to, yet completely independent of, reality, could it serve as a source of objective knowledge. Surrendering either part of the theory would fatally weaken the case for objective knowledge. Thus, Hume can candidly admit that the model is incongruous with experience while still feeling that the model itself must be defended.

Memory in its context

Hume's conclusion is paradoxical. If we really believed that our memories are accurate transcriptions of real experiences, we would display far more confidence in them than we actually do. We would probably also be much more troubled by the fact that we forget. For, much of our everyday experience never seems to be properly 'transcribed' at all. Yet, in normal circumstances, our memories serve us very well; we remember without even being aware that we are doing so. What the failure of empiricist endeavour to discover a truth-guaranteeing mechanism inside the mind implies is that the 'copy and store' model does not really correspond to our experience of memory. It does not imply that our everyday

---

[6] Sorabji 1972. It is not clear whether the empiricists' doctrines on memory were influenced by Aristotle's specific writings on memory, or by the general theory of perception contained in *De Anima*. On this, cf. McGinn 1982.

confidence in our memories is misplaced. We are simply required to seek the source of this confidence somewhere else.

Much of this confidence derives from the fact that we experience the present as connected to the past. Our experience of the present is thus embedded in past experience. Memory represents the past and present as connected to each other, and consistent with each other, in this way. We have confidence in this sort of memory because it is continually tested in everyday life. This testing frequently reveals inconsistencies as well; when this happens, however, we do not usually have difficulty in confabulating a reason. I cannot find my keys in the place where I remember leaving them this morning. I imagine that either someone else has taken them or I have been even more absent-minded than usual. Neither hypothesis forces me to doubt the connectedness of the past and the present.

Of course, this embedding of memory in present experience can also be at the root of its weakness as a source of knowledge of the past. Memory is strongest in the present continuum, where it is constantly exercised and tested; it can be anachronistic about events outside that continuum. Within the continuum, however, the method of continually validating memory through present experience usually works very well.

If memory is validated in and through actual practice, it must follow, unfortunately, that memory is never absolutely certain. Our knowledge of both the past and present is built on ideas and recollections in the present mind; it can be no more accurate than the ideas and recollections upon which it is built. Our confidence in our memories is limited by the possibility that they will be contradicted by new experience or better ideas. Whether we are aware of it or not, what is valuable about memory is not its capacity to provide an unshakeable foundation for knowledge, but, simply, its capacity to keep us afloat.

The failure of both philosophical and psychological accounts to provide a set of categories for the description of memory that is valid universally shows the functional nature of much of our experience of memory. This is usually an experience which is associated with a specific task; and it makes a difference what sort of task it is. Our experience in remembering semantic information is different from our experience in reminiscing about our early childhood. Both are different from our experience in trying to remember how to dance the tango. These functional differences are, however, also social differences, for it is the world we live in that sets the tasks for our memories, determines the ways in which we must perform these tasks, and even gives us the categories in which we think about them. This is true of individual memory, and it is also true of collectively held memories.

Any set of categories used in the description of memory can have only a relative, rather than universal, validity; and this goes, of course, for the categories used in this book. We shall try to pick categories as general and as neutral as possible; they still remain relative categories. We must also beware of rationalizing memory as we describe it. Memory is fluid, and works in ways in which we are scarcely aware. The categories in which we discuss memory should thus be indefinite enough to avoid any sense of rigid boundaries separating one 'type' of memory from another.

There is, finally, the problem that in discussing memory at all we give it an object-like consistency that it does not really possess. This, however, is a problem that is already present in our everyday habit of using physical analogies to express mental experience. Ideas 'strike' us; we 'search' for answers. What we 'really' mean when we say that 'the penny finally dropped' is that the 'machine' suddenly 'switched on' or, perhaps, that the 'point' of the remark suddenly 'clicked' and 'fell into place'. In explaining one analogy, we have recourse to another, and we seem to be permanently unable to move out of the circle. We shall see later that this tendency to describe mind in spatial analogies is itself significant. Here, however, the point is simply to emphasize that such descriptions are, in fact, analogies. As long as we are aware of that, we can understand that the *homunculi* in front of their control panels are just metaphorical and heuristic 'little men' rather than real mental entities.

The problem of analogy exists at a deeper level as well. Our use of descriptive analogies is influenced by our conception of language itself as a medium of description that is autonomous and separate from what it describes. It is this that renders Arthur Koestler's 'ghost in the machine' analogy for describing our minds so obviously heuristic. Yet we also see that the distinction between 'word' and 'thing' is not naturally present in our memories; nor do people of other cultures always experience this distinction in precisely the manner that we do. This means that in moving the discussion from the general problem of how we are to discuss social memory to that of the actual description of other people's experiences of memory, we must be careful how we describe the 'ghosts' in other people's 'machines'.

In principle, we can usually regard social memory as an expression of collective experience: social memory identifies a group, giving it a sense of its past and defining its aspirations for the future. In doing so, social memory often makes factual claims about past events. Sometimes we are able to check these factual claims against documentary sources; sometimes we cannot. In either case, however, the question of whether *we* regard these memories as historically true will often turn out to be less important than whether *they* regard their memories as true. Groups may regard their traditions as a set of amusing stories, possessing, perhaps, a moral lesson to teach, but still only fictions. Yet, in other cases, groups may regard their traditions as authoritative. In these latter instances, it is important to ask how and why they do so; for it is not to be supposed that any group regards its traditions as merely the retained sense data of its ancestors.

Social memory is a source of knowledge. This means that it does more than provide a set of categories through which, in an unselfconscious way, a group experiences its surroundings; it also provides the group with material for conscious reflection. This means that we must situate groups in relation to their own traditions, asking how they interpret their own 'ghosts', and how they use them as a source of knowledge.

Recognition, recall, and articulation
We can return to the description of memory with a simple observation: memory is complex. Behind the term stands a cluster of mental acts. Often associated with memory are, for example, recognition, recall, and articulation. Recognizing means identifying something or someone from previous knowledge or experience – usually, a 'something' that is before us. Presence is not necessary for recall; this term implies, rather, bringing something back into mind. In contrast to recognition, which usually involves perception, recall is therefore a purely internal act, involving some form of mental representation. When we reminisce, communicating what we recall to others, we carry memory a stage further – articulation. This implies expression, which, though usually an externalization of memory, can be a purely internal process as well.

This gives us three categories – recognition, recall, and articulation. We might wonder whether these three categories are parts of a single act, or three distinct acts. In so far as they might be distinct, moreover, we might wonder in what precise sense we should separate them.

According to P.D. MacLean, we can think of our conscious memory – memory, that is, associated with the frontal lobes of our brains – as having evolved in three stages. The first stage represents the development of the reptilian brain, what we might call our 'crocodile consciousness'. Here memory exists purely at the level of recognition. The presentation of a recognized stimulus sets off a course of action that is already, in some sense, programmed in the animal. The second stage is the palaeomammalian stage, or our 'horse consciousness'. This consists in the ability of an animal to form a connection between a presented stimulus and one not present. Thus, the animal does not need to be in the presence of the stimulus itself – food or something it fears – in order to react to it, but only in the presence of something associated with food or fear. This is enough to enable the animal to 'envision' what will come next, and to behave accordingly. The third stage is neomammalian. This is us. In this stage the 'animal' has the ability not only to follow a train of associations, but also to represent or somehow articulate what it remembers (cited in Fischer 1979: 34).

All such theories on the origin of consciousness are extremely speculative: we cite this one merely as an example. It has the advantage of conveniently presenting the three categories of memory as evolving in three, neurologically distinct stages. If we accept the theory, we thus accept that recognition, recall, and articulation can be neurologically distinguished. Does this mean that we can distinguish them in purely psychological terms as well? The point of the example is to show that this does not necessarily follow. Certainly, we can distinguish recognition, recall, and articulation as three different types of behaviour. But neither the possibility of a neurological distinction, nor that of a behavioural distinction, establishes that we also make a distinction purely in terms of mental experience. At this level there is little to separate them. There is nothing, for example, subjectively primitive about recognizing, no feeling that a reptilian part of our brains is relaying its message to our more highly evolved reasoning centres in the cerebral cortex. Nor, for example, when we see a stop sign, do we have any feeling that the recognition of the word comes from one memory 'system' while the recognition of the colour comes from another.

The physical location of memory (or 'memories') may be a pertinent neurological question. This does not make it a psychological one; for wherever this location may be, we do not experience our memories as coming from a 'here' rather than a 'there': we just remember. We 'just remember' because we are so placed in regard to our own thoughts that we have no way of, so to speak, 'looking over our shoulders' to see where 'they' are coming from. As a consequence of our awkward placement, our accounts of mental happenings are rarely more than analogical descriptions. We map out mind by projecting the perceived categories of mental behaviour onto it. Yet these categories, are, for the most part, functional. We define the parts of our mind in reference to what we do with these 'parts'. In this way, social experience is remapped as mental topography. We might go a little deeper into this with the aid of a rudimentary thought experiment.

We can imagine an expert rose grower with a stock of, say, 100 types of roses. If asked to name and describe all his roses, he might be able to do so with ease. Presumably, he would have a great deal of connected knowledge inside his head of types and subspecies, with their various characteristics and histories. Once he started to recall, a natural chain of association would make the rest of his specialist knowledge available to him. Even without the aid of mnemonic formulae, bodies of knowledge are structured in sequences of related concepts. This considerably facilitates their recall.

This connectedness of knowledge not only aids recall; it facilitates articulation as well. Sequences of related concepts are usually in part semantically structured. Such sequences are comparatively easy to articulate because memory already preserves them in a syntactic form. Language is a natural *aide-mémoire*; it organizes our knowledge in conceptual categories that are immediately available for articulation.

We might, however, for the purpose of the experiment, wish to make the mnemonic task harder by introducing the opposition of semantic to sensory. We could ask the rose grower to represent to himself each of the 100 types of roses without articulating in words – not even to himself. In other words, we would be asking him to recall to himself a series of things in purely sensory terms. Solving this task might involve, on his part, an imaginary perambulation round the rose beds, picturing to himself each rose as he came across it. Such a mental operation, deprived of the short cut that language provides, would take longer; we saw that visual, thing-to-thing memory is more cumbersome than word-to-thing memory. Still, it is not impossible. Indeed, the idea of a mental perambulation through a series of visual images was the principle behind the memory theatre.

We might now go a further step, and introduce the distinction between sensory memories which are inherently spatial and those which are not. We might deprive the rose grower of the support of imaginary space, asking him to remember each of the 100 roses by their smells alone, without recalling their names, and without even remembering their images or their locations in his garden. We would, in other words, be asking him to remember a series of unnamed and unlocated odours, a series that was neither logically, semantically, nor spatially organized. This task might well prove impossible. The poor rose grower might not even know where to begin.

Like the distinction between the 'memory of words' and the 'memory of things', the distinction between semantic and sensory is a genuine one. Neither, however, represents simple natural oppositions. They are both ways of interpreting and categorizing experience which developed gradually in Western society. Our experience of memory, however, interlocks with the ways in which we use memory. These distinctions thus influence the way we actually use our memories.

Memory is flexible; we are perfectly able to distinguish abstract memories from memories of perception and of feeling, if we want to. If the rose grower remembers knowledge destined for articulation in semantically structured concepts, he does so because it is more efficient to retain information which eventually needs to be articulated already in semantically structured forms. The reason is functional. The fact that the rose grower articulated his memory in semantically structured concepts does not, of course, mean that he lacked other sorts of memories. He was able to remember his roses as a visual sequence as well. The fact that he observed a distinction between semantic and sensory in practice shows that he knew how to adapt his memory to his purposes.

To put this more generally: it is possible to remember 'pure semantic information' – information, that is, encoded in a string of semantic symbols, linguistic, mathematical, or whatever. This is memory encoded as a disembodied string of symbols. This is what a computer does, and, to a much more limited extent, this is what we do too. The fact that we do find it convenient to remember semantic information in this decon-textualized form illustrates the advantage of words as the medium for the preservation of the 'memory of things'. Typically, when we order our memories into chains of purely semantic concepts, our associative field will, itself, be semantic. One semantic chain leads to another. Chains of semantic concepts are thus embedded in a larger semantic field in which sensory recall is avoided almost entirely.

It is often advantageous for us to remember textual or scientific information in precisely this way. This information is 'objective'. Recalling it does not require us to recall where and when we learned it, for these circumstances have no bearing on the information itself. It is usually more efficient simply to forget these circumstances whenever we can do so without losing the information itself. In this way of remembering, semantic concepts function like 'signifiers' without their 'signifieds'.

As useful as this semantic chain might be for the retention of pure information, however, it was of no use to the rose grower when we required him mentally to perambulate his own garden. Requiring him to forego semantic concepts threw him back onto sensory memory – the 'memory of things'. Significantly, it also threw him back onto personal memory, for he was able to undertake his mental perambulation only through recalling personal experience. This helps establish an important point: sensory memory and personal memory are naturally linked; falling back into one requires falling back into the other.

This link of the sensory and the personal is, of course, nothing more than an effect of the continuity of mind and body, and of memory and perception. It is on the basis of these continuities that memory is able to provide us with that coherency which underpins our sense of self. Providing us with this coherency is, we have said, the main task of memory in our normal lives. Thus, the source of our confidence in the working of memory lies in the continuity of mind and body, and with our personal and sensory memory, rather than with our semantic memory. This stands the textual paradigm of memory on its head: semantic memory is not the canonic, normal form of memory, but the exception. This is not, of course, to underrate the great power and convenience of semantic memory, or to deny that it is principally through such memory that we are able to remember information outside the present continuum. Indeed, if we do not remember semantic information, we tend to complain that 'our memory is failing'. Yet it is still the case that we could not be embedded in the world in the way we are unless semantic memory were continually underpinned and complemented by personal and sensory memory.

The fact, finally, that the rose grower might not be able to recall a purely olfactory series does not mean that he did not remember the scents of his roses. Presented with the scent of a particular rose, he might immediately recognize it. What is more, the instant he recognized the odour, the name and the image of the particular rose might pop into his head. The grower was simply unable to recall these odours in a clear enough way to employ them in a mnemonic sequence.

This helps make a further point. In assuring us that we are attached to the world, all the senses no doubt play a role. None the less, seeing and hearing seem to be the two senses that most characteristically lend themselves to the sort of mnemonic sequencing essential to recall. Smell, taste, and touch also occur in space and time; yet we do not typically use olfactory images as a means of sequencing our memories. Thus, although we recognize by means of all our senses, we typically recall sights and sounds more easily than smells, tastes, and feels. We can represent visual and acoustic images easily to ourselves, while this is more difficult with the other senses. Our ability to recall and fantasize in spatial and acoustic images (even imagining our own minds as 'places' containing 'ghosts' and 'memories') shows that sensory memory of space and sound is no less conceptual than is our abstract memory of

meanings. Space and sound characterize the world as we represent it to
ourselves in our imagination in a way that smells, tastes, and feels do
not.[7]

Extending the notion of 'conceptual' to include visual and acoustic
images means rejecting a notion that limits the conceptual to ideas that
are semantically organized. In terms of the working of memory, recalled
sensory images are no less conceptual than are semantically organized
concepts. Defining recalled visual and acoustic images as 'concepts'
means returning, in part, to Locke's notion that anything that can be
represented in mind qualifies as an 'idea'. We can accept this as long as
we do not have to accept a 'copy and store' model of either memory or
perception. Memory entails a degree of interpretation. Our memories no
more store little replicas of the outside world made out of mind stuff
than do the backs of our televisions (cf. Marr 1982; Kosslyn 1980).

Remembered visual concepts

We can illustrate the notion of a 'visual concept' with a simple experiment by the art historian Ernst Gombrich. Gombrich asked an eleven-
year-old child to make an exact copy of Constable's *Wivenhoe Park*.
The result was a highly simplified representation. Constable's mottled,
grassy lawn was reduced to a patch of flat green; the delicately toned
clouds were turned into a uniform, light-grey area. The animal and
human figures were either brought forward and drawn disproportionately large, or simply dropped from the picture. Constable's carefully
observed study of nature was thus translated into a set of visual concepts
(Gombrich 1980, facing p. 50).

As a concept, grass is a 'green thing', just as sky is a 'blue thing', and
an apple is a 'red thing'. Empirically, of course, grass, sky, and apples
can be any number of colours. If children usually paint skies blue and
apples bright red, it is not because they suffer faults in their vision or
memory; it is, rather, because it is easier to achieve a recognizable like-
ness by painting the concept.

Similarly, the concept of a human being is of something with legs,
arms, hands, fingers, eyes, ears, nose, hair, etc. Empirically, of course,
human beings are frequently located in our field of vision in such a way
as to make many of these details invisible to us. To a child, however, it

---

[7] Oliver Sacks' *Seeing Voices* (Sacks 1989) presents some marvellous descriptions of the
inner worlds of the congenitally deaf. We do not know if anyone has seriously studied the
possibility of ordering memory by smell and the tactile sense alone (see Baddeley 1976:
262–4, for some experimentation). There is, however, a highly entertaining fictional
account in Patrick Süskind's novel *Perfume* (Süskind 1986).

may seem conceptually incorrect to represent a figure in this way (Piaget and Inhelder 1956). Hence, the figure may be disproportionately enlarged and rotated so as to be frontally presented. This gives the child room to include all the essential details. Where this cannot be done, the figures may be simply ignored.

There is always a tendency towards simplification and schematization in memory. Conceptualization means that memory is stored in some 'conceptual' form, as concepts are easier to remember than full representations. The simplification that results from conceptualization can be drastic. Spatial relations in a visual image are apt to be modified so as to make temporal or logical relations of consequence appear more clearly. Occasionally, the spatial arrangement of the figures in the image is even reconstructed so as to manifest relations of cause and effect that were not originally present.

Bartlett and the 'effort after meaning'
We argued that, in our everyday activities, sensory memory and semantic memory are bound together in a complementary fashion. Using the above idea of a visual concept, we can begin to explore how this takes place.

It is difficult to observe conceptualization in a psychological experiment, for the simple reason that it is much easier to observe and record memory 'coming out' than memory 'going in'. Gombrich's example must stand for an entire class of psychological experiments. Significantly, almost all of these were conducted by psychologists specializing in perception (cf. for example, Allport 1955; Gibson 1950). It is easier to observe perception 'going in' than memory. This suggests that, for the purposes of psychological experiments, memory might be treated as an extension of perception. This approach has its dangers: forgetting, for example, is not really analogous to not perceiving. Still, treating memory on the analogy of perception at least gives some indication of some of the distortions that are likely to arise through conceptualization.

The problem of observing memory both 'going in' and 'coming out' was first tackled by the German psychologist Ebbinghaus in the 1880s. He placed his experimental subjects in complete isolation and made them remember strings of nonsense syllables. In the 1930s the Cambridge psychologist Frederick Bartlett studied Ebbinghaus's experiments. In his opinion, the results, though interesting, were limited. The experiments were too artificial. Ebbinghaus had tried to solve the problem of memory by isolating it as far as possible from its context in daily life; yet, Bartlett argued, the most important feature of memory, in the way we actually use it, is that it is never out of context (Bartlett 1932: 3–5).

Bartlett's point of departure for his own experiments was the French psychologist Binet's notion of a 'governing idea'. Bartlett conceived of memory as an 'effort after meaning', where meaning was attained by sequencing what was to be remembered in a clear, comprehensible, and – consequently – easy-to-remember pattern. Bartlett wished to investigate the ideas that governed the formation of these sequences (see Bartlett 1932, for this and all that follows).

In one experiment, Bartlett showed his subjects five line-drawings depicting military faces, and asked them to commit these faces to memory. As he suspected, the subjects picked out salient features in the drawings – hats, insignia, beards, pipes, etc. – as the 'governing ideas' that helped them sequence their perceptions in memory. In discussing this with his subjects, however, Bartlett discovered that they used a number of other techniques as well. Some of the subjects performed complicated mental operations, rotating or reversing certain images, in order that certain visual patterns would appear more evident. Others invented semantic schemes as *aides-mémoire*. One favourite technique was to 'bring the faces alive', imagining them as real people and inventing little stories about them.

These experiments supported some general observations about the use of memory. The first is that the effort after meaning was both a conscious and an unconscious process. Whether the subject approached the task by consciously devising a strategy, or failed to do so, the fundamental approach was still the same. Subjects always tried to observe a pattern in the material, reduce it to a pattern, or impose a pattern upon it, in order to render it capable of being memorized. In other words, before they could memorize the material, the subjects had to 'map' it out.

The patterns with which the subjects mapped the material were of broadly two sorts – semantic and sensory. Some subjects tended more to project semantic patterns onto the material; others to see visual patterns. No subject, however, remembered in either exclusively semantic or exclusively visual patterns. In fact, most of the patterns themselves were both semantic and visual. Thus, one subject who remembered faces by bringing them alive started by employing a visual strategy. Yet, as she explained to Bartlett, as soon as she had brought the face to life, she would fix it in memory by assigning a name to it. Such 'jumps' between semantic and visual were common and experienced as natural. Subjects invented semantic clues to recall visual images, and used visual images to focus semantic descriptions.

Furthermore, subjects did best when they used a variety of techniques together. No single technique gave consistently successful results, for, as Bartlett was fascinated to discover, subjects tended to be misled by the very techniques they employed. Semantic techniques, recalling the information through a verbal pattern, preserved the information only in the verbal pattern itself. Once the verbal pattern had been formed and committed to memory, the signifier was, so to speak, cut adrift from the signified. This meant that once the sensory information had been verbalized, it was effectively forgotten. Subjects could not check back into their visual memory and perceive mistakes. Significantly, however, this did not mean that verbalized memory was unaccompanied by visual images. Inevitably there was a visual image attached to the verbal clue. What is more, this visual image tended to correspond to this clue, whether or not the verbal clue was mistaken. In other words, Bartlett's subjects frequently found themselves in Goethe's dilemma of having no way of telling whether a remembered visual image was real or fancy.

Visual techniques retained an image that could be introspectively consulted. Thus, visual techniques preserved the information in fuller form. None the less, visual techniques tended to preserve the images in an unstructured form. This made them harder to recall. Nor were visual images free from distortion. Concentrating on an image could not, it seems, really be done without fantasizing about it. Thus, the subjects who brought the faces alive tended to reconstruct their images of these faces according to their imaginations. When Bartlett showed one of his subjects the actual drawing of the face about which she had given a very circumstantial, though inaccurate, account, she thought that he had substituted a new drawing.

Bartlett was intrigued by the way in which semantic memory and visual memory complemented each other, even when both were wrong. He suspected that even when memory seemed semantically organized, there might still be a strong visual component in the experience of remembering itself. Visual memory, he noticed, tended to fix on details, which were remembered accurately, while perspective and relations in the visual field were not. This made him wonder about the effect of these vividly remembered details on semantic memory. He had observed that visual memory compensated for a mistake in the semantic pattern by producing a visual image that confirmed the pattern. Could this work the other way round? Would semantic memory accommodate itself to remembered visual details?

To explore this question, Bartlett devised a rather diabolical experiment. He chose a story and gave it to his subjects to remember. He did not expect his subjects to memorize the entire text; he simply asked them to retell the story in their own words. Typically, the experimental conditions were informal; the subjects seem to have all been his acquaintances. They read the story through twice, and were given time to think about it. Bartlett tested them immediately afterwards, and, thereafter, at irregular intervals depending on when he ran into them (he encountered one subject on the street six years after the test and immediately asked for the story).

What Bartlett did not tell his subjects, but what makes the experiment particularly interesting, is that the story is unintelligible. Bartlett had chosen an American Indian tale recorded by the American anthropologist Franz Boas, entitled 'The War of the Ghosts'. The story, however, had been removed from its context. In Boas's text, it is not at all clear who the ghosts are or whom the war is between. As Bartlett foresaw, the radical ambiguity of the story forced his subjects to intellectualize. In their 'effort after meaning', they were forced to map out the story, prior to remembering it, through providing some interpretation that would render it intelligible.

These interpretations were many and varied. The most common approach was simply to rationalize the ghosts away, interpreting the reference to 'ghosts' as denoting some Native American clan or tribe. Not surprisingly, however, in the Cambridge of the classicists F.L. Cornford and Jane Harrison, a number of bizarrely imaginative interpretations were proffered as well. One subject remembered the story in terms of the ancient Egyptian death ritual. Another rationalized the living characters away, interpreting the story as a nature myth.

Bartlett was interested to confirm his hypothesis that memory conforms to interpretation. When the memory was still fresh, subjects were frequently aware that there were possible discrepancies between the story as they remembered it and their interpretations. Later, though the memory of the interpretation remained, the memory of those parts of the story that did not fit this interpretation tended to fade. Subjects might still remember that the story had been ambiguous; they forgot, however, what, from their perspective, had been the discordant bits.

Bartlett was not, however, interested in his subjects' interpretations as such. The ambiguity of the story had forced them to semanticize their memory of it. Bartlett wondered whether this high level of semanticization would inhibit the formation of visual images. If, as he suspected, it did not, he wondered what sort of role the visual images would play.

Again, Bartlett's choice of text was cunning, for though the story made little sense, it still contained a number of vivid visual images. Bartlett suspected that a remembered visual detail often served as the 'governing idea' for a semantic reconstruction. One cannot observe a visual mnemonic image at the point of articulation; one can only observe it, introspectively, at the level of recall. Thus, Bartlett could confirm his hypothesis only by asking his subjects to discuss their experiences. Bartlett did this, and discovered that, indeed, in a number of cases, a remembered visual image did initiate and govern a remembered chain of semantic association.

Bartlett could conclude that behind memory at the level of articulation, which could only be semantically organized, there was a subjective experience of memory which was less semantic. Although, at the level of recall, the degree of semanticization could vary considerably, it was exceptional that recall would be completely semanticized without any accompanying sensory images. In accounting for the distortions in the content of memory, as observed in articulation, one had to take into account the form in which memory was patterned in each subject's mind. Content and form were complementary: the form into which memory was sequenced reflected the intention of the remembering individual; but this intention was itself formed with reference to the content. Individuals usually were not fully aware of their intentions, however, for it was apparent from the experiments themselves that many of the choices about the form into which the material was patterned were spontaneous – techniques that simply presented themselves when the individual sought to remember.

Culture and the sequencing of memory
Bartlett discovered that the form in which a memory might be sequenced not only was a reflection of content, but was also determined by the intentions and predispositions of the remembering individuals. Different individuals remembered differently, using different details as their governing ideas and differing strategies to memorize them. This brings up a final question. To what extent are the strategies that we, consciously or not, adopt in remembering determined by our culture and our particular education? It seems likely that the forms in which lawyers remember legal documents and painters remember paintings are, to some degree, determined by their professional training. Is it possible to extend this and to contrast the general way in which literate cultures sequence their memories to the way in which non-literate cultures do?

The American philosopher Charles Peirce argued that the state of mind most conducive to creativity was that of 'Musement' or 'Pure Play' (in Sebeok and Umiker-Sebeok 1983: 26). The argument is in the spirit of Montaigne: a powerful, active intellect needs to range freely and widely, and thus be relatively unencumbered with the sort of purely passive knowledge that can be looked up if necessary. We can probably take these observations as personal – Peirce is describing his experience of his own mind – and use them to define what, in the experience of one highly intelligent individual, memory looks like. It is typically abstract, highly semanticized, and structured in a network of causal and logical categories. It is also highly personalized, for individuals are able to order their imaginations to suit their tastes. This structure is also loose and informal. The sequencing techniques employed would permit the maximum possible breadth and the maximum possible freedom of association.

The opposite of this sort of memory might be that of a small, isolated, culturally homogeneous, non-literate group. If the hypothesis is correct, their memory would be less semantic; it would also be thing-orientated and less structured in abstract, logical, and causal connections. Their memory would also be narrower, less personal, and more rigidly sequenced. This, indeed, seems often to be the case.

The Jörai, a small tribal group living in Vietnam, have been studied by the French ethnographer Jacques Dournes (Dournes 1976). Dournes describes the mnemonic culture of the Jörai as not only well organized, but also, indeed, hyperorganized. The discourse of the Jörai is highly conventionalized. There is a great deal of homogeneity in the ideas expressed; unconventional ideas are liable not to be understood at all. Thus, for the Jörai, intelligence is manifested not by enunciating new ideas, but by using the traditional stock of proverbs and sayings in telling ways, and by composing songs whose form and content are strictly governed by tradition.

Dournes analyses the sayings or expressions that make up the better part of Jörai conversation. These are set phrases, made more memorable by assonance and rhythm. The Jörai use a wide range of acoustic resources in these sayings – rhythm, rhyme, assonance, and alliteration. Jörai dialogue consists of exchanges of sayings, one of which may bear a relation of assonance with the next. The highly patterned nature of Jörai conversation does not preclude narrative; but, even here, narrative takes off from the exchange of sayings, with the narrator taking both roles in the conversation, and longer passages of monologues gradually replacing the mimicked dialogue. Auditory sequencing thus plays a strong role in underpinning Jörai social memory. In fact, achieving a pleasing acoustic effect in the exchange of sayings seems to express what Dournes calls the Jörai sense of 'bon ton' in personal relations.

Auditory sequencing is not the only way that the Jörai preserve their social memory; there are conceptual sequences and sequences of images as well. In this way, Jörai social memory seems to be very much predetermined by a set of highly conventionalized mnemotechniques. This makes it particularly interesting that the Jörai deny that they use mnemotechniques at all, or at least attach little importance to them. They are very much aware of using rhythm and assonance in order to make their speech more pleasing to the ears. They do not admit to using these means, however, as a way of fixing the saying in their memories. The very idea seems absurd to them, for what their structured, highly conventional, and acoustically embellished sayings seem to them to express is simply the world as it really is.

The British anthropologist Evans-Pritchard observed of the Azande in Africa that they view their world through a 'web of belief'. They do not see this, however, for they take their perception of the world to be simply a representation of the world as it is. They thus 'cannot get out of the meshes' because they never imagine them to be there in the first place. A Zande does not see tradition as 'an eternal structure'; rather, 'It is the texture of his thought, and he cannot think that his thought is wrong' (Evans-Pritchard 1937: 194; Horton 1967).

Like the Azande, the Jörai do not 'see the meshes'. Like the Babylonian scribes writing in cuneiform, they frequently fail to see that a 'word' is different from a 'thing', and that the order of words is governed by semantics and syntax rather than by the world 'as it really is'. Like Tulving, finally, they fail to understand that what they observe is not necessarily the world as it is, but their own projected concepts. We saw in Bartlett's experiments that individuals 'correct' their sensory memory to conform to their general interpretation, even where this interpretation is wrong. We shall see in later chapters how the coherence and support provided by socially held memories can often be strong enough to override and disguise glaring contradictions between memory and reality.

Of course, none of this is to say that the Jörai have bad memories, or are any less intelligent than we. They simply use their minds in a different way. Dournes emphasizes that the Jörai are remarkably adept at remembering all that they want and need to. They remember, however, in a cultural milieu in which the problem of memory as a source of true knowledge simply could not arise. The problem of the coherency of the world in mind with the world outside mind does not exist for the Jörai.

The Jörai express their own conception of the connectedness of mind and body, and of the person to his or her social milieu, by means of a ceremony. Shortly after birth, a Jörai baby has its senses 'awakened' by blowing over a ginger root into them. As the midwife blows into the ears of the infant, she invokes memory. The senses are each enjoined to 'remember': to remember their work; to remember their teaching; to remember the duties to the family. The senses are thus commanded to 'look sharp', in order to recognize the ideas present in the newborn baby's culture (Dournes 1976: 213–15).

Forgetting

Mary Warnock remarks that memory is the only one of our mental faculties that we accept as working normally when it malfunctions (1987, introduction). The remark is deliberately ironic, yet, like Montaigne's remark on the frequent conjunction of good memory and weak intellect, it goes to the heart of the problem. What philosophical and psychological accounts of memory often overlook is that forgetting is normal. Forgetting is, of course, socially embarrassing at times; yet, as the troubled life of the mnemonist described by the Russian psychologist Luria illustrates, it is far more debilitating never to forget (Luria 1975; cf. Borges 1956: 117–27).

What the purveyors of the '10 Steps to a Powerful Memory'-type literature are thus offering is not a means of insulating us from ever forgetting anything, but rather the traditional techniques whereby the process of remembering and forgetting can be brought under some degree of conscious control. This, as we have seen, is merely an extension of the sorts of conscious techniques we often seek to master to make our memories more efficient in our daily tasks. Yet our conscious control of our memories is never more than partial and limited. Our memory keeps us afloat in our daily lives in ways that we are hardly ever aware of.

Our memories express the connectedness of our minds to our bodies, and our bodies to the social and natural world around us. Yet this continuity is the source of normal forgetfulness as well. If I turn the same light switch on and off four times a day for ten years, I do not retain in my memory an ordered sequence of 4×365×10 separate memory traces; for, in the case of habitual actions, the repetition effaces previous memories. This successive 'blotting out' of repeated instances of habitual events is normal, yet it may also have unexpected results. We do not perceive the changes in the face we see in the same mirror each morning. Yet, if unexpectedly presented with an old photograph, we may be surprised to see how the process of change has crept up on us. We fail to perceive the changes not simply because they are, from day to day, too small to be noticed; the habitual nature of the action blots out our previous memory. Unless there is some special association that causes the memory to stick, we may find that we are simply unable to remember looking at ourselves in the same mirror a month, a year, or ten years ago.

What is true of the memory of individuals is true of social memory as well. Roman Jakobson, in describing the oral transmission of folk-tales, describes how a story, in passing from generation to generation, is successively altered. Yet this process of change may be unsuspected in an oral society itself. Without written records to freeze a version at any stage of transmission, there is no basis for comparison. The version as told by the storyteller seems the same as the version learned by the storyteller many years ago. And this version, in its turn, seems identical to the version first told, many generations ago, when the supposed event was still fresh in everyone's mind. There is no perception of the process of change, for this process obliterates itself in passing (Jakobson and Bogatyrev 1973).

We have tried in this chapter to rescue memory from the problems of the theory of knowledge, so as to reveal its subjective and conceptual character. Memory is ordered not like a physical text, but, for all the difficulties that may ensue from acknowledging this, like thinking itself. It is not a passive receptacle, but instead a process of active restructuring, in which elements may be retained, reordered, or suppressed. In the next chapter we shall look at how this process works.

2
The Ordering and Transmission of Social Memory

> A fellow of the King's whose head was a storehouse of the storied verse, whose tongue gave gold to the language of the treasured repertory, wrought a new lay made in the measure.
>
> The man struck up, found the phrase, framed rightly the deed of Beowulf, drove the tale, rang word-changes. He chose to speak first of Sigemund, sang the most part of what he had heard of that hero's exploits.
>
> *Beowulf* (lines 866–75)
> (trans. Alexander 1966: 52–3)

Oral memory

The memory of words

The song of the 'fellow of the King's' extolling 'the deed of Beowulf' seems spontaneous: the words just come to him. The warriors are riding back from the mere where the monster Grendel has died from the wound inflicted by Beowulf. They are happy, and as they race their horses over flat stretches, Beowulf's deed is 'much spoken of'. 'Many said' that 'no other man beneath sky's shifting excelled Beowulf.' It is almost a description of a crowd walking home after a game. Suddenly, one of the men, someone clearly well known for versification and song, 'struck up'. He 'wrought a new lay' in praise of Beowulf's deed, comparing it to the deeds of the great heroes of yore.

Compare this picture with the romantic image of the nineteenth-century *poète maudit* in his garret. The self-conscious and rather anti-social activity of a literary poet stands in contrast to the easy sociability of the illiterate Anglo-Saxon *scop*. Yet this contrast is misleading. The skills of traditional poets in non-literate societies were underpinned by knowledge, practice, and, in many cases, intensive formal training. Lacking the capacity to order his words in writing, the poet had to carry out oral composition in his mind: the only space available to shape the words was his own skull. To acquire these techniques, the oral poet trained his memory.

In principle, scholars have always been aware of the special character of poetry in non-literate society. They knew that an Anglo-Saxon *scop*, like the comparable figures in other 'heroic' cultures, was a master of the word hoard. He was also a master of 'measure', capable of improvising a poem within whatever metre, rhyme scheme, or pattern of assonance and alliteration the traditional culture demanded. Yet, tied as they were to their own text-based habits, scholars before Parry (and many after him) failed to perceive any real difference between a *scop*'s use of the language and measure of heroic verse and that of, say, Tennyson: it was really only a matter of style. They thus failed to understand that metre and the auditory structure in general of many types of oral poetry, along with their repetitive, formulaic nature, were not merely stylistic conventions, but also functioned to provide the regularities which helped the poet remember.

The insight that the structure of oral poetry reflected the need for an oral reciter to remember came from the American Homeric scholar Milman Parry in the 1920s. Before Parry, the 'Homeric question' had been a scholarly argument over how the supposed 'text' or 'texts' of the Homeric poems fitted together. Parry cut through these problems by arguing that it was not a question of one or many texts underlying Homer, for, in reality, there were no texts at all. Instead of texts, there had been recitals – moments when the stories of the Trojan war and of Odysseus's return were sung by poets (Parry 1971; Lord 1960).[1]

Parry and his followers pointed out that oral poetry is typically performed in a set and traditional auditory structure. 'Auditory' here stands for anything – metre, cadence, rhyme, assonance, alliteration, performance style – that may affect the sound of the poem as speech. The formality of the auditory structure helps an oral poet remember and compose by allowing him to 'feel' the shape of the cadence that he is about to fill even before he chooses his words. An oral poet thus knows the shape of his verse before he begins to recite it. This, in its turn,

---

[1] Our descriptions of oral poetry, it should be stressed, specifically relate to epic verse; there are other types of oral poetry that are much more stable than Parry and Lord recognized, sometimes even consisting of (usually relatively short) composed and remembered texts. See Turville-Petre 1976; Finnegan 1988: 86–109; and, for a relatively stable epic tradition in India, Smith 1977.

influences the choice of words themselves. As Parry wrote of the Homeric poems, the choice of words and word-forms depends upon the shape of hexameter verse (Parry 1971: xix). This means that the poet must have at his disposal a vast stock of ready-made phrases. Many of these words and word-forms are, in their turn, parts of stock formulae and epithets. Many are metrical variations of names of things and simple expressions, allowing the poet to place a name or specific reference wherever he wants in the hexameter. A mastery of these formulae allowed the preliterate Greek poet to knit his hexameter together semantically without falling into metrical difficulties.

These formulae exist on a larger scale as well. Not only does the oral poet have a large stock of synonyms and epithets; he has a stock of longer phrases too. Though our text of *Beowulf* was certainly reworked at the stage in which it was committed to writing, it still betrays its preliterate origins; many of its half-lines can be matched, wholly or in part, by half-lines existing elsewhere in our – comparatively meagre – corpus of Anglo-Saxon verse (Magoun 1953). These half-lines represent standard ways of describing a character, introducing a scene, or carrying forward the action. As Parry's student, Albert Lord, pointed out, these formulae are, in their turn, grouped around larger themes – the warrior's challenge, the fight, the council, etc. – whose pattern of action is, itself, standardized (Lord 1960: 68–98).

The result is an underlying structure which provides the singer with clues, helping him to remember and compose. There is an internal pattern of assonance which, allied to the poet's feel for cadence, gives him a clue to what must come next in the poetic line. In association with metre and the pattern of assonance, there is also a principle of attraction of words to other words, or phrases to other phrases. This, too, provides mnemonic clues that facilitate composing. Tied to this, finally, is the pattern of succession of units of meaning. In oral poetry, metrical units correspond to syntactic units: each completed stanza, or each completed line, corresponds to a unit of meaning. Therefore, from the smallest poetic units to the largest, from the basic auditory structure to the syntax and the structure of meaning, the form of poetry in oral societies is ordered so as continually to provide the reciting poet with signposts showing him the way to proceed.

The above passage from *Beowulf* portrays this process of composition. The *scop* is extemporizing a 'new lay'. Although this 'new lay' may have been improvised on the spot, it was largely made up of tried and true formulae. The song was 'made in the measure' and 'framed rightly'. The poet 'rang word-changes'. This is a description of oral composition. But in what sense is it also a description of the *scop* remembering? The training in rhyme and metre, the knowledge of words and stories, help the poet compose his poem. How do they help him remember it? What did the poem 'look like' inside the poet's memory?

The question is clearest in the case of Homer. His verse is complex; it is richer and more polished than Anglo-Saxon poetry. Although the Homeric poems seem to possess many of the characteristics of oral verse, it has appeared impossible to many scholars that these poems could be nothing more than rough improvisations. Could it not be that, if not the entire poems, at least large sections of them, were committed to memory and transmitted verbatim from one generation of *rhapsodes* to the next?

The objection to this is not that memorizing the *Iliad* and the *Odyssey* was a task beyond anyone's mnemonic powers. It is a difficult task, but one that was regularly accomplished by professional reciters in the classical period. The objection is, rather, that, until the poem had been written down, no one would have known for sure whether a particular recital was a verbatim repetition of an earlier one or not.

This may seem an odd objection. We have a clear idea of what verbatim repetition entails. We also have written texts for reference, however; and that is the difference. Without the control of a written text, it is difficult, in the event of doubt, to establish what the 'original' was. There is only memory to go on. Literacy helps create the idea of a written text as a copy, in written form, of speech. It is this idea of written text that provides us with our particular notion of the original and authoritative point of reference. Without the idea of a written text, the idea of the verbatim repetition of a recital will always remain extremely vague. It is this that makes it unlikely that large sections of Homeric 'text' were ever memorized and transmitted in preliterate Greece.

To test this hypothesis, Parry and Lord taped, or had copied out, the performances of Serbo-Croat epic singers (Lord 1960). They discovered that although the singers frequently insisted that they had not changed a word between one performance and the next, the transcribed tapes showed otherwise: invariably there were numerous changes. The singers' knowledge and skill were such as to enable them to 'generate' a poem upon a specific subject. They did not memorize a text, but recomposed an epic tale in a way which, though very similar, was never identical to an earlier version.

In the last chapter, we compared semantic memory with visual memory. Parry's theory allows us to extend the discussion to include auditory memory as well. The mnemonic skills of an oral poet are comparable with those of a classical orator trained in the memory of

places. The difference, of course, is that classical mnemotechnology was based on the *eye*, while the skills of oral poets are based on the *ear*. Parry's work and that of his many followers illuminate, in fact, a general, and very important, network of connections between sound and memory. The skills of oral poets derive from a perception of speech not as sight, but as sound. Metre is an auditory pattern imposed on speech. Before metre can be exploited in the composition of poetry, however, the presence of auditory regularities in speech must first be recognized and understood. Poets can compose in metre because they can 'hear' speech as abstract sound, and imagine the various patterns into which this sound may be arranged.

This internal 'hearing' presupposes the conceptualization of speech as sound. This form of conceptualization does not lead to an intuition of language as text. None the less, it still forms the basis of very effective mnemonic techniques. The lack of a visual conception of language helps explain why the memory of language in preliterate cultures is so rarely verbatim and decontextualized. The presence of an auditory intuition of language, however, explains why preliterate cultures sometimes are able to remember so much. Preliterate cultures commit to memory poetry, as well as prayers, incantations, and ritual formulae that are often structured like poetry, and, indeed, examples of prose such as lineages, dynastic lists, titles, and even legal codes (cf. for example, Duverdier 1971).

The ability of a society to transmit its social memory in logical and articulate form is thus not dependent on the possession of writing. The question is far more complex. The transmission of articulate memory depends, in a more general sense, upon the way in which a culture represents language to itself. It depends on the extent to which a society can perceive language as a vehicle of expression and communication independent of immediate social context. It depends also on the group's conception of the knowledge it remembers: does it regard this knowledge as images or texts to be analysed, or merely as sequenced patterns of sound to be committed to memory? These are all capacities that vary considerably from group to group (and from individual to individual). Certain oral societies, such as the preliterate Greeks and Polynesians, or the Celtic tribes of north-western Europe at the time of the Roman conquest, possessed a highly developed auditory intuition. These societies were capable of accomplishing remarkable mnemonic tasks. Not coincidentally, these societies possessed highly developed poetic traditions.

For this reason, it seems misleading to make the difference between preliterate and literate cultures stand for the distinction between

'prelogical' and 'rational' mentalities, as writers even now sometimes do. Describing the activity of oral poets as 'prelogical' simply obscures a perfectly rational process whereby they are able to conceptualize language as both sense and sound, and use these intuitions as the basis of their poetic skills. Indeed, one can go further. Not only does this argument obscure the element of rationality in preliterate memory, but it also obscures the element of continuity between the mnemonic habits of preliterate cultures and our own. The mere fact that a society has acquired the ability to represent its knowledge in written forms does not mean that that society has ceased to be an oral culture as well. We remain an oral society, and the ways in which we pattern our social memory continue to reflect, albeit in altered forms, the same practices and thought processes of preliterate cultures. Writing may absolve us of the need to learn complex mnemotechniques; it does not absolve us of the need to speak.

What kind of memory, then, does Parry's account describe? Certainly, a very agile one: in the Parry theory, memory is active. An oral poet does not 'read' a 'text' stored in memory, but creates it as he goes along. In the epic singer's mind are not entire texts, but lines, images, stanzas, formulae, themes – the stock in trade of the poetic craft. There are stories as well, along with the images and ideas, that define and characterize these stories. The *Iliad* is a story of the fall of Troy; before a poet can improvise an epic on this theme, he must know the story. The 'singer' must put this all together: small pieces – such as stock phrases and line fillers – fitting into larger units – such as motifs, stock situations, acoustic and visual images – and finally emerging as a structured and ordered story.

This is what oral memory 'does'. What, however, does it 'look like'? How does the 'memory' of a story differ from the poem as realized in performance, or on the printed page? We saw in the last chapter that, characteristically, we memorize by conceptualizing. Our memories hold concepts rather than sense data. We need now to examine what these concepts are made of: how they are structured, and how they are ordered in memory. We have already seen that memory can be examined only after it has 'come out'. The relation between memory as internal representation and memory as articulated representation is always difficult to determine. In this respect, however, the Parry theory is extremely helpful; for, in describing the relation between the memory of the epic poet and the recited poem, the theory provides an insight on the internal structure of memory. More than that, however, the theory provides an insight on the transmission of memory as well. What is transmitted, as the poem passes from one reciter to the next, is not so

much text, but, rather, an idea of the story along with certain of the images and phrases that accompany it. It follows that reconstructing the actual process of transmission, while observing what is retained, what is added, and what is dropped, is one way of discovering the shape and structure of an idea in memory.

Images and memory

A memory can be social only if it is capable of being transmitted, and, to be transmitted, a memory must first be articulated. Social memory, then, is articulate memory. Articulation does not always imply articulation in speech. Jan Vansina, among others, has shown how a great deal of African social memory is preserved in rituals; here the meaning is not put into words, but is acted out (1955). We transmit manual skills more by showing how than by explaining how; much of our memory of gesture and bodily movement is articulated non-verbally (Connerton 1989). Still, the importance of articulation puts a premium on words, and, in this chapter, we shall look at social memory in the form of narrative.

Does the importance of communication mean that social memory is more semantic than individual memory? It is, after all, easier to communicate a semantic message than a sensory image. In fact, however, the need to communicate does not reduce the sensory quality of social memory at all. We saw that an oral poet's memory of the poem as sense – that is, as telling a certain story – was not separated from that poet's memory of the poem as sound. Sensory and semantic were interlocked in his memory. We also saw in Bartlett's experiment that visual images usually accompany semantic memory, and that the interpretations offered by his subjects were often founded on remembered sensory images. This is no less true of memories which are collectively held; they, too, are patterned in ways that are both semantic and sensory. Thus, as in the case of individual memory, the images held in social memory are composite: they are composed from a mixture of pictorial images and scenes, slogans, quips and snatches of verse, abstractions, plot types and stretches of discourse, and even false etymologies.

Social memory is thus not limited to the memory of words. The higher level of articulation necessary in social memory does not make it more semantic than individual memory. It does, however, make it more conceptualized. Images can be transmitted socially only if they are conventionalized and simplified: conventionalized, because the image has to be meaningful for an entire group; simplified, because in order to be generally meaningful and capable of transmission, the complexity of the image must be reduced as far as possible. Individual memories include remembered personal experience, much of which is difficult to articulate. Thus, the images in any individual's memory will be richer than collective images, which will be, by comparison, more schematic. None the less, this schematization does not require a loss of the images' sensory quality: the images and ideas of social memory still retain a composite semantic and sensory character.

We saw an example of this composite character in the discussion of ancient mnemotechniques (above, p. 12). In our example, the orator was advised to remember the presence of a witness (Latin: *testis*) by incorporating a pair of ram's testicles into the scene. The connection between the particular image and what it refers to is here largely fortuitous: there is no conceptual relationship between the two – just a similarity of sound. This, however, has no effect on the effectiveness of the image as a mnemonic aid. In fact, the fortuitous connections between the mnemonic images and the ideas they represented probably simplified the orator's task. The images were no more than signposts, and the best images were those that point to their meanings by the fastest possible route. Beyond serving as signposts, these images had no further function, and no meanings in themselves.

This brings out a point that is very simple, but easy to overlook: concepts are not like material objects. An image held in memory is a concept; as such, it interacts with other concepts in a conceptual, rather than in a concrete fashion. A relation between concepts can be established on any basis, however fortuitous or eccentric, for the relations between concepts in our minds need not reflect relations in the world. In so far as memory is conceptual, then, it does not make the slightest difference whether its concepts are sequenced so as to reflect real links between real things or only imaginary ones.

This arbitrariness in the relation between images in memory and the meanings to which they are connected is not, however, of itself apparent. There is nothing in the remembered image itself that informs us whether or not it refers to something real or something imaginary. Thus, Goethe was unsure of the real source of his vivid childhood recollection. Normally, of course, we assume that our memories are real. We assume, that is, that if we retain images of events in our past, these images refer to, and even directly derive from, a real event. If we have a memory of an event, then that event happened: we could hardly think otherwise.

This assumption may be generally valid with regard to our personal memory; here, we usually, though not always, have means of contextualizing isolated memories in other memories. This usually allows us to go back to the circumstances to which the memory is connected. This is not so easy in the case of social memory, however. Here, the images often refer to circumstances that we have not witnessed ourselves, and, thus, we have no means of recovering these circumstances by contextualizing the images in other memories. We shall see that the images of social memory are comparatively 'disembodied'. They are often decontextualized, and, in a radical sense, we may have no real way of knowing whether they refer to something real or something imaginary. Of course, the normal assumption will continue to be made: members of any given social group will imagine that if their tradition preserves the memory of a certain event, then that event must have happened. Yet the group is merely assuming that their traditions must refer to something real; they have no way of knowing that this is so.

The relation between a remembered image and the meaning or event to which this image supposedly refers is inherently arbitrary; yet, nothing in the nature of the remembered images themselves gives this away. We saw in Bartlett's experiment that all of his subjects employed associative strategies for fixing the material to be remembered in their minds, but that these subjects were only partially aware of using such strategies. Some associations just seem to arise spontaneously. This, of course, happens to everyone. We shall find that in articulating traditions concerning the past, social memory, groups may sometimes assert very odd connections. Were we to assume that all traditions must have some real, tangible basis, we might arrive at some bizarre reconstructions of the histories of these groups.

Narrative and memory
The twelfth-century abbot, Suger of Saint-Denis, observed, in a famous verse: '*Mens hebes ad verum per materialia surgit*' (cited in Panofsky 1970: 164). The sense is that uncultivated minds rise to truth through the help of concrete images. This idea was a commonplace in medieval writing,[2] and reflected the consciously didactic intent in much of the visual arts of the period. Etienne Gilson has described the techniques used in a medieval sermon (1932). The central images were drawn from sacred scripture, and this automatically gave these images authority. These

[2] Panofsky further comments that the passage is 'nothing but a metrical condensation of John the Scot's "impossibile est nostro animo ad immaterialem ascendere caelestium hierarchiarum et imitationem et contemplationem nisi ea, quae secundum ipsum est, materiali manuductione utatur" ("it is impossible for our mind to rise to the imitation and contemplation of the celestial hierarchies unless it relies upon that material guidance which is commensurate to it.")' (1970: 165). The imagery goes back to Gregory the Great; see further on the issue Kessler 1985, who develops the sixth-century context.

images were fixed in the listener's mind by rendering them as vivid, even as gruesome, as possible. A medieval sermon was like a fresco or a stained-glass window: it taught through a succession of visual images.

Thus, we can take the reference to *materialia* as indicating primarily visual images – either in the strict sense of paintings, sculpture, and stained glass, or, as in a medieval sermon, as verbal descriptions of scenes and events. In either case, the visual effect of the images was heightened as far as possible, either by the skill of the artists or by the skill of the speaker. The images themselves were signposts, constructed with the precise purpose of guiding the 'sluggish of mind' to higher 'truth'. The *verum* in this case is Christian doctrine as expressed in sacred narrative, for, as Gurevič has observed, the medieval church consistently expounded its doctrines and teachings in the form of stories (1986: 8).

This illuminates an important connection between visual imagery and narrative. A story can be depicted or mimed. The story may be heightened by accompanying visual or auditory images, or by the performance of the narrator. Yet a story needs to be nothing more than plain words. As recounted, a narrative is primarily a story in words. Does it follow that narrative memory consists of nothing more than plain words as well? Medieval practice indicates otherwise. The church's use of visual images to fix sacred narrative in the minds of the laity shows that, for the church at least, images and stories went together. This attitude was typical. In folk-tales, in oral poetry, and, more generally, in situations where knowledge is transmitted in an informal and predominantly oral setting, narrative often moves through a succession of visual images. Thus, visual imagery is one aspect of narrative memory.

What, then, is the role that the memory of words plays in the memory of stories? In simplest terms, it is that of ordering and connecting the images. In this sense, a story is a sort of natural container for memory; a way of sequencing a set of images, through logical and semantic connections, into a shape which is, itself, easy to retain in memory. A story is thus a large-scale *aide-mémoire*. We do not, of course, learn stories in this way. We rarely, in fact, 'learn' stories in a conscious fashion at all; we simply listen to them or read them. We also make them up about ourselves and about others. In this sense, stories appear to us as just a natural way of thinking about things, a way of ordering our knowledge (or our castles in the air), and representing them in our minds.

The fact that we assimilate stories so readily, accepting them as representations of reality (even when we know that they are fictions), renders their function as containers of memories all but imperceptible. When we listen to a story, or when we fantasize, memory is just there. We rarely need to make an effort. Yet the function of memory in stories is all the more important for being so largely invisible. Stories do more than represent particular events: they connect, clarify, and interpret events in a general fashion. Stories provide us with a set of stock explanations which underlie our predispositions to interpret reality in the ways that we do. As we shall see in the last chapter, memory is not merely retrospective; it is prospective as well. Memory provides a perspective for interpreting our experiences in the present and for fore-seeing those that lie ahead.

Thus, images and words are two of the most important components in our memories of narrative. Of course, they are two components that work together, for, as we saw in Bartlett's experiment, we are rarely conscious of the distinction between semantic and sensory in the every-day use of our memories. Still, for the purposes of illustration, it will be helpful to separate them to some extent, considering sensory memory in narrative first, and logical and semantic memory second. We can begin with an example in which the relation of visual images to the story itself is particularly clear and well defined, the medieval epic of Roland; for our discussions of 'logical' memory, we shall turn to fairy tales.

Narrative memory

Roland

We know little concerning the background and composition of *La Chanson de Roland*, *The Song of Roland*. Our earliest text probably dates from the closing years of the eleventh century, three centuries after the events it purports to describe, and we do not know how much this text represents a transcription of an oral performance and how much a writ-ten composition. The composition, however, in whatever case, certainly reflects oral practices, and for this reason little hangs on the question for our purposes here (see further below, p. 158). Our written text probably represents the last stage of a long chain of oral transmission. The composition of the poem betrays this: it is intended for an audience of listeners, not readers.[3]

---

[3] See ch. 4, n. 8, for editions, translations, and commentaries on the poem, and also the next note. Here, all translations are our own. Our treatment of the poem is indebted to Auerbach's discussion of the 'figure' in Dante, and in medieval literature in general (Auerbach, 1953).

By the middle of the poem, Roland and his men have been ambushed by a vast Saracen force at the pass of Roncevaux. Although they fight valiantly, repeatedly putting the Saracens to flight, they are hopelessly outnumbered. By *laisse* (stanza) 163, the only French remaining on the field are Roland and Archbishop Turpin. Roland, himself wounded, carries the body of his friend Oliver to the archbishop to be shriven. The archbishop, however, is himself wounded; when he attempts to fetch water in Roland's horn, the effort is too much for him. He collapses and dies. The death of the archbishop sets the scene for the description of Roland's own death.

Roland, wounded and exhausted, takes his horn Oliphant and his sword Durendal and, walking in the direction of Spain, mounts a hill where stand a tall tree and four marble stones. Here he faints. A Saracen, feigning death amidst the other bodies, arises and tries to despoil Roland of his armour and sword. Roland opens his eyes and, discovering the Saracen stealing his sword, rises up to strike and kill him. Yet Roland is growing steadily weaker, and has now lost his sight. He manages to struggle to his feet and vainly seeks to smash his sword against the stones, all the while praising it for the victories it has won and the relics it contains.

At *laisse* 174, Roland feels the approach of death. He goes to a pine tree, and kneels beneath it, with his sword and Oliphant. He beats his chest, praying God to forgive him his sins. He extends his right hand to God, and then lets it fall. God sends His angels to carry him to paradise.

The action itself can be quickly summarized; yet, like the heroes and heroines of grand opera, Roland takes his time in dying – 138 lines to be exact. It is the climax of the poem, and the 'author' – the enigmatic Turoldus of the final line – draws it out for all it is worth. Employing a variety of poetic and rhetorical devices, he shapes the death of Roland into a sequence of sharply focused and vivid images.

The language is often formulaic, sometimes in the strict sense of the Parry theory, with pat epithets that seem to serve as line-fillers. On other occasions, *The Song of Roland* employs a another auditory device, typical of oral poetry – making the first line, or lines, in a *laisse* echo the last line, or lines, of the preceding one. This connects the two verses acoustically, though not semantically; it does not, in other words, establish any sense of continuity between the two *laisses*. The echoing of the end of one verse by the beginning of the next may thus only help to fix a certain verse order in the narrator's memory.

A number of typically oral devices, such as line-filling epithets and assonance between *laisses*, can therefore be found in the poem, and these no doubt formed part of the mnemonic armature of the poem at an oral stage. None the less, the instances of repeated lines or half-lines do not always seem to be vestiges of oral composition. Many séem to be functioning more as part of a technique of emphasis through echoing. There are many examples of this in the poem, especially in the more dramatic moments. Here their function seems rhetorical.

As is normal in oral poetry, metric units in *The Song of Roland* correspond to units of sense. Each unit conveys its own image, and each image is free-standing. There is no syntactic connection between units; thus, there is little way that the poet can indicate a logical or causal relation between one unit and the next. In this context, the rhetoric of repetition can even substitute to some degree for the missing syntax. It cannot establish specifically syntactic connections between the images; it can, however, throw certain images into relatively high relief.

There are a number of examples of rhetoric taking on the task of syntax. Instead of echoing the last verse of a preceding *laisse*, the poem often establishes a connection by echoing successive first verses. Thus, the scene of Roland's death begins, in *laisse* 168, with line 2259: '*Ço sent Rollant que la mort li est pres*' (Now Roland feels that death is near to him). This is echoed in the first verse of *laisse* 170: '*Ço sent Rollant que s'espee li tolt*' (Now Roland feels that his sword is taken from him); in *laisse* 171: '*Ço sent Rollant la veue ad perdue*' (Now Roland feels that his sight is lost); in *laisse* 174: '*Ço sent Rollant que la mort le tresprent*' (Now Roland feels that death is passing through him); in *laisse* 175: '*Ço sent Rollant de sun tens n'i ad plus*' (Now Roland feels that his time is up). Here the echoing has a clear, rhetorical effect. Roland collapses in a succession of stop-action images. The formulaic 'Now Roland feels ...' marks off each successive stage. The use of this formulaic language may still be mnemonic; but it is mnemonic less in helping the singer to remember as he improvises, than in fixing the images in the memories of his audience.

Thus the repeated opening, '*Ço sent Rollant ...*', serves as a signpost, introducing images of Roland's progressive collapse. None the less, these images are not always sequential. Sometimes the action is repeated. Thus, '*Ço sent Rollant ...*' in *laisse* 171 introduces the image of Roland striking the stone with his sword. This action is repeated in *laisse* 172, and again in 173. This repetition is itself marked by echoes in the opening verses of these two *laisses*: '*Rollant ferit el perrun de sardonie ...*' (Roland strikes the stone of sardonyx ... 172); and '*Rollant ferit en une perre bise ...*' (Roland strikes upon the grey stone ... 173). The effect is not to carry the action forward, but to telescope scenes, and scenes within scenes. The technique is cinematographic: the repeated '*Ço sent Rollant ...*' passages mark the changes of shot, while the two

'*Rollant ferit* ...' passages introduce changes of camera angle within the same shot. The full effect of these stop-action images is achieved at the beginning of *laisse* 177, where the formula is suddenly varied: '*Morz est Rollant, Deus en ad l'anme es cels*' (Dead is Roland. God has his soul in Heaven).

This technique of using repeated lines to frame dramatically repeated images of action occurs especially in the central section devoted to the battle: in *laisses* 83 to 85, Oliver entreats Roland three times to blow his horn; in *laisses* 129 to 131, Roland proposes the same thing to himself three times. He blows the horn repeatedly in *laisses* 133 to 135. These triple repetitions do not move the story along: quite the contrary, they stop the action. In doing so, however, they heighten the impact. Just as in a medieval sermon, or in a scene in a stained-glass window, they focus attention. The technique of intercutting long shots and close-ups, and signalling changes of shot and camera angle through the rhetorical use of repeated phrases, is reminiscent of Eisenstein's *Battleship Potemkin*, or televised football.

The images of Roland at the point of death are highly dramatic. He extends his gloved hand, commending himself to God. The archangel Gabriel takes the glove. Then, joining his hands in a gesture of reverence, Roland lets his head fall upon his arms. Cherubin and St Michael arrive to join Gabriel. The three of them then take Roland's soul to paradise. The two *laisses* that describe this scene are clearly describing a succession of poses. The succession, however, is not described in strictly chronological order in the verses themselves. *Laisse* 175 finishes in lines 2373–4 as Roland extends his right glove to God, and angels descend. *Laisse* 176, however, jumps backwards and starts with Roland extending himself under the pine. The *laisse* then has him recall his past, and, once again, beg for God's mercy. Only in line 2389 does Roland, once again, extend his right glove to God. This time, Gabriel is not made to descend again: he is already waiting to accept Roland's glove. This allows the poem to move to the next pose – that of Roland with his hands joined and his head collapsed on his arms.

The poem narrates the death of Roland purely as a succession of images. Erich Auerbach describes this sort of succession in the roughly contemporary *Chanson de Alexis*. Each image, he observes, 'contains one decisive gesture with only a loose temporal or causal connection with those that follow or precede. [...] Every picture has as it were a frame of its own. Each stands by itself in the sense that nothing new or unexpected happens in it and that it contains no propulsive force which demands the next. And the intervals are empty.' (1953: 115).

The technical term for this type of narrative is 'paratactic'. In paratactic narrative, the images are only strung together like beads on a string. They succeed each other in a rough temporal order (Bauml 1980). There is little or no syntactical connection between one image and the next, and often, as is frequently the case in *Roland*, none even between lines within the *laisse*. The syntactic simplicity of paratactic narrative made it an appropriate vehicle for oral poetry. The poet could concentrate on generating a succession of images, which he endeavoured to render brilliant and striking, without having to embed these images in a syntax which articulated logical and causal relations.

What exactly is *The Song of Roland* about, and why is it told in the manner in which it is? Were it an account of a real eighth-century battle at Roncevaux, the answer to this last question would be 'this was the way that things actually happened'. Were *Roland* instead a story entirely invented by a poet, the answer would be 'this is the way the author wanted to narrate them'. In the present case, however, neither answer would be correct. *The Song of Roland* tells the story neither of a real event, nor of a fiction that simply came out of the storyteller's head. The poem instead narrates a tradition that, in some form, had been transmitted orally for centuries. In this sense, the poem refers to a collective memory.

By the twelfth century, the story of Roland was already traditional, widely known, and accepted as a true account (see below, p. 159). The poem thus refers to a traditional story of Roland as it had been remembered and transmitted orally. The poem's audiences accepted the lack of syntactic articulation in the poem, partly, no doubt, because they were accustomed to this as a narrative technique. In any case, the lack of syntax would hardly trouble them, as they knew the story anyway, and could reconstruct the relations of cause and effect through their own memory of it. This is an important point. The extremely low level of syntactic articulation, together with the extremely high level of rhetorical heightening, makes sense if we regard the poem as reminding the audience, in ways pleasing both to the ears and to the imagination, of a story they already knew.

A twelfth-century audience would probably have regarded the story as true, and would have accepted any narration as correct so long as it kept to the outline of the story as they remembered it – Ganelon's betrayal, Roland's death, and Charlemagne's revenge. The audience would, no doubt, have been familiar with some of the details as well – the friendship of Roland and Oliver, the blowing of the horn, the striking of the rock – and would have expected these to be included in any narration as well. We have no way of knowing all the images and themes associated with the story of Roland in oral tradition, but it seems probable that among the most important of these were those images that our text takes special care to underline through the rhetorical device of threefold repetition.

The triple repetition allows the audience to linger over these images. The device is thus not mnemonic in the sense that it helps the audience remember previously unknown images; rather, it is mnemonic in the sense that it enables the audience to visualize a remembered detail of the story in a vivid way. Saying that the images that comprise the story of Roland are remembered images is also to say that they are conceptualized images. Although the audience may have believed that they were hearing a description of real events, what the audience was remembering were merely their own memories, brought to life in poetry. The fact that the point of reference of the poem was not real happenings but conceptualized memories helps explain the occasionally striking lack of 'realism' in the story itself.

We have seen that the images of Roland follow a temporal sequence. The reason for this is mainly simplicity: a more complex sequence would have needed the addition of syntax. Despite this temporal simplicity, however, there are any number of examples of the poem's violation of the principle of strict chronology. Does Roland really blow the horn Oliphant three times? Does he really strike the stones with Durendal three times? Although, in all such cases, the poem describes the action three times, the effect is not of succession but rather of superimposition.

Like the sudden jump backwards at the moment of Roland's death, the departures from strict temporality of these images can be explained as enriching an image by repeating it. Yet this technique might be confusing if the audience did not already know what these images were. *Laisse* 87 opens with the line, *'Rollant est proz e Oliver est sage'*, which can be translated as Roland is 'valorous' or 'worthy' while Oliver is 'wise' or 'experienced'. Yet nothing in the poem so far justifies such a contrast. Roland and Oliver have so far been presented as equal paragons of knightly virtue. Indeed, *laisse* 87 continues by making just this point: saying that Roland and Oliver are equally brave, valorous, and lofty in speech.

The meaning of the contrast is, however, clear in narrative context. In *laisses* 84, 85, and 86 Oliver has entreated Roland to blow his horn and Roland has refused. The audience knows well what the consequences of this refusal will be. When *laisse* 87 starts with *'Rollant est proz e Oliver est sage*' no listener could have doubted the meaning of the contrast. With respect to forthcoming events, which the audience foresees, Roland has been rash to refuse his friend's wise counsel.[4]

The contrast of '*proz*' to '*sage*' was probably traditional in the story of Roland by the time the poem was composed. Roland and Oliver are linked in the memory of the story, and the '*proz*'/'*sage*' contrast was probably also remembered as a tag. In whatever case, this contrast certainly passed into the memory of Roland afterwards. From Ariosto to de Vigny, no later treatment fails to dwell on the rashness of Roland and the prudence of Oliver.

Not all the departures from strict temporality can therefore be attributed to rhetorical heightening. Some represent the characters in ways that are, strictly speaking, inappropriate. Again, we must understand these discrepancies from the perspective of an audience which already knows the story. Early in the poem, Ganelon proposes to Charlemagne that Roland take the rearguard. Charlemagne reacts fiercely and reproaches Ganelon for this, saying: '*Vos estes vifs diables. El cors vos est entree mortel rage*'. (You are a living devil. Into your heart has entered mortal rage.) Charlemagne, however, has no reason to suspect Ganelon of treachery at this point. If he did so, moreover, it seems strange that, having reproached Ganelon, he did not reject his treacherous suggestion as well. Instead he accepts it, as does Roland, though both, somehow, seem to know that the proposal will lead to fatal consequences.

Thus, Charlemagne seems to have foreknowledge; yet he does nothing. He behaves like this on a number of occasions. During the battle, which is fought as he is leading the main body of the army back over the mountains, Charlemagne is represented as continually on the point of turning back with the main French force to save Roland. He never does, but rather remains in an indecisive posture throughout the battle scene, arriving punctually in the verse that follows Roland's death.

The behaviour of Charlemagne has often troubled commentators; yet it is not to be explained by any weakness in his character. It is the *audience* that already know that Ganelon's proposal conceals treachery; they also already know that Charlemagne will not arrive in time to save Roland. The inexplicable behaviour on the part of Charlemagne thus does not display foreknowledge on his part, but on the part of the audience.

As we shall see in chapter 4, the character of Charlemagne as

[4] This is the traditional interpretation, and one which we continue to accept. It has, however, been contested, most recently by Brault (1978: e.g., 179–86) and Cook (1987), who maintain that there is a positive side to Roland's refusal to blow the horn.

portrayed in *The Song of Roland* does not conserve the memory of a real, historical person. What the twelfth-century French knew about Charlemagne, they knew in large part in relation to their memory of the story of Roland. In the context of this story, their memory would be governed by the precise role that Charlemagne plays. This role is to arrive too late, to display unbridled grief at the death of the twelve peers, and to wreak terrible vengeance on the traitor Ganelon. As long as Charlemagne acts in a way consistent with this role, the audience will perceive him as acting in character. This is true even when he acts 'in character' before the events in the plot have made such action appropriate.

We saw in the first chapter that there exists a 'reversion to the conceptual' in memory. Constable's sky and fields were reduced to concept-signs: flat green grass, flat blue sky, flat white splodges for clouds. This tendency exists in the memory of narrative as well. As ideas held collectively in social memory, the characters and images of a remembered narrative tend to simplification and conventionalization. What is more, as concepts, the characters are linked to other concepts through their meanings. This conceptualization of characters in collective memory is shown whenever these characters behave more like embodied meanings than like flesh-and-blood beings. Both Charlemagne and Roland are linked to meanings or events within their stories; this linkage is conceptual, not empirical.

We also saw that, in continuous experience, memory overlays memory. The transmission of narrative is marked by this process as well. It is a process, however, which covers its own tracks. The stages through which the memory of real events becomes a set of images is not usually visible in the finished product. The very existence of this process of conceptualization is itself hidden. Successive superimposition conceals that the process has taken place at all. All that remains is the latest set of images, and these may seem lifelike and real. What the twelfth-century audience of *The Song of Roland* heard and saw in their imaginations were images of a battle between the French and the Saracens. There was nothing in the images to tell them that this battle never really took place. Though what is remembered are just memories, not retained perceptions of real events, this is hard to recognize. The images seem real.

In this way, the process of change during the transmission of social memory is equally a process of conceptualization. Unless a society possesses means to freeze the memory of the past, the natural tendency of social memory is to suppress what is not meaningful or intuitively satisfying in the collective memories of the past, and interpolate or substitute what seems more appropriate or more in keeping with their particular conception of the world. Thus, medieval Western European social memory at the time of the Crusades remembered that Charlemagne had fought the Saracens at Roncevaux, while the written words of early ninth-century chroniclers, closer to the original battle in 778, tell us that he had, in fact, fought the Basques.

If we look at *The Song of Roland* as a record of real events preserved in social memory, then we can conclude only that memory is indeed a weak and fragile faculty. If we look at it as story, however, we are forced to come to a a very different conclusion. The memory of the story of Roland is as tenacious and stable as the memory of the actual events of Roncevaux is fragile. As we shall see, the memory of Roland continues to thrive in many parts of the world today. The process of conceptualization, which so often disqualifies social memory as an empirical source, is also a process that ensures the stability of a set of collectively held ideas, and enables these ideas to be diffused and transmitted. Social memory is not stable as information; it is stable, rather, at the level of shared meanings and remembered images.

Fairy tales
Like any folk-tale, a fairy tale is a conventional narrative. Its language is often formulaic, but the function of the formulae here is often merely to locate the listener. The 'once upon a time' opening of fairy tales is not a line filler; it serves rather to tell the audience that they are about to be led into the particular world of a fairy tale, in which all sorts of fairy-tale-like things can be expected to happen. The phrase thus transports the audience into a particular imaginary world, in which the audience will remain until the conventional 'and they lived happily ever after' brings the story to its close.

This imaginary world is, in its turn, a conventional one. Characters are simple, and props, scenes, and setting are all stereotyped. This simplicity helps create a familiar, and, hence, recognizable landscape. This is equally true of fairy-tale plots. Typically, these plots concern the adventures of a child, who attains a wish; who is rescued, rewarded, or punished; or who fulfils a task, often against the hostility of his or her parents or stepparents (Propp 1968). The formulaic language and the conventionality of characters and plots all combine to establish a world which, though totally make-believe, is bounded and recognizable. This world forms the backdrop for the story itself.

Between the conventional opening and the conventional happy ending, there unfolds a succession of incidents – problems to be solved, tasks to be accomplished, obstacles to be overcome. These problems and obstacles can only delay the ending, however; eventually all will be resolved, and the story will end happily. Since we can already foresee the happy ending, the interest in a fairy tale lies mainly in the nature of the obstacles and the ruses or magic help that the hero or heroine employs in negotiating them. The art of fairy-tale invention lies here – in filling the space between the two fixed points, providing the audience with as much excitement and amusement on the way as possible.

As with situation comedies and serialized adventure stories, new fairy-tale plots are created by recycling old material. New stories are generated by recombining old themes in a new way, or by grafting a sequence of themes from one story into the plot of another. The composition of new stories from old reflects a logic of recombination in which the storyteller's skill is manifested in an ability to get the most from the themes employed. The themes themselves are usually conventional. Cultures, and storytellers, possess not only a repertoire of stories, but also a repertoire of motifs from which new stories can be constructed. Both stories and motifs are passed on from one storyteller to the next, evolving and changing over time.

This skill of the storyteller in the invention of new stories cannot, of course, be displayed if the storyteller merely reads the stories from a book. We must not forget that until comparatively recently the typical context of fairy-tale narration was oral. Fairy tales themselves evolved in oral storytelling traditions; all our classic fairy tales were once oral narratives.

In its original setting a fairy tale was not just a story; it was also a performance.[5] An oral storyteller had many ways of bringing an old story to life and making it seem new – using weird language; giving detailed description of settings or magical props; using verbal emphases and different voices; making salacious or satirical comments and jokes; drawing an appropriate moral; or using any assortment of crashes, booms, growls and teeth-gnashing, scary faces, and creepy shadows on the fire-lit wall. A storyteller adapted the tale to suit the age, sex, and mood of the audience. Our notion of fairy tales as classics, specially suited for children's bedtime, is a very recent one. Many of our classics have had to be considerably tidied up before they became 'fairy tales'.[6]

---

[5] Finnegan 1977, Vansina 1985, and Tonkin 1991, among others, rightly emphasize the performance element in storytelling, and in recitation in general. A great deal of information about the oral narrative of fairy tales in our culture is contained in the Opies' books, e.g., Opie and Opie 1988. See also Falassi 1980. Nor is this 'synaesthetic' heightening limited to traditional or preliterate cultures, for we are just as likely to dramatize our narratives today as plays or films.

[6] A good example is 'Little Red Riding Hood' ('Le Petit Chaperon Rouge'): see Verdier 1978; Darnton 1984: 9–13. The Grimms considerably prettified 'Goldilocks' as well: Tatar 1987.

As in epic narrative, the teller of a fairy tale knows that much will be familiar to the audience. None the less, there are important differences between the way in which an audience remembers an epic and the way it remembers a fairy tale. The social memory of epic is focused on the images of the heroes or heroines as the central ideas. The various deeds in the epic are remembered as attached to the memory of the hero that accomplishes them. The story of *Roland* tells of Roland and his deeds, just as the story of *Beowulf* is the story of the deeds of a man called Beowulf. The audience, in all likelihood, regarded these figures as real, historical persons, and the deeds described in the poem as real deeds. Epics are thus *chansons de geste*, commemorating the deeds of heroes.

In fairy tales, by contrast, the specific identity of the characters is much less important. They are less likely to be considered real. The hero or heroine of a fairy tale may, in different versions of the same tale, be introduced as the son or daughter of a great king or of a poor wood-cutter. The change of setting makes little difference to the development of the plot. These heroes can, moreover, be given various names, or, in many cases, no names at all. They may be called simply 'the prince' or 'dumbkin'.

Our reliance on books as the source of 'classic' fairy tales often makes us see fairy-tale characters as more defined than they really are. The girl who flees from the murderous intentions of her wicked stepmother and finds herself under the protection of seven dwarfs can be none other than Snow White, and her wicked stepmother can be only a queen, not a woodcutter's wife (as in 'Hansel and Gretel') or a merchant's wife (as in 'Cinderella'). Yet 'Snow White', 'Rapunzel', 'Sleeping Beauty', 'Cinderella', etc. are not really the names of individuals at all; they are the names, rather, of particular folk motifs with which the hero or heroine is associated in the particular story.

Given that today a storyteller usually reads fairy tales rather than improvises them from memory, it is not surprising that we should look at the stories themselves as fixed texts. Thus, Cinderella appears to be no less the literary child of Perrault than Oliver Twist is that of Dickens. Yet Perrault did not invent the story, which had existed in oral traditions for centuries, perhaps many centuries, before Perrault composed his particular adaptation (Dundes 1982). Perrault defines what, for us, is the standard version of the story. Yet his version is no more authentic than the rather different versions of the Brothers Grimm or of the seventeenth-century Neapolitan, Gianbattista Basile. They are all variants of a much older, and extremely wide-spread, oral tradition that we, for the sake of having a label, call – rather improperly – the story of 'Cinderella'.

In 1893, Andrew Lang, the classicist, folklorist, and anthologist of fairy tales, remarked: 'The *märchen* is a kaleidoscope: the incidents are the bits of coloured glass. Shaken, they fall into a variety of attractive forms; some forms are fitter than others, survive more powerfully, and are more widely spread' (Lang 1893a: x). This is an apt description, and helps make clear the difference between an epic and a fairy tale. A fairy tale appealed to the audience's intellectual curiosity. For both the narrator and the audience, the hero's quest could be treated as a puzzle. The themes through which the quest evolved were linked in relations of consequentiality: each new theme, introducing a new obstacle or new magic helper, was presented as the direct consequence of the theme that preceded it. The quest moved through a series of these consequentially sequenced obstacles until the resolution of the final problem set up the happy ending. In this way, there is an easily perceptible logical strand running through each fairy tale.

This thematic logic may be of a very simple sort: as soon as Bluebeard tells his new bride that she may go into any room in his castle but one, even a small child immediately suspects that she is going to break this prohibition and that the fairy tale will tell how she manages to avoid the consequences of her disobedience. Still, the fact that there exists a thematic logic in fairy tales means that the social memory of fairy tales is different from the social memory of epics. A fairy tale is not narrated paratactically; its themes are not so many free-standing units, arranged in rough chronological sequence. Instead, they are interlocking units, arranged in a consequential order. Remembering a fairy tale requires remembering these relations of consequence.

We can start the discussion with the images themselves, identifying a specific motif and seeing how it came to be incorporated into a fairy tale. This image can play the role of a trace element, allowing us to observe a process of transmission, diffusion, and internal evolution characteristic of the social memory of fairy tales.

The tree, the bones, and the beast

During a trial for witchcraft at Modena, in northern Italy, in 1519, a certain Giovanni da Rodigo testified that at the witches' sabbath 'he had also seen [...] many others there who were eating and drinking. Among other things, they were eating an ox, onto whose skin they all threw their bones. At the end, there came the Lady of the Sabbath who struck the skin with a staff, and the animal returned to life.'

The vicar of the Inquisition, the Dominican Bartolomeo Spina, was so startled at this detail that he asked the witness whether he was joking ('*diceret hec serio vel potius ioco*' – the comment in the original Italian was probably a good deal sharper). Spina's astonishment is understandable.

What disturbed him was not the strangeness of the story, but, on the contrary, its familiarity. In 1523, in his *Quaestio de Strigibus*, Spina returned to this testimony, adding that in performing this 'miracle' the Devil had evidently intended to imitate St Germanus of Auxerre, a fifth-century saint, who had brought back to life a calf whose bones had been collected on its skin (Bertolotti 1979).

What, Spina wondered, could an incident from a saint's life be doing at a witches' sabbath? What Spina did not recognize was that the detail is a folk motif: as such, it can crop up in rituals, myths, or any other form of narrative. The story of the beast resuscitated from its skin and bones appears in each of these contexts. It appears, for example, in the *Gylfaginning* section of the *Edda* of Snorri Sturluson, of around 1220–30. Here, Thor resuscitates two goats, on whose flesh he had banqueted the night before, by touching, with his hammer Mjollnir, their bones, bundled in their skins (Faulkes 1987: 37–8). Turning to Stith Thompson's *Motif-Index of Folk-Literature* (Thompson 1955–8), we see that there are a number of close correspondences in folk-tales as well: E 32 – resuscitated eaten animal; E 32, 3 – dismembered pigs come alive again only if bones are preserved; E 33, 3 – resuscitation with missing member. Thus, the theme of the resuscitated beast provides an example of an image, stored in long-term social memory, functioning in narrative.

We can illustrate this with a familiar fairy tale. In this tale, the theme appears in an altered, though still wholly recognizable form (in the interests of brevity, the parts in brackets represent summaries of the text we are using):

[Once upon a time, there lived a rich man with a beautiful wife, but, although they prayed night and day, they had no children. In front of their house was a juniper tree.] Once, in wintertime, the woman stood under the tree and peeled herself an apple, and as she was peeling the apple she cut her finger and the blood fell onto the snow. 'Ah,' said the woman and sighed a deep sigh, and she looked at the red blood before her and her heart ached. 'If only I had a child as red as blood and as white as snow.' And as she said it, it made her feel very happy, as if it was really going to happen.

[In this manner, a child was conceived. The woman's pregnancy followed the cycle of the tree: she swelled as its fruit swelled. At seven months, however, she was seized by a sudden greed and ate so many juniper berries that she became ill. At eight months she realized her illness was fatal. She told her husband to bury her beneath the juniper tree. When her pregnancy came to term, she gave birth to a boy and died. Her husband placed her body under the juniper tree.]

[Later, the father married a woman with a daughter. The stepmother hated her stepson. One day, the stepmother offered her stepson an apple from a chest. As he leaned over the chest to take his apple, the stepmother slammed the lid, decapitating him.]

[The stepmother took the decapitated body and propped it up on a chair, placing the head back on. She told her daughter, Ann-Marie, to give her stepbrother an apple. Angered by her brother's silence, however, Ann-Marie slapped his face, knocking off the head. Terrified, she told her mother that she had killed her stepbrother. The mother replied that it would be best to cut up the body and cook it into a 'sour broth' to serve to the father. When the father arrived, he ate it with relish.]

And he ate and ate, and threw the bones under the table, and finished it all up. But Ann-Marie went to her chest of drawers and took her best silk scarf out of the bottom drawer and fetched every little bone from under the table and tied them up in the silk cloth and carried them outside, weeping tears of blood. Then she laid them under the juniper tree in the green grass, and as soon as she had laid them there she felt so much better and didn't cry any more. But the juniper began to stir and the branches kept coming out and coming back together again, just like someone who is really happy and goes like this with his hands. And then there was a sort of mist coming out of the tree and right in this mist it burned like fire and out of this fire flew this lovely bird that sang, oh so gloriously sweet and flew high into the air ...

[The bird, charming people with his beautiful song telling of how he was murdered, obtained a golden chain, a pair of red shoes, and a millstone. He returned to his house, and perching on the juniper tree, sang this same song. When the father went out, he dropped the golden chain around his neck. When the stepsister went out, he threw the shoes down to her. When the stepmother went out, however, he dropped the millstone on her, crushing her to death. He then descended and became a little boy once more.]

This story, for those who have not already recognized it, is number 47 of the Grimm brothers' collection, 'The Juniper Tree' (trans. Segal 1973). It provides more than enough folk motifs to keep any number of comparative mythologists or Freudian critics busy. We shall simply try to show how some of its themes were remembered, ordered, and transmitted.

A fairy tale such as this was fashioned piece by piece. Although the audience knew that convention required a happy ending, they did not always know how this would be brought about. The storyteller was free to lengthen the quest of the hero or heroine by adding new trials, new adventures, new helpers, and new magical objects. The storyteller could not, of course, add new themes arbitrarily; the sequence had to make sense. This meant that each theme had to be introduced in a way that made it appear as the consequence of the theme that came before it.

This necessity of consequentiality affects the characters as well. In *The Song of Roland*, we saw that the fact that the characters existed in the audience's memory as concepts related to a particular story explained why these characters sometimes display a curious omniscience – seeming to know what is about to happen as well as the audience. The characters in fairy tales are sometimes even less realistic. They seem to have no minds of their own, and to perform actions which are totally lacking in motivation. This is because fairy-tale characters are often simply the embodied causal agents of the themes used in the story. It is the logic of the themes, rather than the will of the characters, that determines the course of the action.

In 'The Juniper Tree', the mother does not ask how and why she has become pregnant, nor how or why she is to die in giving birth. Similarly, there is no particular reason why Ann-Marie gathers her brother's bones and buries them under the juniper tree; she just does so. The father is given no personality at all; he merely serves to accomplish the thematic business of eating the 'beast'.

This motivelessness is typical. The behaviour of fairy-tale characters is governed by a set of themes which specifies the way in which a particular series of actions must be performed, and it is this thematic logic, rather than a character's psychology, that is frequently behind the character's action. Even though there is nothing in the story that gives Ann-Marie reason to know this, she must bury her brother's bones at the foot of the tree that marks his mother's grave because this is the way the particular narrative motif works. Unless the bones of the slaughtered beast are gathered in its 'skin' and placed beside its mother, it cannot be resuscitated.

Fairy-tale characters are thus, as Propp put it, 'functions' (Propp 1968). They are embodied functions, however, for, as Greimas observes, all relations of consequentiality in a fairy tale must be embodied in some real thing – a character, an animal, or a magical object – rather than be left abstract (Greimas and Courtès 1976). We saw that characters such as Charlemagne functioned, in part, as 'embodied meanings'. The behaviour of fairy-tale characters, by contrast, arises from the fact that they, in part, function as 'embodied causes'.

Nor can the set of causal relations set up by the themes be sequenced in a haphazard fashion. They are, rather, linked to form stories. Stories, in fact, serve as the vehicles for the remembrance of themes. None the less, typical sequences often appear in more than one story. Something of this should be evident even in the above, truncated fairy tale. The beginning of the story, for example, can be broken down into the following succession of themes:

One: mother conceives child while eating apple under tree; she cuts her finger and wishes the child to be as red as blood and white as snow.
Two: pregnant mother feels urge to eat juniper berries; she eats them greedily, falls ill, and dies.
Three: mother buried under juniper tree.
Four: father remarries, stepmother favours her own child while being cruel to her stepchild.

Although we tend to treat the story as a fixed text, none of the themes listed are particular to this story alone. The first theme of the mother's cutting her finger and wishing for a child white as snow and red as blood is a theme that 'The Juniper Tree' shares with 'Snow White'. The second theme of the sudden urge of a pregnant woman to eat some specific food – berries in this case – and the eventual loss of a mother that results from this provides the opening motif of 'Rapunzel'.

We should not speak of 'borrowing' here, as if a certain theme was the personal property of Snow White or Rapunzel. Bartolomeo Spina may have thought that the theme of the resuscitated beast had been 'borrowed' by Satan from St Germanus. Yet, as Delehaye remarks, even in the lives of saints, the hagiographic attribute is not something that can have a particular owner (Delehaye 1961, cited in Gurevič 1986: 78). This is even more true of folk-motifs in fairy tales. They are not the personal property of any folk-tale character. A storyteller does not borrow, but, rather, recycles.

Nor is this recycling arbitrary. Certain thematic sequences evolve, and these tend to be used repeatedly at similar points in fairy tales. Thus, in both 'Snow White' and 'The Juniper Tree', the cut or pricked finger prefigures the birth of a child to a hitherto barren woman. In both 'Rapunzel' and 'The Juniper Tree', the act of gluttony during pregnancy sets up a chain of events that leads to the elimination of the mother: Rapunzel's mother is forced to yield her daughter to the care of a witch; the boy's mother in 'The Juniper Tree' sickens and dies, and her place is taken by a wicked stepmother.

In all three cases, moreover, the opening sequence of themes serves the important narrative function of introducing the protagonist of the story: a child who has lost its mother, and who is placed in the care of an evil substitute – evil queen, witch, or wicked stepmother. At this point, 'The Juniper Tree', 'Snow White', and 'Rapunzel' are all roughly the same story. The opening themes establish that this is going to be a fairy tale about the adventures of an abandoned or mistreated child. The precise identity of this mistreated child will soon be made clear: in one story, the mistreated child will run off into the forest to be befriended by seven dwarfs; in another, the child will be imprisoned in a tower.

Yet even these opening themes cannot be entirely reduced to a formal device. They have an important plot function as well. The audience foresees that the story of the unhappy child will end well. In order to reach the happy ending, however, the child may need magical help. The best help that a child can obtain is often that of its dead mother. This is true in the case of 'The Juniper Tree'. Here, the opening motifs do not merely introduce the protagonist; they introduce two other important 'characters' as well – the dead, real mother and the juniper tree.

The mother conceives under the juniper tree; she dies from eating the berries of the juniper tree; she is buried under the juniper tree. Later, the same juniper tree receives the 'skin' and bones of the murdered child, and from this tree the child is reborn. In this way a series of connections is established. The juniper tree is associated with the slaughtered child. It is also directly associated with the mother at the moments of conception and of death. In this way, it serves as a connecting link between these two characters. In fact, the juniper tree provides a strand of connectedness that runs through the entire story. In the final scene, the bird returns and sits on the juniper tree before flying down and transforming itself back into the murdered child.

Before considering the mother's role, it is worth pausing to ask what the juniper tree might 'mean'. The Russian folklorist Vladimir Propp devoted a special study to the magic tree on the grave (Propp 1975). According to him, the folk motif of the resuscitated beast was regularly combined with that of the magic or wish-granting tree. Propp traced the origin of this pair of motifs to primitive hunting rituals. In these, the bones of a sacrificed beast were placed in its skin, and put at the foot of a sacred tree, on whose branches were also hung the trophies and spoils of war. The purpose of this ritual, Propp argued, was to ensure a plenitude of game.

This is very interesting. None the less, such an explanation tells us little about the use of the paired motifs in 'The Juniper Tree'. Propp's conclusion that the purpose of the ritual was to ensure the plenitude of game is a functionalist explanation, and, as such, can be true only within a given social context. Yet the paired motifs appear in more than one social context. They continue, in fact, to be transmitted through the centuries, despite radical changes in external, social context.

The meaning of the paired motifs can only be their meaning in context. Out of context, the themes of the resuscitated beast and the wish-granting tree are nothing more than narrative motifs. They are part of the storyteller's stock, and have little inherent meaning by them-selves. It is this, in fact, that facilitates their passage from one social context to another, or from one type of social activity – such as ritual – to another type – such as folk narratives. The meaning that they take on in these successive contexts will always be a meaning in reference to that context. What Propp did was to give us, as it were, an 'etymology' of motifs by discovering their meaning in context at their hypothetical point of origin. This can establish only what their earliest meaning was then: it does not establish an intrinsic meaning for them. Propp could have pushed his investigations back to the Old Stone Age and beyond, but all he would have discovered is a series of earlier and earlier meanings in context, not the 'real' meaning of the themes.

This helps illuminate an important point about the transmission of social memory. Where meaning is related to context, the memory of meanings will tend to be lost as the context changes. Granting for a moment that the original meaning of the paired motifs was, as Propp argued, to ensure the plenitude of game, social memory would tend to conserve only this meaning as long as it remained associated in actual practice with a hunting ritual. Once such hunting rituals had dis-appeared, or once social practice no longer associated the paired motifs with them, there is no reason to expect that social memory would retain the association.

This, however, brings up another question. If they had lost their 'orig-inal meaning', why should social memory retain the paired motifs at all? The answer is probably that they are retained and transmitted simply because they are narrative motifs, kept alive in the memory of stories. This narrative social memory preserves the themes in a relatively decontextualized form, however – simply as narrative motifs. They are whittled down to a series of actions that are consequentially linked. The 'meaning' is not retained, for it is not necessary to remember this mean-ing to use the themes in a narrative. In this form, the themes are also easier to remember. They are clear and simple. It would be difficult to remember them if their memory required retaining a lot of information about social practices that were no longer current. Thus, narrative memory conserves the paired themes in a way typical of social memory in general: it simplifies them.

The lack of inherent meaning of the paired themes, and the fact that they are retained in narrative in a relatively decontextualized form, does not, of course, prevent the storyteller from adding meanings during a retelling. The theme of the resuscitated beast, for example, requires that the flesh of the slaughtered beast/child be entirely consumed, leaving nothing but the skin and the bones. In 'The Juniper Tree', this task falls to the father. A real storyteller's audience might, at this point, be led to imagine a gargantuan meal, especially large as the son's identity has been disguised by turning him into a 'sour broth'. In the interests of psychological plausibility, to say nothing of filial piety, we might hope that the storyteller would make the father say, 'Ah, wife, I do not know why, but your sour broth repels me!' This is not about to happen, however, for the storyteller and, presumably, most of the audience as well already know that the father will not be given any option: he is required to eat his son, every bit of him. Even the somewhat priggish Brothers Grimm describe the father's mealtime behaviour like this:

> With that he began to eat and said, 'Ann-Marie, what are you crying for? You'll see, your brother will be back.' Then he said, 'Ah wife, what good food this is! Give me some more.' And the more he ate the more he wanted, and he said, 'Give me more. You can't have any of it; it's as if all of this were for me.' And he ate and ate, and threw the bones under the table, and finished it all up.

There is, in fact, no real reason why the father has actually to enjoy the meal. He could perfectly well fulfil his role as an embodied cause in a more decorous silence; he does not have to make a pig of himself. In reality, it is probably the storyteller that is enjoying himself (or herself) rather than the father. The obligatory scene of paternal cannibalism provides a first-class rhetorical image, as striking as many in *The Song of Roland*. A real storyteller might well pause to draw it out – in this case, by embellishing the scene with appropriate gastric effects – grunts and burps, smacking, gnashing of teeth, and licking of chops, all the while describing poor Ann-Marie as she is sent flying back and forth to the kitchen with furious roars of 'More! More!'

It is not inconceivable that such a vivid performance would lead some member of the audience to ask 'Why?' What is the 'reason' that the father should eat his son with such relish? The honest reply would, of course, be that there is no real reason for the father to act in this way; it just makes the story more entertaining. Yet an audience might not accept this answer: they might experience the story as real, and thus demand a 'real' reason for the father's behaviour. A good storyteller might be forced to invent some explanation. The explanation would have no bearing on the story, however. Indeed, in the course of many performances of the same story, the teller might be asked the same question a number of times, responding with explanations that ranged from the mundane to the Freudian. None of these explanations would change the story itself in the least.

A fairy tale is no more than a story; it is remembered and composed as a simple narrative. As social memory, it has no intrinsic meaning. If the story is told well, the audience will experience it as real. This may induce them to ask for all sorts of explanations. Yet any such explanation will be gratuitous, for the story is not real. It remains just a story. Themes, such as the resuscitated beast or the wish-granting tree, are the building blocks from which the story can be assembled. That is really their principal, and in many cases only, function.

Is the juniper tree, for example, a 'symbol' for the child's mother? The Grimms make some effort to establish such a relationship. Ann-Marie places her stepbrother's bones under the tree, and 'the juniper tree began to stir and the branches kept coming out and coming back together again, just like someone who is really happy and goes like this with his hands.' The 'goes like this with his hands' calls for a gesture on the part of the storyteller – waving hands about for joy, or, perhaps, cradling an imaginary baby. In the next sentence, however, a mist comes from the tree and it burns like fire, and, finally, a lovely white bird flies out of the tree. This bird will turn into the murdered boy. Does this mean that the tree has 'given birth' to the bird? If so, how are we going to explain the birth of the child in the beginning of the story? Although the juniper tree is represented as somehow involved in the conception of the child, it cannot possibly, at this juncture, symbolize the mother.

The juniper tree is, in fact, less of a symbol than a connecting thread in a series of metamorphoses. It is, somehow, the 'cause' of these metamorphoses. How does the juniper tree cause these miraculous happenings? We are not specifically told. We simply know that the tree can behave in the way it does because it is a *magic* tree. Why is the tree a juniper tree in the first place? The juniper is an evergreen shrub, with prickly leaves and branches reaching down to the ground. It is hard to imagine how anyone could even crawl down under it, let alone eat an apple there. It is equally difficult to imagine anyone gorging on juniper berries; they are simply not that kind of fruit. An apple tree would have been much more appropriate. After all, the mother was peeling an apple when she cut herself, wished for a child, and somehow became pregnant. The little son was murdered while reaching in the chest for an apple. Yet, had the storyteller identified the tree as an apple tree, the beginning of the story would have been virtually indistinguishable from 'Snow White'. One suspects that the significance of the juniper tree is (in part at least) to remind the storyteller not to tell 'Snow White'.

It is always possible, of course, to narrate 'The Juniper Tree' in a way which makes clear and coherent the exact role – causal, symbolic, magical, or botanic – that the tree plays in the story. Yet this is not necessary. All that is necessary is that the audience grasps that the tree is a magic tree. Once the audience sees this, it no longer matters exactly how the tree does what it does – it simply does it by *magic*. Nor does it matter what particular species the tree belongs to – apple in 'Snow White', hazel in 'Aschenputtel', rose in 'Beauty and the Beast', or juniper here.

'The Juniper Tree' is a story of a chain of magical happenings, all of which are 'causally' linked to the magic tree. Yet these links are not 'causal' in the sense that the story gives us any information about real meanings or real causes. The causes are all fairy-tale causes. They exist only in reference to the events in the story; they have no meaning outside this point of reference. Just as the temporal sequencing of *The Song of Roland* does not refer to 'real' time, so the causal sequences in a fairy tale do not refer to 'real' causes. They are really a sequence of narrative links that allows the story to be remembered as a story.

Narrative social memory
The thematic memory of fairy tales is a decontextualized memory. The fairy-tale narrator remembers themes primarily as a means of recovering stories, of composing new versions of old stories, or of inventing entirely new stories. The Russian version of 'Cinderella', 'The Beautiful Vassilissa', incorporates a visit to Baba Yaga in the forest. Baba Yaga was a familiar figure in the Russian folk-tale tradition, and many of the Russian versions of the classic fairy tales include a Baba Yaga episode. Thus, fairy-tale narrators worked like the epic poets described by Parry and Lord, lengthening or altering their tales, or interpolating specific themes from their repertoire to fit the taste of their audience.

In a manner reminiscent of that of the memory of places in classical rhetoric, the fairy-tale narrator also remembers themes simply in order to tell stories rather than in order to retain meanings and historical information associated with these themes. Like the memory of 'pure semantic information' discussed in the first chapter, the memory of fairy-tale themes is a memory of 'signifiers' without their 'signifieds'. Narrators may remember themes and stories without having to remember the circumstances in which these themes and stories were learned. Meaning is added in the retelling. This decontextualization of narrative memory exists, however, only in reference to the contextual meanings of the themes; narrative memory is not decontextualized in the sense that the themes may be remembered in any order and in any combination. On the contrary, the themes of fairy tales are linked in relations of consequence. This consequential logic needs to be mastered if the narrator is to articulate the themes properly. The memory of the proper order of consequences is thus part of the memory of the themes themselves.

For this reason, it is convenient to distinguish between an external or social context, which is regularly lost during transmission, and an internal context, which tends to be preserved. Using this distinction, we might put Jakobson's observation (above, p. 40) into a more precise form. What governs the process of 'blotting out', as one version of a tradition covers over the version that preceded it, are, in the first place, changes in surrounding context. Information that is context-dependent – information, that is, that derives its meaning from a specific social context – will tend to be lost whenever that context changes. Working against this, however, is the ability to reinforce memory by conceptualizing its images and themes in ways which are not context-dependent. What can be freed from surrounding context, and remembered on its own, will tend to pass intact from one social context to another.

We have been examining two common ways in which this conceptualization takes place – visual images, as in epic, and causal motifs, as in fairy tales. In narrative memory, stories themselves can serve as internal contexts, fixing the memory of images and links in a properly consequential order. A fairy-tale plot is a sequence of linked themes; the memory of such a plot requires the memory of both the themes and their successive links. This memory is mutually reinforcing. In this sense, a plot functions as a complex memory image, and learning a repertoire of plots is equivalent to learning a large-scale mnemo-technique that permits the ordering, retention, and subsequent transmission of a vast amount of information. Remembering in visual images, syntactically linked and articulated in causal and logical relations, we make up little stories. This is a 'mnemotechnique' we constantly use without being aware of it.

The intuition of a plot as a chain of consequentially related themes, and the committing of that plot to memory, entail conceptualization. Conceptualization here shades into memorization; the sharper the conceptualization, the easier it is to memorize. This does not mean, in the case of a folk-tale, that an image has to be reconceptualized by every individual who learns the story, for the conceptualization is already implicit in the image as it is retained in its internal context. The magic tree of indeterminate species which so helpfully brings about transformations in fairy tales is a highly conceptualized image, and, in such a form, has been transmitted in narrative memory for many centuries.

The conceptualization is already there; all we have to do is to know how to use it.

In this way, the blotting-out process during transmission is not just a general and gradual loss of factual information – though it is certainly true that social memory is not always very good at conserving facts. Facts are lost or retained in specific circumstances and in specific ways. They are lost whenever, in a new external context, old information is no longer meaningful; or, alternatively, because they do not fit into the new internal context designed to hold the information. Conceptualization requires simplification, and adaptation of details to fit into the story as a whole. Thus, in the memory of the story of Roland, the Saracens were substituted for the Basques because this fitted better. We must always remember that memory is an active search for meaning. Sometimes social memory does not so much 'lose' specific information as intentionally disregard it.

This helps us perceive a general pattern in remembering and forgetting. If, in certain situations, memory seems fragile and volatile, it is because so much of our memory is the memory of context-dependent information. As long as we remain in these contexts, we remain surrounded by clues which prompt our memory. Here, in what we earlier called our 'present continuum', the external environment itself takes over the job of ordering memory into a sequence: we remember things in the order in which they habitually appear. This is memory at a low level of conceptualization: little more than simple recognition. Take away the external, material support, and the memory of the ordered sequence tends to fade. If memory at other times seems, by contrast, stable and tenacious, it is because we have ways of freeing memory from this dependence on external context. Committing something to memory thus means conceptualizing it and encoding it in an internal context, as this enables us to retain the memory regardless of changes in the external environment. This tenacity can have a number of consequences when a group continues to 'relive' its past in the present.

Facts are typically lost quickly at early stages of social memory. To be remembered and transmitted at all, the facts must be transformed into images, arranged in stories. Internal contexts, such as narrative genres, exist as the typical patterns in which we experience and interpret events of all kinds. Accommodating remembered facts into predisposed internal contexts may impose a radical reordering of that memory at the outset. The conceptualization that occurs when memory is transformed into a story to be transmitted is an independent movement. Facts lost at this moment are lost not simply as the result of the quick fading of the factual content of memory, but also because facts that are not in harmony with our predispositions tend to be filtered out in transmission.

Once memory has been conceptualized into a story, the process of change and of factual loss naturally slows down. Remembering within an internal context gives the memory the support it needs to be retained. Individual narrators may expand or embellish the story in whatever way they wish; they will still tend to adhere to the plot as the group recognizes it. For the narrator's community, this stabilized version is 'the story', and they may often refuse to accept any major variant.

Folklorists have a term to express such a locally standardized species – 'oikotype' (home type). In any community, standard versions tend to emerge. These are the versions that are 'oikotypical' for that community. It is thus the remembering community which decides which version is acceptable and which not. In his account of a *veglia*, or storytelling evening, in Tuscany, the Italian folklorist Alessandro Falassi describes a storyteller trying to splice two different tales into one. On this occasion, the audience of adults and children simply would not accept it. They knew the stories too well themselves, and, when the storyteller stopped, they told them 'correctly' (Falassi 1980: 54–70). An allegiance to an oikotype reflects a habit of thinking. The group knew that the stories were simply fictions; yet this made them no less clear and concrete in their minds.

We saw that Andrew Lang remarked that some of the 'attractive patterns' into which fairy tale themes may be ordered are 'fitter than others'. These 'survive more powerfully'. This Darwinian language may have been inadvertent; it is not wholly inappropriate. The existence of oikotypical variants demonstrates that fairy tales do evolve. Evolution here is a process of transmission and diffusion. There are, for example, hundreds of oikotypes of the story of Cinderella existing all over the world. The earliest known comes from ninth-century China (Jameson in Dundes 1982). Although we cannot always establish the chain of transmission and diffusion in detail, we sometimes know enough to sketch it out. We often, in other words, can trace certain paths by which the story, or a new version of it, diffused from one group to another. We can also trace lines of transmission showing how a single tale broke up into related 'species' (Rooth in Dundes 1982).

We might put this distinction between transmission and diffusion in narrative memory in a more general form: transmission is an internal, diachronic process; diffusion, by contrast, is external and synchronic. Thus, diffusion changes social memory from the outside. It is like a case of infection: stories 'infect' other stories. As we shall see, this sort of change through diffusion is very common in social memory.

Oral tradition

Ethnohistory
Fairy tales possess a remarkable durability. They resist the onslaughts of both the well-intentioned bowdlerizer and the searcher for deeper truths. A mark of this durability is the stability of fairy-tale themes and plots. One reason for this stability is that the stories are set in the world of 'once upon a time'. As a genre, fairy tales are fictions: since we do not believe they really occurred at all, we are unlikely to alter their plots to reflect our changing perceptions of the real world. External circumstances would have to change radically before we felt it necessary to change the way in which we told 'Rumpelstiltskin'. Fairy tales are thus a narrative genre relatively immune to influence from the real world.

Occasionally, however, fairy tales do become 'infected'. In 'The Juniper Tree' the wicked stepmother can be only a stepmother, for the plot opposes her to the real mother. In other stories, such as 'Snow White' or 'Hansel and Gretel', there is no structural reason why the children should suffer at the hands of a stepmother instead of a real mother; nor do they in many variants. Yet there may seem a moral reason. All their proclaimed reverence for the folk tradition notwithstanding, the Brothers Grimm evidently baulked at presenting so many scenes of maternal cruelty. They transformed the cruel mothers in 'Snow White' and 'Hansel and Gretel' into wicked stepmothers; and it is in this form that they have become fixed in our own oikotypical versions (Tatar 1987: 37–8).

Fairy tales have always been susceptible to this sort of manipulation. As they came to be perceived as a genre of fiction, distinct from folktales in general, and especially intended for children, narrators, authors, and anthologizers began to see fairy tales in a new light. Fairy tales needed to provide a lesson. Thus, from Perrault's *Contes de ma mère l'Oye* of 1697 onwards, there arose the practice of appending morals at the end of the stories.

The morals appended to Perrault's fairy tales are, in the most obvious of ways, an attempt to provide a new meaning in context. This is a very venerable practice in the transmission of social memory. The medieval church preserved pre-Christian folklore and ritual by placing it in Christian contexts. In the ancient world, the Stoics and the Neoplatonists reinterpreted classical mythology in allegorical and pseudo-historical terms. In each case, the stories were retained by transferring them into new contexts or into new narrative genres. However, this transfer from one context or genre into another entailed a reinterpretation and rearranging of the original memory. In this way, a changing social perspective can require recontextualization into a new genre, and this can initiate a set of changes within the memory itself. As we shall see, this recontextualization can also mark a change in perspective on the part of the remembering group, showing how groups attempt to come to terms with their traditions in changing circumstances.

In his inaugural lecture on African history at the University of Birmingham in 1965, John Fage argued that the existence of oral traditions showed that preliterate African societies had a sense of history comparable to that of literate societies. These societies, he continued, had 'developed formal oral records of their past and elaborate methods of maintaining these records for their posterity'. By 'formal oral records', Fage meant king lists, genealogies, and other items of lore and legend that were carefully preserved by oral tradition. It followed that historians, often called 'ethnohistorians', specializing in the history of preliterate peoples might make legitimate use of these 'oral records' as a historical source. Of course, these records needed to be used critically; to be 'sifted, correlated, and cross-checked as any other evidence until a residuum is obtained which is acceptable as "truth"' (Smith 1988: ix).

We are not concerned here to evaluate the work of ethnohistorians as a whole, but, rather, to examine the sort of problems that arise from their treatment of oral tradition.[7] It is worth noting, however, that where historians and ethnohistorians have been able to evaluate and control these traditions through other sorts of historical evidence, oral traditions have indeed revealed themselves as a valuable historical source. In this way, a study of oral traditions has helped in reconstructing the respective histories of societies inhabiting the West African coast, the kingdoms of the Niger, the kingdom of Rwanda, and the Zulu people (Vidal 1971; Wilks 1975; Smith 1975; Peel 1983; Smith 1988; to mention just a few).

---

[7] There has been no lack of debate over the use to which ethnohistorians put oral tradition. Anthropologists have been particularly critical (Beidelman 1970; Willis 1980). The reaction of other historians has been more mixed; they seem less interested in criticizing the use of oral tradition in itself than some of the specific methods and conclusions that ethnohistorians have reached (e.g., Vidal 1976). David Henige has examined orally transmitted chronologies, concluding that very little faith may be put in them (Henige 1974; cf. 1982). For an overview, see Cohen 1989 and Salmon 1986; see also Miller 1980b for a good discussion of the whole problem.

In the above cases where oral traditions were successfully used as historical sources, the historian had other sources to go on. In certain instances, the sources were the medieval Arab geographers; in others, early European explorers; in still others, colonial records. The reliability of these written sources was variable, and there were occasions in which the historian might choose to follow oral tradition even when contradicted by the written word. Yet the very existence of these written sources was in itself significant. Even when they seemed unreliable, they could still put the oral traditions into perspective.

The problem of perspective is, of course, common to all historians. Sources must be located and put into focus. To do this, however, the historian needs more than one. For all the valuable information that a single source may contain, as long as it cannot be placed in perspective, it is difficult to know what the information means, or, sometimes, even what it is referring to. A second source throws the first into relief. Even if the second source is of dubious veracity, it may still help in identifying the standpoint of the first.

Oral traditions are hard to put into this sort of perspective. Like folk-tale themes, oral traditions are often decontextualized in social memory. Regardless of the number of variants that an oral historian may collect for a certain tradition, the tradition as a whole still resembles a single source. A group's oral tradition may affirm, for example, that there was a king, having a certain name, and coming from a certain place, who ruled about 500 years ago. Without the sort of evidence that can place this tradition in perspective, the historian has no way of knowing whether the tradition is genuine, stemming from a real event, or merely a legend; nor of knowing whether the figures referred to in the tradition are real or mythical; nor even of knowing whether the tradition really 'belongs' to the group which now transmits it, or whether it is a tradition 'borrowed' from a neighbouring group. The historian, in short, does not know what the tradition refers to. The historian cannot establish this for the simple reason that the group which remembers the tradition has no real way of establishing it either. It is often remembered as a decontextualized story, whose entire history of thematic ordering, transmission, and diffusion has been blotted out.

We saw earlier that the connection between a mnemonic image and its meaning or external point of reference is arbitrary. The connections are simply conceptual connections, not real ones. We also saw, however, that there is no reason that the remembering group might suspect this arbitrariness; it is not apparent in the tradition itself. The story in the *Chanson de Roland* probably seemed real to a twelfth-century French audience; most of them would probably never have asked whether or not it referred to an actual event. This is not, however, to say that it was impossible to challenge a traditional story. A literate listener to the *Chanson de Roland* might have observed that the story was just a poem in the vernacular; it lacked, therefore, the authority of a Latin text, or, in particular, the authority of the Scriptures. This is an important argument. For us, questions of historical authenticity are usually decided by documentary evidence. This was not often possible in non-literate societies. Here, the question of whether or not to accept a certain tradition or version of that tradition was, to a large extent, a question of authority. This could mean the authority of the speaker. Yet it could also mean the authority of the genre itself.

In non-literate (and indeed, not seldom, literate) cultures, decisions whether to regard traditions as a source of historical truth or merely as fictions are often made simply in reference to their genre. As a genre, fairy tales are fictions. They are remembered and transmitted, but not considered to be historically true. Other genres, king lists, for example, may, however, be regarded as historical. Still other genres, such as sacred myths, may be regarded as canonical and authoritative. The contextualization of certain types of social memory into certain genres, and the varying degrees of truthfulness or authority which the group assigns to these genres, are all reflections of culture and social practice, not reflections of where historical truth lies. The group which arranges its social memory into different genres is usually in no position to know what is really fictional and what really historical. The arrangement merely defines the historical status of the tradition as it exists in people's minds. It reveals what the group's feelings and beliefs are, rather than what the past itself was. Ignoring this distinction can lead to disastrous results.

In 1966, in his study of the kingdoms of the savannah, the Belgian ethnohistorian Jan Vansina wrote: 'Around 1500, [when] the area between Lake Tanganyika and the upper Kasai was organised into a multitude of smaller chiefdoms ... a great immigrant named Kongolo [or Nkongolo] was to become the founder of what has been called the first Luba empire.' Vansina continued his account of the reign of King Nkongolo with other items of information drawn from oral tradition, finishing with a description of his death, at the hand of his nephew, Kalala Ilunga, founder of the 'second Luba empire' (Vansina 1966: 71–2).

Vansina was nowhere claiming that all the information garnered from oral tradition was true, or even credible. Still, it is clear that, for Vansina, the point of reference of this entire tradition is probably an actual king named Nkongolo, whose reign he fixed to 'around 1500'. In 1972, however, Vansina's colleague, the anthropologist Luc de Heusch, in his study of Bantu mythology, interpreted the figure of Nkongolo as the rainbow-serpent who 'binds' the heavenly waters (de Heusch 1982: 8–75). In other words, de Heusch interpreted Nkongolo as a completely mythological entity. Much subsequent scholarly opinion has tended to agree with de Heusch, and, although we cannot go into the debate here, his approach has the merit of taking the oral tradition as a whole into consideration.

Vansina has been a leading, and even emblematic, figure in ethno-history, and it would be very unfair to single him out for criticism, especially as this example is unrepresentative of much of his later work. Nevertheless, there is a general problem at stake here. Ethnohistorians have sometimes taken extremely complex and highly ambiguous bodies of oral tradition and attempted to reduce them to a 'residuum' of histori-cal facts. They have defended this procedure as a form of textual criti-cism, arguing that, for the purpose of historical analysis, it is irrelevant whether the sources are texts or oral traditions. Until the late 1970s, Vansina was a leading proponent of this method. Yet all this method-ological rigour is of no avail unless ethnohistorians can first demon-strate that the traditions themselves are about 'something' at all.

Many of the techniques that ethnohistorians have developed, as well as the arguments they have advanced, are in themselves interesting. African societies preserve their oral traditions through a variety of mnemotechniques. Ethnohistorians argue that the fact that certain types of information are mnemonically reinforced or associated with import-ant rituals demonstrates that this information is socially relevant to that group. This is a good point. Vansina himself has done a great deal of research into the study of the dynamics of their transmission (Vansina 1966; 1985). He shows, for example, how the memory of oral tradition is supported by formal mnemonic techniques or by being contextualized in important rituals. Certain types of information, such as king lists, genealogies, clan names, honorific titles, legal precedents, etc., are often carefully fixed in memory, to be later declaimed on solemn occasions. A familiar figure in many traditional African societies is the *griot* – 'lore master' or 'praise singer'. Such people are specialists, very much like the Anglo-Saxon *scop* or the Greek *rhapsode* we described earlier. Thus, Africans possess the sorts of mnemonic techniques that help ensure that their corpus of oral tradition remains stable.

This stability is still, of course, no guarantee of truth. In fact, the stab-ility of, say, genealogical memory is, in many respects, similar to the stability of thematic memory in folk-tales. This means that mnemonic reinforcement decontextualizes the information as it preserves it. The information is retained without the accompanying contexts that would put this information into perspective, and allow us to evaluate it as a historical source.

If memory is to be preserved beyond the present continuum, it must be conceptualized and fitted into an internal context. These internal contexts are not naturally presented to us, however; they must all be created. The internal contexts that a particular group develops will naturally tend to reflect that group's culture. Preliterate cultures cannot, for example, employ many of the simple devices we use in writing. We would not expect a praise-singer to retain a list of kings in alphabetical order. Nor would we expect a preliterate society to organize its traditions into the sorts of logical categories employed in an encyclopaedia. This is, no doubt, an elementary point; but it is one that bears emphasizing. Preliterate cultures need to devise conceptual receptacles which order and store memory. They need, in other words, to make out of conceptualized time and space 'maps' in which social memory can be organized. A genealogy is one example of this type of map. A genealogy maps out the idea of 'succession'. The succession that any particular genealogical tradition preserves may, of course, be a real succession of historical figures; equally, however, a genealogical tradition may map out a set of purely symbolic categories.[8] In order to use a particular genre of oral tradition, such as genealogy, as a historical source, it is obviously important to know what it is doing. Until we can discover what sort of knowledge the genealogy preserves, a genealogical tradition is of absolutely no value as factual evidence. Ethnohistorians sometimes seem to plunge into their process of textual criticism without ever seriously examining the question of why they consider that some genres are more 'historical' than others.

De Heusch has commented that ethnohistorians often 'briskly' excise

---

[8] Edmund Leach has observed that it is hardly by chance that genealogies in preliterate societies include mythological ancestors (1964; 1969; see also Sahlins 1985, ch. 2, for a similar argument). These lineages and genealogies function not only as a source of information about 'real' ancestors, but also to situate a group as a clan or kinship group in relation to other such groups. In other words, lineages and genealogies also situate a group within a system of symbolic classification represented by totemic and mythological figures. We must remember that groups such as the Jörai (above, pp. 37–9) lack the means whereby they might either verify or disprove their traditions, and thus, as interesting as the question of the factual accuracy of these traditions may be to an ethnohistorian, it is a relatively uninteresting question to the preliterate group itself. The ancestors do not have to be strictly mythological to be, in effect, mythical: in the specific instance of western and central Africa, conversion to Islam has frequently led to 'lineage amelioration' in the form of posited connections between local clans and *shurfa* lineages, families claiming descent from the Prophet (Conrad 1985; see also Curtin 1975), and parallels to this are widespread.

anything that they regard as a 'mythological excrescence on the body of narrative history' (de Heusch 1982: 8). That is, their methodology is one of a preliminary sorting: anything that might contain a kernel of historical truth is saved for further consideration; anything that seems purely mythological or fictional is discarded at the outset. This is a methodology that is unfortunate in many respects. Myths, genealogies, folk-tales, etc., are nothing but genres in which social memory is retained and transmitted. The fact that we might regard certain genres as inherently more plausible, and thus more likely as historical evidence, is no demonstration that this is the way they really function. We have no way of knowing, a priori, where, in oral tradition, historical facts are likely to lie.

Having isolated a certain body of traditions as possible sources of fact, the ethnohistorians proceed to sift and cross-check these traditions to reveal a 'residuum'. This procedure itself, however, does not demonstrate that the 'residuum' they end up with is historically true. The sifting method only succeeds because ethnohistorians assume that kernels of historical information are there in the first place. They are in no position, however, to demonstrate this assumption. To do this, they would have to show that a certain genre preserves true information (rather than merely mnemonically stable information). They would also have to show how and why true information is preserved in certain genres and not others. This would necessitate considering the cultural functions of the various genres in relation to the corpus of oral tradition as a whole. They would need, in short, to put their evidence into a larger context. Yet by their preliminary division of oral tradition into plausible and implausible parts, ethnohistorians have decontextualized their evidence. This makes it unlikely that the kernels that their sifting process will inevitably bring to light can be defended as factual truths. All that can really be said is that this sifting reveals the lowest common denominator of the traditions. In the case of genealogies, this is likely, often enough, to be a set of mythological ancestors (Horton 1971: 73).

Ethnohistorians have sometimes defended their procedures and conclusions with another argument. Their interpretation of oral tradition, they observe, often seems plausible to the remembering group itself. This may often be true; but, in a sense, all this argument is saying is that certain remembering groups share the ethnohistorians' low opinion of myth as a historical source. None the less, this argument about the apparent plausibility of certain versions, rather than others, is significant. Ethnohistorians' choices about which traditions to discard and which to accept are, in many cases, reflections of the opinions of the remembering group on the matter. Thus, it may be sometimes the preliterate culture itself which has performed the task of briskly excising 'myth' from its 'narrative history'.

Why should a particular group excise what it considers myth in this way? This question is similar to the question of why European social memory has not preserved a set of mythical and ritual meanings which, if we accept Propp's reconstruction, were once associated with the motif of the resuscitated beast. In this case, the original meanings were associated with practices which were no longer current, and, therefore, no longer meaningful. In European social memory, when mythological themes survive in oral memory at all, they often tend to survive as simply the raw material for fiction. The case of oral tradition in Africa is somewhat different. What could be happening in this case is that myth is recontextualized as genealogy. The memory of mythological figures, such as Nkongolo, survives only in so far as it can be accommodated into what the group regards as its more plausible body of narrative, genealogical tradition.

Examples of this sort of recontextualization are by no means rare; in traditional African societies, mythological figures regularly double as founding ancestors. There is no inherent incompatibility between mythology and genealogy, or, indeed, between either of the two and true narrative history. We should remember that 'myth' and 'mythology' are our terms, not theirs. As a rule, oral tradition combines mythology, genealogy, and narrative history rather than holding them apart. This means that king lists are often spliced onto stories of mythological ancestors, and clan origin myths are embedded in stories of tribal movements (Beidelman 1970; Pender-Cudlip 1972). This makes it comparatively easy for either the remembering group or the historian to rationalize this body of tradition into a seemingly plausible story of folk movements and dynastic succession. All that is necessary is to arrange the legendary and genealogical information into a coherent form, while suppressing the 'mythological excrescences'.

The very notion that oral tradition is a source of factual information may sometimes blind ethnohistorians to the real structure and historical significance of the traditions they study. What is the significance of a shift from one pattern of remembering to another? It may reflect the group's changing perceptions of their own past, or, as in the changes in fairy tales, their changing perception of what is socially acceptable. It is striking, in this instance, that Vansina's treatment of the oral tradition of the Luba not only rationalizes this tradition into a succession of historical figures and events, but also 'euhemerizes' the tradition.

Euhemerism, which takes its name from Euhemerus, a Greek mythographer of c.300 BC, is the doctrine that 'the gods had been recruited from the ranks of mortal men' (Seznec 1972: 11). As a theory itself, euhemerism is usually dismissed out of hand (Kirk 1970: 1–2). Yet its significance perhaps lies less in its theoretical value as such, than in the historical fact that it provided a vehicle for the recontextualization and transmission of much of classical mythology. In the ancient world, the euhemeristic interpretation of mythology developed in conjunction with the allegorical interpetations of the Stoics and the Neoplatonists. These two strategies of interpretation provided a means of recontextualizing classical myths into pseudo-historical genealogies and stories with allegorical meanings. This recontextualization provided ancient peoples with both a way of preserving their mythology in a way that seemed rational, and a way of the giving to this mythology an ethical meaning acceptable to a literate, classical culture.

The subsequent history of the doctrine that the gods were once mortal men is no less interesting. The doctrine was quickly adopted by the Fathers of the Church, who used it as a weapon against pagans: 'Those to whom you bow were once humans like yourselves' (Clement of Alexandria, in Seznec 1972: 12). Gradually, however, with the spread of Christianity, the euhemerist tradition lost this polemical function, being retained simply as a means of ordering information concerning pagan history, both classical and then, later, Celtic and Germanic. In his *Chronicle*, written in about AD 300, Eusebius identifies the Babylonian god Baal as the first king of the Assyrians, and dates his reign to the time of the war between the Cyclops and the Titans. Isidore of Seville codified this tradition into the universal history of the world divided into six periods. This periodization was, as Seznec remarks, 'rudimentary', but it was enriched 'with a wealth of marvelous detail' (1972: 14). From here, the euhemerist tradition passed into the Middle Ages, where it served as the basis for innumerable chronologies and universal histories.

Although the euhemerist tradition was only pseudo-historical, it could still serve as the vehicle for erudition. Scholars in the Middle Ages, 'sifted, correlated and cross-checked' the various universal histories, 'as any other evidence'. The tradition grew in richness, detail, and complexity. Since they based themselves almost entirely on late sources already in the tradition, there was no reason that these scholars would suspect that the tradition itself was spurious. Had medieval Western Europe been visited by a party of extraterrestrial ethnohistorians, they would not have lacked a corpus of plausible stories, king lists, and genealogies describing the far distant past from which to draw their 'residuum' of historical fact.

For all its inanity as a theory of mythology, the euhemerist tradition marks a historical stage in the development of European social memory.

It is a development, moreover, that reflects a general process of social and cultural change. In this sense, the recontextualization of social memory has a wider historical significance. Where one is in a position to trace the development of memory as it preserves, yet transforms, itself in moving from one genre to another, one has the opportunity to study this process of social change in contemporary experience. This is one of the senses in which social memory is truly a witness from the past, and a historical source.

We can give an example of how such evidence might be used by returning to fairy tales. The successive recontextualizations of the themes connected with the 'resuscitated beast' motif is suggestive (above, pp. 67–8). If we accept Propp's study, the earliest instances of the motif are in the context of hunting rituals. If we accept, too, that, despite its late date, Snorri's *Edda* preserves pre-Christian traditions, the next appearance of the theme would be in Nordic mythology. After this, the theme appears as a hagiographic motif in the life of St Germanus of Auxerre. Next, it appears at a witches' sabbath. (There are numerous other examples of this; see Farinelli and Paccagnini 1989: 15–97 and notes.) Finally, the theme appears in a fairy tale.

As this historical itinerary proceeds, the theme itself changes in a marked way. In the first two instances, the theme has specifically masculine connotations. It is part of a hunting ritual; it is associated with the god Thor. In the witches' sabbath, however, the theme has acquired a specifically feminine association. Although the Inquisitor insisted that the sacrificed beast could be resuscitated only through the intervention of the Devil himself, the witness's testimony clearly stated otherwise: it was the Lady of the Feast who accomplished the deed. This feminine association is strengthened as the theme passes into fairy tales, for here both the magic tree and the resuscitated beast meet at the tomb of the mother.

How are we to account for this change of gender? The first reference to the theme in a hagiographic context is in the ninth-century life of St Germanus by the monk Eiric. The specific way in which the theme is used here is interesting. The story describes the saint's visit to Britain. In the course of this visit, Germanus arrived at the door of a petty king and asked for shelter. Being 'barbaric both in body and soul', the king refused him hospitality, and Germanus was forced to seek refuge with the king's cowherd. Impressed by Germanus's saintly demeanour, the cowherd not only offered him shelter, but also served the saint his only calf as the evening meal. Germanus accepted it; after the meal, however, he requested that the bones of the calf be collected in its skin. These were then placed in a manger before the calf's mother. When this was done, the calf returned to life. The next day, the saint deposed the barbaric king, placing upon the throne in his stead the good cowherd, whose descendents continued afterwards to reign in Britain (*Miracula Germani*, quoted in Bertolotti 1979: 478).

The exact words of the text seem to give a clue to the precise meaning in context of the theme in this particular version. We read that the saint ordered the skin and the bones to be placed in a manger in front of the mother: *ante matrem in praesepio componat*. The Latin word '*praesēpe*' – like the English word 'manger' – is strongly associated with the birth of Christ. Interpreting the detail as containing a reference to the Nativity helps explain the rest of the story. The barbaric, pagan king is dethroned, and the cowherd takes his place. St Germanus has evidently converted the cowherd, for the story mentions that he founds a line of Christian rulers. The cowherd, like his calf, is thus 'reborn'; and this makes it hard to take the communal meal made of the sacrificed, and later resuscitated, calf as not containing a reference to the Eucharist. Thus, in a manner very typical of early medieval saints' lives, a set of pagan motifs is reinterpreted in the light of the central symbols of the story of Christ. In this particular case, however, this also meant bringing these motifs into contact with the figure of the Mother of Christ. This may help explain the change in sexual connotation in the themes themselves.

This is speculative. If we wished to construct a historical argument about the influence of Christianity in the recontextualization of folk motifs, we would need to amass a great deal more evidence and consider the matter in a variety of different guises. At this stage, we have only the beginnings of a hypothesis. This, however, is not the point of the example; we have included it here not to make any specific empirical claims about it, but rather to show how the idea of recontextualization can help us to understand the processes of cultural change.

The violent amputations that ethnohistorians occasionally inflict on oral tradition are often undertaken in the belief that these traditions can be used by historians only as the repositories of historical fact. What this notion ignores, however, is that the process of transmission and diffusion of oral tradition is itself historical. It is historical, moreover, regardless of whether the information it contains consists of kernels of true fact, or merely folk motifs. Accompanying the process of transmission of oral tradition is a process of reinterpretation. Every time a tradition is articulated, it must be given a meaning appropriate to the context, or to the genre, in which it is articulated. This necessity to reinterpret often lies behind changes within the tradition itself. These changes may be small in scale, or they may be large-scale recontextualizations of the entire tradition. In whatever case, the process of reinterpretation reflects real changes in external circumstances as well. It may sometimes be the case that a motif retained in a special way in the oral memory of myth or folk-tale may provide us with an important clue concerning the nature of these changes. But here we move from the issue of the structure of narratives to the issue of their meaning for specific social groups. How such groups construct themselves through remembering is the theme of the next chapter.

3
Class and Group Memories in Western Societies

The peasants of Gagliano were indifferent to the conquest of Abyssinia, and they neither remembered the World War nor spoke of its dead, but one war was close to their hearts and constantly on their tongues; it was already a fable, a legend, a myth, an epic story. This was the war of the brigands. Brigandage had come to an end in 1865, seventy years before, and only a very few of them were old enough to remember it, either as participants or as eye-witnesses. But all of them, old and young, men and women, spoke of it with as much passion as if it were only yesterday. When I talked to the peasants I could be sure that, whatever the subject of our conversation, we should in some way or another slip into mention of the brigands. Their traces are everywhere; there is not a mountain, gully, wood, fountain, cave or stone that is not linked with one of their adventures or that did not serve them as refuge or hideout. (Levi 1948: 137)

The peasants of 'Gagliano' (Carlo Levi's pseudonym for Aliano in Basilicata, the instep of Italy) in 1936 remembered the days of the brigands in the 1860s because they had some meaning for them, whereas World War I had none; the latter was just another mortal affliction imposed by the government, but the brigands had fought for them, against the newly formed Italian state, in the peasants' last resistance to the modern world. That is to say, even the Risorgimento of 1859–70, in Levi's time the mythic historical moment for Italians as a whole, particularly the middle classes (cf. below, p. 128), was simply remembered by these peasants as something that had to be opposed. We have seen that social memory exists because it has meaning for the group that remembers it. But the way this meaning is articulated is not a simple one. We have been concentrating on narrative context as a guide to how the forms of memory can be structured, and therefore unpicked. What sorts of things are remembered in the first place, and why, is an equally important issue, however. Events can be remembered more easily if they fit into the forms of narrative that the social group already has at its disposal; many peasantries, for example, have well-established ways of recounting local revolts against the state, just like Aliano's brigands, as we shall see. But they tend to be remembered in the first place because of their power to legitimize the present, and tend to be interpreted in ways that very closely parallel (often competing) present conceptions of the world. Memories have their own specific grammars, and can (must) be analysed as narratives; but they also have functions, and can (must) also be analysed in a functionalist manner, as guides, whether uniform or contradictory, to social identity, as we shall see in this chapter. These two procedures are not really distinct, but each of them needs to be analysed on its own terms before they can be combined, as they will be in the two chapters that end this book.

The essential subjectivity of memory is the key issue to begin with. Of course, memories about the past can themselves change across time, but, even when they do not, they will certainly be selected, out of the potentially infinite set of possible memories, for their relevance to the individuals who remember them, for their contribution to constructing personal identity and relationships. This is true both when individuals recall their own personal experiences, and when they remember episodes from the stock of memories that are collectively held. But the relevance of memories to others is, obviously, particularly relevant when they are articulated; *shared* memories, indeed the sharing process itself, that is to say, the production of spoken or written narratives about the past, will take form within the framework of the meaning given them by the group inside which they are told. (Many of Carlo Levi's peasants had experienced World War I, but even among ex-combatants, it seems, this experience was not given enough meaning for it to be talked about; it was on the way to being socially, even if not individually, forgotten.[1]) These points have been widely discussed, above all in the last decade or

---

[1] The alternative reading is that they did not want to talk to Levi about it – that the social group that could be constructed by a (presumably hostile) commemoration of the war did not include him. We shall see examples of such patterns later in the chapter, but we might doubt it in this instance, for Levi seems to have had a close relationship to the Alianesi. Rural communities elsewhere in Italy, by contrast, as, for example, in parts of Piemonte, identified much more closely with the war, and their male members, at least, remembered it very clearly sixty years later (Revelli 1977).

so, at least on a theoretical level.[2] What has to be done now, however, is to use those memories about which we have documentation in order to give concrete examples of how social identities are actually constructed through this or that version of the past; and this is a much harder task. In part, this is because of the conceptual difficulties involved; indeed, not even the theorists of the process have all managed to present detailed research that really illuminates it. In part, however, it is a simple question of evidence.

This last statement may appear surprising. After all, even if we do not have much direct evidence about the social memories of people who lived before our generation (although, as we shall see, something can be said about the memories of European peasants and town-dwellers going back into the seventeenth century, and sometimes even the fourteenth), we have now the wealth of recollections that has been collected in the last two decades, above all by oral historians. But not all oral historians have been very interested in analysing memories for their social meanings, rather than as life stories, that is to say individual commemorations consisting of more or less true statements about the lived past. Indeed, not all oral historians have been very interested in analysis at all, until very recently; as we commented earlier (p. 2), many of their projects have been aimed more at constituting archives of living testimony, normally by the oldest members of a society, who have the longest personal memories and are therefore in some sense more 'authoritative' than younger people (the latter being, furthermore, more likely to have their memories 'spoilt' by outside influences, such as books or TV). Such archives are often themselves *acts* of commemoration, monuments to the past, as well as (or, sometimes, rather than) the complex historical sources that they can be when they are critically analysed.

One can see why these patterns have developed. In part, they derive from the original interest that these memories had for most researchers, which was precisely and legitimately the memorialization of those people whose experience and whose voice could not be found in documents, which is the great bulk of us; as well as – and by extension –

---

[2] Examples include Tonkin 1991; Samuel and Thompson and Tonkin in Samuel and Thompson 1990; Dakhlia 1990; Passerini 1988; Thompson 1988: 135–49; Debouzy 1986; Grele 1985; Joutard 1983; Johnson et al. 1982; Portelli 1981a; 1981b; Bouvier et al. 1980, which give clear discussions of what can be called the 'anti-positivist' wing of oral history; see Collard 1989, Price 1983, Rosaldo 1980, MacGaffey 1970, for anthropological approaches. The clustering of references round the end of the decade is not chance; there seems to be a sea change in methodological awareness occurring right now. References from after 1989 have not been fully incorporated into our text.

the finding out of things about the past that could not be discovered in written texts. In part, they result from a defensiveness that many oral historians have had about their material, a felt need, in the face of attacks by more 'mainstream' historians that have been little short of hysterical, to justify oral sources as potentially 'reliable', or at least as reliable as documents are (Thompson 1988: 67–71, 101–17). They may often also derive from a feeling that the alternative way of looking at memories, as statements that, whether they are true or false represent-ations of the past, have a meaning in the present, has not seemed to many historians to be sufficiently 'historical' as a method. As the dates on which informants were recorded begin to recede into the past, this sense of embarrassment may lessen a little.

But, in the meantime, we have a problem. These archives essentially exist on tape; they have rarely been published, and never published in full. They have been used, sometimes with little explicit critical control, as sources; and extracts from them, often lengthy ones, can be found in books. But these extracts are almost always taken out of context, in the sense that they tend to cut out interviewers' questions, periphrases, repetitions, chronological disorganization, and conversational moves towards or away from topics – as well as, almost inevitably, tones of voice and other elements of the performance that are inherent in any oral narrative: the very features that provide the setting for the way people speak about the past, and that can tell us how the past is structured and commemorated by them. (For all this, see Passerini 1988, e.g., 131, and Tonkin 1991; for more imaginative transcription patterns, see Bosio 1981, and Tedlock in Grele 1985.) Worse: many such narratives have in reality been entirely patterned by the questions of the interviewer; in such cases, the conversational context that would allow us to give individual memories their meanings could not be found even on the tape. (See, for a good discussion of this, Ivey 1970.) Had Levi, for example, simply wanted to know about World War I, and specifically interrogated his peasants about it, he might never have noticed that they wanted to talk only about brigands. These distortions have the ironic result of undermining a pillar of the positivist defence of oral history, the possibility of evaluating a source's empirical reliability. Many oral sources genuinely cannot be criticized as tightly as documents can. This is not the case, fortunately, for all such material; as we shall see, some recent oral historians are highly rigorous and highly sophisticated. But in other cases, for all these reasons, we shall have to use our sources with some caution. A great deal of further research will have to be done (or published) before we can proceed more easily.

Returning to Levi's comments on Aliano, we can see that the key feature of the Alianesi that struck him in his description was that they had a different view of the relative importance of past events than he had, as he could tell from the ways, the contexts, in which they commemorated brigands. Many of the most fruitful analyses of the meaning of memory have derived from this simple realization (see, for example, Collard 1989); indeed, informants who think about the past *just like* outside observers have often, rightly or wrongly, been treated as a little suspect. This is a good place for us to start as well, through the question, 'Why do different social groups remember this rather than that?' Social groups, are, however, very various indeed, and we cannot even begin to look at them all. In this chapter we shall concentrate on modern Western Europe and, to a lesser extent, the European colonies in the Americas. In this context, we shall give brief discussions of four broadly drawn types of group memory: the memory of peasants (by which we mean all settled subsistence cultivators, whether with landlords or not); that of working-class communities; that of 'national' communities, which are not always nation-states, but which certainly almost always represent the group memories of a bourgeois intelligentsia; and that of women, that is to say, the issue of how far the social memory of women is differently structured from that of men (for most of our sources for the other groups are, in practice, going to be the voices of males). The most familiar of these types will probably be national memories, but we shall argue that nations are just like social groups of any other kind; national views about what constitutes relevant history are certainly not more significant (still less, more objective) than anyone else's. It follows from what we have already said that we shall be relatively detached about the empirical accuracy of such memories, for it is the function of commemoration rather than the truth about what is commemorated that is our chief interest. We shall not normally, or even usually, doubt their accuracy, however, although it may be remarked that inaccurate memories do shed a more unmediated light on social memory than accurate ones do: they are not, so to speak, polluted by 'real' past events. We shall discuss, as well as different group criteria for the importance of past events, different conceptions of time and of legitimization, all of which can serve to delineate the social nature of memory and its meaning for specific social groups – both those we have selected and the very many others that we cannot include. These discussions will in turn serve as a basis for putting narrative forms and narrative contents together in our last two chapters, which deal, respectively, with medieval narratives and images of the *mafia* in Sicily.

Peasant memories

In the late 1960s, Philippe Joutard, a historian of early modern France, while studying the Camisard revolts of 1702–4 in the Protestant areas of the Cévennes mountains of the south of France, began to ask contemporary peasants from the area about it (Joutard 1977a). He was amazed to discover an extremely complex memorialization of the Camisards – the richness of which, indeed, turned him into a full-fledged oral historian with his own research group in Aix-en-Provence. Protestant Cévenols can easily, and love to, recount a great deal about the Camisard past. What sorts of things, though, and why?

The Camisard wars were a violent reaction among Protestant peasants to local enforcement of the Revocation of the Edict of Nantes, Louis XIV's outlawing of Protestantism. This reaction was largely stirred up by local Messianic preaching. The Camisards had several heroic leaders, such as Jean Cavalier, Pierre Laporte (called Roland), and Henri Castanet, and for two years they kept Royalist troops out of the central Cévennes by guerrilla tactics and the occasional pitched battle, until they were eventually overcome. In the century that followed they were condemned as fanatics not only by Catholics but even by Protestants of the literate elite, until their rehabilitation by Romantic, Protestant historians of the nineteenth century, who wrote enthusiastic accounts of Camisard leaders and their battles; indeed, the late nineteenth century saw a wave of formal commemorations of the uprising, and the building of memorials to it in most villages. Modern oral accounts, however, while owing something to the histories, which most informants have read, and indeed to the memorials as well, frequently focus on altogether more 'minor' affairs – a village skirmish, or, very often, the personal fortunes of a family ancestor. These accounts are essentially structured by village and family memory, even though it is clear that all informants see the wars as being experienced by the Protestant community as a whole; they are in this respect independent of nineteenth-century historiography, and many of them seem indeed to derive directly from eighteenth-century experience, which had remained underground, commemorated in oral culture, until its rehabilitation over a century later.

Traditionally, Camisard stories have been told to children in the Cévennes in the same way as folk-tales are told elsewhere (and, indeed, some folk motifs survive in Camisard stories). They constitute a symbolic past that dramatizes and romanticizes Cévenol Protestant resistance to the state, and are in this sense what anthropologists call a 'mythological charter', a founding image that justifies all forms of local resistence. The stories are not for that reason necessarily unreliable. Here, as elsewhere, many of them are 'verifiable', in that they are backed up by eighteenth-century documents; indeed, some of them can be accepted as adding to (or, in some cases, correcting) our knowledge of the wars as derived from written texts. Other stories derive from such documents themselves, or, more often, from the historical rewritings of them dating from the last 150 years. Still others are largely or entirely invented. But all of them have the same function: that of constituting the Protestant community's identification of itself as a community of resistance, which is partly backed up by and partly creates a tradition of resistance that has continued to exist in the area until today. (For all this, see Joutard 1977a: 279–356; and, further, Joutard 1977b; Pelen and Joutard in Joutard 1979; Poujol 1981; Pelen 1982; Lewis 1985.)

Many of the Camisard memories are essentially geographical: this pass, this cave (caves were Camisard hideouts), this assembly spot. Just as in Levi's Aliano, Cévenol geography acts as a sort of memory theatre, in the sense given to it by the sixteenth-century mnemotechnicians: a direct aid for the recall of the past. It is clear that such an importance attached to local geography presupposes a stable population, which has existed in the mountains until after World War II; in the equally Protestant plains below the Cévenol highlands, memories of the uprising are much more sketchy, because there has long been more geographical mobility there (and indeed, with industrialization around the plains centre of Alès, even the geography has changed: Joutard 1977a: 289, 318–20; Lewis 1985: 165–73).[3] It is not surprising that Joutard and his associates found the detail of Camisard memories lessening in the 1970s, as mountain society became more mobile, and it is likely that the complexity of commemoration of the wars of the 1700s required for its survival a continuity of community high by the standards even of nineteenth-century, let alone twentieth-century, France.

The complexity of Camisard memory has had an important result: other memories of the historical past have become 'camisardized'. All other forms of Protestant affirmation are remembered as Camisard, including the eighteenth-century clandestine preaching known as the

---

[3] A good parallel for this use of landscape is the strong geographical sensibility shown in the historical narratives of the Ilongot in the Philippines (Rosaldo 1980); see further below, p. 1. Outside one's own personal environment, mental geographies can be more mutable as mentalities change: the classic example is Halbwachs' study of the changing sacred topography of Palestine in the imagery of successive Christian communities in the West (Halbwachs 1941).

Desert, which at the time was very hostile to the resistance tradition. So, sometimes, is the White Terror of 1815, the Catholic Royalist revenge on (often) Protestant Republicans, which was strong in the Cévennes. This and later moments of religious tension have also been remembered through stories of Protestants finding their houses marked to distinguish them from those of Catholics, an image taken from accounts of the St Bartholomew's Day Massacre in Paris in 1572, and thus signifying a feared Catholic pogrom. (This imagery is legendary too; it probably comes eventually from Exodus. Cf. Joutard 1976; 1977a: 312–14.) And those historical points of reference that are not remembered as Camisard are explicitly seen as analogous, such as the local support for Dreyfus, and the local activism of the World War II Resistance. Both of these are structured by an explicit pro-Judaism (on the grounds that both religious groups have been victims), but during the Resistance it could also be said – and not wholly wrongly – that the Maquisards were 'reliving' the Camisard period: *noms de guerre* such as Roland and Castanet were common, and so were eighteenth-century songs, reused Camisard hiding-places, and even remembered military tactics. That is to say, not just other memories of the past, but even perceptions of the present were seen in a perspective governed by memories of the eighteenth century. The Camisard past determined a continuity of political stance: in support of Revolution, Republic, and eventually the Left. This pattern has also structured, in reverse, the memories of the Catholic minority in the mountains, who remember the French Revolution as Camisard, and maybe the Wars of Religion of the 1560s as well, and who recall their opposition in 1906 to the official separation of Church and State with the same pride in resistance that their Protestant neighbours have (Joutard 1977a: 297–8, 320–2). The Camisard wars dominate the past for all inhabitants of the central Cévennes, Catholic and Protestant alike. But only in the core areas of the 1702–4 revolt do Catholics have a highly articulated sense of past 'historical' events at all: elsewhere, they are more likely to recount tales of wolves.

This sort of commemoration of a period of past opposition, physical or moral, can be found, in some other Protestant areas of rural France, to work in similar ways. One such is the mountains of the Drôme, east of the Rhône, above Valence (Reverchon and Gaudin 1986). Here, there was no Camisard war, and memory has focused on the Desert, which has produced a symbolism less of resistance than of persecution. This symbolism has a very similar structure, however. Here, the nineteenth-century analogue is not Dreyfus, but rather the local revolts against Napoleon III's *coup d'état* of 1851, although the dominant theme in people's memories is the subsequent repression rather than the resistance itself. The memories are family-focused once again, and are also explicitly patterned by geography, with Protestant landmarks acting as guides for Maquisard strategies, as well as for modern Protestant assemblies, which consciously replicate those of the Desert. In the Drôme, however, one single event has not wiped out all preceding ones – Protestant repressions are remembered back into the seventeenth century or before; there is room for more flexibility, at least inside the basic format.

On the other hand, one should not forget that such imagery in French peasant societies is not confined to Protestant areas, or to the Left. Even the Camisards had no greater impact on the memory of the Cévennes than the Revolutionary armies of 1793–6 had on the Vendée in the west of France (Martin 1984). The Vendéens have a right to remember this, for, in the civil war between the armies of the Revolutionary government and the local Catholic and Royalist resistance, perhaps a sixth of the local population died (Jones 1988: 225–30). But the resultant commemoration has been systematic and long-lasting, sanctioned both at the official and Catholic level (monuments and ceremonies) and – linked to this, but with its own autonomous roots – at the level of family recollection, with the mixture of oral-derived and text-based memory that we have already seen for the Cévennes. That is, the *Vendée militaire* structures local popular consciousness in exactly the same way, and with the same sorts of touchstones, as the Camisards do. Other acts of Vendéen resistance against the nineteenth-century secular state have been absorbed into the traditions of 1793, too, as have some from the Wars of Religion of the sixteenth. Vendéen local consciousness has even had economic results: local inhabitants have tended to avoid migrating to towns outside the region, and in recent years, under the aegis of the Church, have developed their own rural industries, which themselves have then reproduced the region in its own specificity. This has survived; Vendéens may not remember the 1793 massacres as well as they did a generation ago, but there were certainly no tricolours out in 1989 (R.J. Holt, pers. comm.).

Several points follow from these characterizations. One is, as we have emphasized, the obvious conclusion that within these communities, events have a hierarchy of importance different from that familiar to outside observers. The Camisard obsession led Cévenols to say relatively little about the French Revolution, though they supported it. And elsewhere in peasant France, most obviously in the areas of the south-east studied by Joutard's pupils and associates in Aix, precise memories about the Revolution seem equally rare – at Arves in the Savoy Alps and Lus in the eastern Drôme (a Catholic village), informants tended to have much more to say about the evil deeds of the lords of the *ancien régime* (this tends, here as elsewhere, to focus on the droit de seigneur: Collomb 1982; Bouvier 1980: 145–52). Other omissions are equally alarming for the well-brought-up French historian: nothing on Napoleon, very little on World War I, almost nothing on the Popular Front. (This last event certainly held more meaning in towns, which have a separate sensibility to the past, as we shall see; it was not always remembered even there, however.) Such forgetting, in cases such as the Cévenols, is clearly a matter of choice, however, given the wealth of information available about earlier periods.

This is important, for several reasons. For a start, it emphasizes that the 'Great Events' of the past are designated as such by people external to most local societies, and certainly all peasant societies. This is indeed true everywhere, and not only in France, though such events are very clearly characterized there. The resistances of 1851 are not always counted among the major events of mid-nineteenth-century France by historians; and, similarly, Carlo Levi was slightly patronizing about the Alianese interest in brigands. None the less, just because historians regard Napoleon as worth remembering and discussing, other people are not required to think in the same way, or, indeed, to commemorate any Great Events at all. (This is certainly true as far as peasants are concerned, for, as we shall see, they tend to stress their social identity through images of resistance to the state, which are peculiarly unlikely to get into Great Events history.) There is a more specific reason why such choices are important, too: they show that these differences in commemorations are internal to communities, and not imposed from outside, whether by literature or schooling or the media, which would all have made memories more homogeneous, and would scarcely have failed to stress the Revolution and Napoleon. This cannot be repeated too often: however much a novel or a schoolteacher's story can affect the *content* of a memory of an event held by an individual or even a social group, it will have much less effect on which *sorts* of events social groups will characteristically choose to commemorate, which are linked to deeper patterns of identity.

This brings us to a second, connected point, one already referred to in the previous chapters: the differences between oral and literate cultures. All the societies we shall be looking at in this chapter were, at least in part, in touch with the world of writing, which, from the sixteenth century (and in some areas before), began to spread from the clerical, aristocratic, and bourgeois elites to the peasantry in the countryside and the poor in the towns: it spread at different speeds in different countries, but everywhere more quickly after 1850 or so. (See, e.g.,

Burke 1978: 250–8.) More people are better documented thereby; but it is also true to say that more memory comes to be structured through a dialectic between written and oral narrative. It has been argued by many theorists that there is a fundamental divide between oral and literate societies in their forms of organization and the ways they develop their world-views. (Classic examples are Ong 1982; Goody 1968; 1977; 1987 – the latter being the most nuanced.) We ourselves do not, in fact, believe this, as we argued above (p. 45); but the issue is relatively unimportant for our purposes here. It should be clear that in the Cévennes as in the Vendée, the former at least a highly writing-orientated society, people use books as only one out of many sources for their representations of the past. Writing on one level transforms memory, by fixing it; but, put as simply as this, such a development evidently has not taken place in the Cévennes, where social memories continue to relate closely to (doubtless changing) collective self-images. A moment's reflection will show why: no society is an entirely literate culture, including our own (and even including the heavily text-orientated microsocieties of academics); and shared memory, whatever its sources, tends to be communicated above all in the arena of the oral, through anecdote and gossip, with narrative patterns that can owe as much to oral as to literate tradition.

Anyway, as, for example, Ruth Finnegan and Elizabeth Tonkin have argued, there are few if any genres that can be regarded as restricted to either oral or literate culture: once writing has appeared, there are no 'characteristically oral' or 'characteristically literate' ways of describing the world (Finnegan 1977: 134–69; 1988: 86–109; Tonkin 1991). At the level of narrative, therefore, oral vs. literate is an unhelpful distinction, especially as it has been too often used by the literate to deny both rationality and legitimacy to oral culture. A better distinction is one found in all societies: that between stable and formal structures of narration and more informal ones. Stable structures exist in many types: the folk motifs indexed by Stith Thompson, the patternings of epic and ballad formulae (see above, pp. 44ff.), the anecdotes of early modern *colportage* literature (Mandrou 1964), the Great Events history of the compulsory schools of the 1870s and onwards (see, for France, Bonheur 1963), historical novels, or, nowadays, the romantic tropes of TV sagas. Each of these may well provide a genre in which memory can be recounted, and may well provide much of the content of the memory itself. But they tend to fit into wider and more fluid conversational discourses; it is these latter that can tell us more about the real meanings they have for particular people and groups.

A third point is the continuity between the past and the present.

People often distinguish between personal memories (or 'life histories') and 'oral tradition', the latter having to do with what is recounted, sometimes by professional remembrancers, of a past too remote to have been experienced by its narrators, or sometimes, as with folk-tales, of a past that is recognized to be imaginary. Indeed, few oral historians in Europe (as opposed, say, to Africa) study the latter at all.[4] The distinction certainly exists; many societies have separate sets of genres to recount each (Vansina 1985: 18ff.). But one could not argue, for example, that personal memories are more (or, indeed, less) 'reliable' than oral tradition, given the subjectivities we have discussed; and both of them, as well as written texts, can be profoundly structured by the same narrative forms. In the Ica valley of Peru, traditions about the 'Andean utopia' and the Inca foundation of the local irrigation system interpenetrate inextricably with memories of peasant struggles of the 1920s (Oré and Rochabrun 1986). In the Cévennes, as well, the two very evidently run into each other: *remembering* the Maquis and *recounting* the Camisards are tightly linked. That is to say, for our purposes, both are patterned by the same choices about social relevance.

There are contexts, on the other hand, in which this distinction has seemed, to some analysts, to be highly important for understanding peasant societies. Not all societies show the complex characterizations of the past that we see in the Cévennes. The distant past, as we have seen, is remembered selectively even there; and other societies seem to lack notions of archetypical events that define them as a historically specific group. Not a few peasant societies have appeared to commemorate the past exclusively through personal memories, and these personal memories often seem to be focused less on 'historically relevant' events than on the recurrent processes of the life cycle of the family, going back at the most to grandparents: daily life, the seasons, festivals, and the world of nature (often expressed in supernatural or folk-tale terms), with life histories superimposed onto and structured by these sorts of memory alone. These memories exist in all societies, of course; Cévenol Protestants have them as much as anyone else, and it is likely that they form the bulk of collective discourses about the past even in the

[4] There have been some accounts of European societies with specialist remembrancers of oral traditions along sub-Saharan African lines, such as that of the Scottish Highlands with its memories of the Massacre of Glencoe, the battle of Culloden, and the Clearances, or that of Serbia with its whole array of heroic verse narratives (Dorson 1971; Lord 1960 – see above, p. 44). For societies with more informal contexts of remembering, however, there seem to be few systematic historical analyses of such traditions outside the Aix-en-Provence school.

Cévennes (Pelen 1983; cf. Thompson 1988: 136). But it has sometimes been argued that memories of this kind are the most *normal* ones for peasants to have; that 'historical' events, whether national or local, tend to be forgotten by them because they are normally irrelevant to their experience, or else they are turned into real myths, such as that of the Golden Age, a past era of justice and happiness. People who argue this often go on to state that peasant societies have little or no conception even of the linear movement of time, but see it rather as cyclical, following the seasons and the family cycle: social change is not, in general, comprehensible to them, except in very schematic patterns of 'before' and 'after' – the appearance of cars, of electricity, or of new kinds of vegetables.[5] Let us look at this argument in more detail.

Françoise Zonabend studied personal memories in a Burgundian village, Minot in the Côte-d'Or, in the 1970s (Zonabend 1984). She noted that the two World Wars were used as dating tools for life histories, but were never discussed in them: war stories were entirely absent, and few other external events were even mentioned. She came to conclusions similar to those we have just described: community and family time were cyclical, outside any linear development, and 'history' was simply avoided. Simultaneously, however, she conceded one point that undermined her whole argument: the Resistance, with the score-settling of the Liberation, like previous political oppositions in the village, was regularly commemorated at least at one point – during elections. The Resistance in Minot was evidently very divisive, and presumably conflicted with the image the villagers wanted to give Zonabend, and maybe even themselves, of a community harmony structured by family cycles. Logically, therefore, they did not discuss it with her. But the memory of it was there, all the same, ready to appear when it was needed, as an alternative set of memories, an alternative community image, functional to some social situations but not others (Zonabend 1984: 196–203; cf. Aschieri 1985: 116–20).

This example shows quite clearly that informants may well not tell observers everything they think; and such a situation may well explain many other peasant communities mysteriously forgetful of major events, too, not least those about which they have opinions at variance with those known (or supposed) to be held by the questioner. Maria Pitzalis Acciaro found in her researches in central Sardinia that villagers would

---

[5] For the vegetables, see Joutard 1983: 179; Zonabend 1984: 27–8. For peasants without history, apart from the examples discussed below, see Le Roy Ladurie 1975: 425–31, for a typical formulation.

flatly deny the existence of local feuds even in the very weeks that their relatives were found shot dead, and we ourselves have had similar personal experiences in both Sardinia and Sicily, with informants implausibly insisting, for example, on the long-standing amity between villages when local tensions were transparent. In central Sardinia, outsiders are potentially spies and emissaries of the *carabinieri* and the state; truth-telling to outsiders is seen not only as informing, but also as a version of lying (Pitzalis Acciaro 1978: 21–6, 86–100). Such caution about talking about community dissensions to outsiders can be found, in less extreme forms, everywhere. And when it comes to community affirmations, at least if they are heterodox ones, caution can be just as great: it is not likely that the Cévenols as yet boasted much about the Camisards to Catholic visitors of the 1750s, or Basilicatan peasants much about about the brigands to inquisitive north Italians as early as the 1880s. The possibility of such diffidence must be recalled in other contexts, as well; and when, as happens in many cases, the whole of local history is constructed socially out of memories of family dis-sensions (see below, p. 112), all commemorations of the past may be invisible to the outsider.

We do not wish to argue that everyone who finds a peasant society which remembers only in terms of family cycles is, by definition, wrong. Sometimes, the transmission of tradition is broken, by some local vicissitude; sometimes, perhaps when it is too negative to be borne, it is better to forget it – though failure, at least if it is heroic, is quite often commemorated; sometimes, with social change, traditions lose their meaning, and are either transformed or simply vanish. If commemor-ation is functionally relevant in order to construct local identity, clearly its survival is less assured when that relevance recedes. But historians have been rather too prone to leap to conclusions about peasant forgetfulness. Sometimes, they have generalized too much from their disappointment at individual examples of the elision of events they themselves considered important (see, for a well-analysed set of such examples, from both peasant and urban sources, Joutard 1983: 174–9). Sometimes, however, they have simply asked the wrong questions.

This brings us back to the distinction between personal memory and oral tradition, for oral historians have tended to focus their interests on the former: on the personally experienced past of their informants; on how they lived; on how they married, worked, brought up children. (For an example of this, see the sample questionnaire in Thompson 1988: 296–306.) Such narratives will always privilege the cyclic, with the outside world impinging externally on memory, rather than structuring it. Indeed, it is not just peasants (or factory workers) who remember the past like this; we all do. No matter how keyed into historical culture one is, one's memories of major events – World War II, for instance – can turn into simple exercises in day-to-day survival, at home or at the front, or sources of isolated anecdotes, whether terrifying, terrible, amusing, or life-affirming. World War II, was, of course, an event which brought personal experience and collective experience together, and thus the relevance of the former to an understanding of the latter has always been clear. But the two are tightly linked in much less dramatic moments in the histories of groups as well; and here the relevance of the personal to the collective (and vice versa) needs to be brought out through more sensitive analysis. Social commemoration can be appreciated, in part, through tighter investigations of the narrative contexts in which the war or other events are talked about by people in their personal anecdotes. But it can also be got at by asking questions about traditions, and not just personal memories. Such questions may and will elicit much 'folklore', but they are the only questions that will produce the genealogy of traditions that we have for the Cévennes or the Drôme or the Vendée, which gain their force precisely because they link the recounted with the experienced past. In truth, we need both kinds of questions; for discussions of traditions, too, may well be misunderstood if they are divorced from the conversational contexts of life histories: the real symbolism of the past may be missed as a result. But one cannot restrict oneself to a study of the one and conclude from that that the other does not exist.

Up to here, the points we are making are relevant not only for peasants, but also for the urban working classes, which have also been regarded as outside the framework of linear time by some observers (see below, p. 123); much the same has been true in the case of traditional writing about women. But peasants have tended to be regarded as, *par excellence*, the social class outside time, and this for specific reasons. Peasants have often been categorized, too often indeed for comfort, as not really part of the cultural world at all: mute, immemorial, forever and unchangingly bound to the cycles of nature (as opposed to the cultural, creative activities of even the most dispossessed artisans), and, as a result, excluded by definition from real historical processes. For all his sympathy for the Alianesi, Carlo Levi discussed his peasants with this sort of imagery in mind, and he had a long literary genealogy behind him: it can even be found in Marx (Levi 1948; Marx 1852/1973: 238–9). It is an imagery that, in a more subtle and attenuated form, one can find in the work of many modern historians and sociologists too, in particular when they argue that peasantries undergo history, rather than acting in it, and that even when peasants take on political positions they do not really understand them, for they interpret them simply in terms of their necessarily limited perceptions of their particular situation.

Peasants do not, of course, always know or understand what is going on; and when their traditional class enemies, landlords, who were at least usually local, were supplemented in the early modern period by equally predatory townsmen (such as wholesalers, or doctors and lawyers), and the distant, unfamiliar, but more and more exigent state, they can hardly be blamed if they reacted in ways that do not always seem to be characterized by historically minded sophistication. But peasants as conscious political actors, with recognizable political perceptions that are based on (true or false) representations of a relevant past, are not in reality very difficult to find. When brigands in southern Italy took up arms against the new kingdom of Italy in the 1860s, they fought in the name of a discredited and reactionary regime, the Bourbon kingdom of Naples, and indeed in the name of 'king' Conradin (d. 1268), who was never more than an unsuccessful claimant of the throne and who thus was, as a ruler, an entirely legendary figure. None the less, this does not mean that they lacked a clear awareness of what they were fighting *against*, for they were also genuinely resisting a foreign power that appeared to them to be (and indeed would become) even more oppressive; their peasant supporters and kinsfolk knew this as well as they did, and remembered them for it thereafter.[6] Perhaps the emblematic example of this dialectic between error, imagery, and authentic group consciousness is the 'Great Fear', which sped across France in July 1789, leading nearly the whole country to believe, always falsely, that brigand armies, probably paid by aristocrats and including foreign mercenaries, were just over the hill, ready to kill and burn in order to put down the new self-confidence of the *Tiers Etat*. The peasants may have been wrong, and often ludicrously so – flocks of sheep, the reflection of the sun in windows, and burning weeds all became brigands somewhere; but they reacted like this because they had a perfectly clear, remembered image of the terms in which aristocrats were capable of

[6] For more sympathetic analyses of the internal structures of the political perceptions of the peasantry, see, as the classics, Hobsbawm 1959; 1972a. One strand that is worth mentioning is the false genealogies that have commonly been constructed by peasants between early rebellions and modern political movements; apart from the obvious example of the Camisards, one could cite Bercé 1974: 673, on nineteenth-century socialists in Périgord as heirs of the seventeenth-century Croquants, or Davis 1974: 45–6, on a socialist leader of the 1920s, in Pisticci in the Basilicata, as being like 'Masianedd di Roma' (Masianello, the seventeenth-century leader of the Naples uprising): as usual, however false, these representations show a fully autonomous peasant perception of their place in historical development.

responding to peasant self-affirmation, and their reactions were of course very closely in tune with the development of events in Paris, which, indeed, they were following with careful attention (Lefebvre 1973; Jones 1988: 60–85).

The most important issue for us is not *whether* peasants (or any other social group) can have a historical consciousness that is separable from the continuous concerns of everyday life, for, clearly, they can, and often do; but, rather, which consciousness, and why, and why individual cases differ. We have already posed the question of why peasants choose to emphasize one event rather than another, but this can now be generalized. To understand the social structures of peasant memory fully, we would have to ask why peasant communities sometimes remember precise and detailed events such as the Camisard wars; why, at other times, they remember much sketchier versions of events in the past, perhaps as vague chronological markers for memories focused on family life cycles; why, at still other times, they talk about 'events' that historians do not see as real at all, such as stories about *ancien régime* lords, or the Roland legend, which is still popular among peasantries of the most diverse types, as we shall see; and why, finally, they sometimes talk in terms of narratives that even the tellers do not see as real, such as 'The Juniper Tree' and the rest of the folk-tale tradition. To consider what each of these can mean for collective identity, we would also have to ask how far back in time events are remembered, how much their recounting owes to formal narrative structures (whether oral or written), and how much these histories are local (of local resistances, say, or of family feuds) and how much non-local (most typically, national). Ideally, we would also investigate the different images of the past of different strata inside individual peasant societies: and, not least, the role of the local 'traditional intellectuals', established mouthpieces of the peasantry who are not, however, peasants themselves – most classically, the priest, the notary, and the teacher (Gramsci 1971: 5–23). Such a list makes it clear that, to do justice to the social function of peasant memory alone, it would be necessary to write a book several times the length of this one, even supposing the relevant research had been done. Here, we shall restrict ourselves to commentaries along these lines, on two or three further empirical examples; let us start with north-east Brazil.

North-eastern Brazilian peasants (Nordestinos) of the dry backlands (*sertão*) tend to look back to a group of early twentieth-century rural heroes, most notably the bandit Lampião (d. 1938), who dominated the *sertão* for twenty years; his predecessor Antônio Silvino (though Silvino's memory has tended to become subsumed into stories about the younger man); and the holy man and political boss Padre Cicero (d. 1934). No one has yet bothered to do much systematic oral-historical study of what peasants remember in this region; but many of their principal points of reference are visible in texts, in particular the still widely circulated chap-book ballads called *literatura de cordel*. These are small, crudely printed (usually) eight-page books (*folhetos*) with titles such as 'The Death of Lampião'; or 'Lampião's Fortress'; or, with a certain imaginative contemporaneity, 'How Lampião met Kung Fu in Juazeiro do Norte' (Kung Fu being transformed into a rival Japanese bandit; Juazeiro is Padre Cicero's cult centre) – as well as titles reflecting less historically specific themes, such as great droughts, magic cows, brave cowboys who fought dragons, girls who dressed fashionably and went to hell, or 'The Ten Commandments of Cane Spirit'. They also feature (as a sort of local journalism) any number of national and international political events, such as the deaths of Sacco and Vanzetti, John Kennedy, or Aldo Moro; innumerable ballads about the Brazilian dictator Getúlio Vargas (d. 1954); texts about the Falklands War (starring 'Dona Margareth, por arte de Satanás [by Satan's Art]': *folheto* by Rodolfo Coelho Cavalcante, 1982); comets; football matches; and so on. To try to understand peasant memory through such texts poses problems, of course. They constitute a literary genre, with its own specific rules; and they are by named authors, who themselves have to be understood sociologically, as a recognizable group of traditional intellectuals: as literate (though not very), and as, for example, critical of local abuses of power rather than the structure of power itself (Cantel 1980: 59). But although *cordel* reflects the attitudes of its authors more directly than those of the peasants, it has to be accessible to the latter, and, at least in part to respect their value systems, because they buy it; peasants buy *folhetos* not only because they are well told (or well sung, often by their author-vendors themselves, at the markets of the northeast), but also because what *folhetos* say has meaning for the members of local society.[7]

It is in this context that it is striking how often the ballads come back to Lampião. He first appeared in *cordel* simply because he was a contemporary figure, like Vargas, who is the central political figure in the

---

[7] The analyses of *cordel* literature that we have found most useful are Lessa 1973, Cantel 1980, and Peloso 1984; we are also indebted, for guides to and discussions of the material, to Paulo Farias and Altamirando Camacám. The easiest parallel is seventeenth- and eighteenth-century French *colportage* literature, the Bibliothèque bleue of Troyes (Mandrou 1964, with the warnings of Ginzburg 1980: xiv–vi); *cordel* is more local and much less obviously didactic than this, however.

history of Brazil this century. But Vargas is by now forgotten by the ballad tradition which was once so full of him, except as an occasional point of reference; Lampião, by contrast, while less local heroes come and go, remains in the centre of local culture, and has new *folhetos* written about him all the time. Reflecting the mixed feelings of the peasants themselves, Lampião is sometimes a devil incarnate, sometimes a hero; his devilry is treated with a certain reluctant respect, however (his violence reflects values that Nordestinos can recognize), and his heroism is clearly directed against the enemies of the peasantry, that is landowners, shopkeepers, tax-collectors, or the army (Peloso 1984: 54–86). So, for example, at the end of José Pacheco's famous 'The Arrival of Lampião in Hell', after a long battle between the bandit and many devils, we find Satan himself characterized as a shopkeeper:

> Houve grande prejuízo / no inferno, nesse dia: / queimou-se todo o dinheiro / que Satanás possuía. / Queimou-se o livro de pontos, / perdeu-se vinte mil contos, / somente em mercadoria (José Pacheco, c.1949).
> (There was great damage in hell, that day; all the money that Satan possessed got burnt, and the account books, and 20,000 *contos* were lost in merchandise alone.)

Lampião was not, in reality, always opposed to the enemies of peasants; like Silvino before him, he was often in the pay of landowners. The reality of his career, as Chandler has systematically shown, was almost without a hint of the positive qualities traditionally associated with the figure of the 'social bandit'. But this is not the point; he is remembered as one. (Chandler 1978; Hobsbawm 1972a; cf. Lewin 1979.) *Cordel* as a genre has made an important contribution to this version of his memory, and did so from the start; indeed, the bandits knew it themselves, and pre-empted the game, so to speak, by making up their own songs about their exploits – in a style different from that of *cordel*, but often demonstrably the source of the latter's detail. Peasant 'memory' of Lampião is thus conditioned by ballads, and indeed, more recently, by TV and radio as well – though radio, at least, can be so local and so amateur as to be virtually a disembodied storyteller. But the continuing relevance of this version of Lampião for a peasant audience is the essential reason why ballads about him stay in the repertoire at all. Lampião remains central to the social memory of Nordestinos, as a resister, and even, to an extent, as one of them, in effect a local boy made good, and they do not need much encouragement to reminisce about him today, either, as anyone who visits the region can discover.

Lampião's image in the *folhetos* has an epic aspect to it, and this is not chance. There are ballads in *cordel* not only about bandits, but also about Roland and Robert the Devil, French epic models with a long history in the popular literature of early modern Spain, Portugal, and Latin America; Lampião is treated in the same way as they (particularly Robert, a highly ambiguous figure in popular tradition). So were Jesuíno Brilhante in the 1870s and Antônio Silvino in the first decade of this century; Silvino, in particular, reputedly a more high-minded man than other bandits, could claim to be 'famous like the great hero of the North [Roland]', or to weep for his men 'as Charlemagne wept for his twelve knights' (Cantel 1980: 42–3; Peloso 1984: 67–8). The imagery of the present day looks back to Lampião, the last great bandit of the *sertão*; but the imagery of the bandit leaps even further back, to the noble heroes of medieval Europe, as popularized in the early modern period. This is significant. We can no longer interrogate Brilhante and Silvino's contemporaries to see what they thought about history; but they presumably did not talk so much about earlier bandits, because, before about 1870 in the north-east there were in fact very few. The earliest cycles we know about concerned (often unnamed) cows and cowboys; the only other points of reference at the end of the century were not Brazilian figures at all, but simply Roland, Robert, and the Empress Porcina, one of the many variants of the 'calumniated wife' folk motif (Peloso 1984: 92–106). It looks as though local historical memory, earlier than the development of the bandit tradition, did not fix upon any indigenous Nordestino or Brazilian events, but rather on these heroes of a legendary European past, who were never, even nominally, rooted in Brazil.[8]

The reconstruction of memory through texts rather than speakers poses more clearly than in our previous examples the problem of how much memory is determined by the characteristic narrative lines of a given genre, as discussed in the last chapter; it also sets into relief the issue of who controls commemoration in any given society, for local intellectuals 'speak for' peasants in societies other than that of north-east Brazil, and usually with more distance from them, too. But the role of the distant and foreign past as a historical (and moral) point of refer-

---

[8] One might have expected to find at least some historical reference points derived from Portugal, but these, too, seem to be absent; there is some evidence for the appeal of Sebastianismo – the messianic belief that the 'hidden' King Sebastian of Portugal (d. 1578) would return – into the 1830s and maybe the 1890s, but not thereafter (Azevedo 1947; Pereira de Queiroz 1977: 217–27; but see Marotti 1978: 153–5). To what extent people believed Roland and the others to be real historical figures is not a problem: they were real points of reference, at least (cf. among others, Veyne 1988).

ence is the issue that is most convenient to develop here, because it has
a number of immediate parallels. It is, in particular, remarkable how
popular Roland and the other Paladins of France have been among the
peasantries of the Romance-speaking world. In the Contestado uprising
of southern Brazil in 1914, the prose narrative of Charlemagne and the
Twelve Peers of France was literally a sacred text for the rebels, whose
leaders, indeed, called themselves the *imperador* and the *doze pares*
(though *par* was understood, in a world far from formal aristocracies, to
mean 'pair', with the result that there were twenty-four of them: Pereira
de Queiroz 1977: 277–9). The Spanish version of the same text was read
by Ezequiel Mendoza, one of the principal surviving participants in
(and oral sources for) the Mexican peasant rebellion of 1926–9 known
as the Cristiada, precisely as a prefiguration of that revolt. South Italian
peasants and bandits read *I reali di Francia* (the cycle of Pipin,
Charlemagne's father), too, and the text was the favourite reading of
the Tuscan mountain messiah Davide Lazzaretti (d. 1878); as we shall
see later, puppet-theatre representations of *The Song of Roland* were
extremely popular among the young *mafiusi* of nineteenth-century
Palermo as well. (Meyer 1974: 273–4; Levi 1948: 165; Hobsbawm 1959:
181–2; see below, p. 194.) The least one could say is that these texts
were very widely available, and had been for three centuries – they were
a major part of the Bibliothèque bleue, for example (Mandrou 1964:
131–47); they were popular for themselves, and over wide areas. They
commemorated groups of young fighters with strong bonds between
them that peasants minded to violence could very easily identify with.
But they were also, very often, so powerful that they, rather than any
more immediate local event or hero, were the models *par excellence* for
peasant images of justice; hence the number of nineteenth- or twentieth-
century risings that seem to have looked to Charlemagne and Roland. It
is evident that such examples show a view of the past different from that
in the Cévennes.

It is not at all easy to explain such a pattern, based as it is essentially
on absences. One may note that some of these peasant societies, those
that had a local image that could operate as a point of reference for
them, like Conradin for the Basilicata bandits, or the Sicilian Vespers of
1282 for nineteenth-century Sicilians (see below, p. 175ff.), used such
images *alongside* Charlemagne and Roland. What peasantries very often
have seemed to need is a point of reference in the past which they could
regard as a time of justice, and which they could perceive in personalized terms – good kings, noble bandits, French Paladins – and thus
through narratives. It may well be that, in parts of colonial Brazil, no
local time of justice had ever been perceived to exist, and that no 'real'

history had ever seemed to peasants worth commemorating, thus leaving
them with the relatively fixed versions of nobility and justice that are
represented by the legends of the Paladins of France. A parallel to this
can be found in the Indian communities of Mexico and Peru studied by
Wachtel, which have nothing relevant to look back to more recent than
the Spanish Conquest itself, which is acted out ritually every year, in
nearly every case simply as a drama of loss and trauma, the incomprehensible end of a legitimate historical past (Wachtel 1977: 33–58; but
compare the more positive use made of similar memories by the peasant
activists of the Ica valley in Peru in the early 1980s: Oré and Rochabrun
1986). Such a wretched role for the remembrance of the colonial period
in Latin America was not, of course, universal, and even in the specific
cases we have cited it is, in part, hypothetical: if the Cristeiros in
Mexico in 1926–9, for example, had had previous local reference points,
these could well have been blotted out of their memories, precisely by
the Cristiada itself. But this absence of legitimacy of the local past is at
least a possible explanation for such a generalized interest in Roland;
and it can certainly be said that when legitimate reference points did
become available, they were swiftly adopted. Indeed, once these modern
acts of defiance had run their course, in each case destroyed by the
armed power of the state, each uprising itself took on the role of a local
mythological charter for future history. The Cristiada, Lazzaretti,
Lampião, and the south Italian brigands put on the mantle of
Charlemagne, and invested him with local meaning, local attributes, and
even a local geography, and it is this which has persisted. A relevant
historical past may not always exist for the abandoned peasant
communities of the world, but it can certainly be *created*. In this respect,
these peasantries do indeed parallel that of the Cévennes: the Protestant
preachers who led the Camisards looked back to supposed local religious
precursors, the Albigensians and Waldensians, rather than to Charlemagne (Pelen 1982: 129 – though one of their generals did call himself
Roland), but their own uprising entirely replaced these distant images –
history in the Cévennes would henceforth 'begin' in 1702.

Peasant revolts and brigands are not the particular theme of this
section, though there may seem to have been a lot of them so far;
peasants do not, unfortunately, spend most or even much of their time
revolting. But revolts are useful for our purposes, if for no other reason
than that it is at such times that outside observers (particularly before
this century) bother to write down anything peasants actually *say*. What
they say about the past at such times tends to fall into certain broad
types. One is the commemoration of past local resistance itself, most
notably resistance against the state (revolts against landlords – which

were anyway often smaller in scale and more temporary – do not seem to produce the same long-term resonance and narrative force in local societies). Another is the remembrance of a Golden Age of just royal rule over the country concerned, in the name of which the peasants are resisting present rulers who are less just. A third is the more legendary nobility of Roland and the others, which can serve as an image of absolute justice, much more divorced from time and place. A fourth, still more distant, is the millenarian image of divine justice at the very beginning of time, set against which no human society can ever be wholly legitimate. We have seen something of the first and third of these rough groupings of traditions; let us now look at the second.

Quite a number of peasant revolts have been in the name of past kings or other rulers. In the Norman Nu-Pieds rising of 1639, for instance, songs invoked the justice of Louis XII (d. 1515), in whose 'golden age' there had not been taxes like those of the seventeenth century, as well as the age of the independent dukes and the rights attached to the Norman Charter of 1315. Here we have a double image, the Golden Age king and the charter of local rights – the latter, in this case, probably more authentic than the former, for, although an older memory on the surface, the Charter was a real guarantee of local privileges, and had only recently been abandoned (Foisil 1970: 188–94; Le Roy Ladurie 1987: 390–1). In this case one may suspect that the songs were not all written by peasants (another song brings in Caesar and Catiline, in a prefiguration of French Revolution rhetoric). But the pattern is common enough: rebels in the sixteenth- and seventeenth-century French south-west, known as the Croquants, looked back to Louis XII as well, and, even more generically, to Louis IX (d. 1270), as just kings who taxed little, and Henri IV (d. 1610) was added in the 1630s; these three came to be the canon, and they recur in the peasant grievances of 1789 (Bercé 1974: 634–6; Goubert and Denis 1964: 41, 48). Conversely, in Gascony, like Normandy an area until recently independent of Paris, contemporary revolts recalled either the privileges of English rule or the franchises that marked its end (Bercé 1974: 658–61). Emblematic just kings, such as Louis IX and Louis XII, could be found in every country in Europe: other examples were the Emperor Frederick II, Mátyás of Hungary, Sebastian of Portugal, and Ivan the Terrible. They permeated an entire popular imagery of the past, which was, in consequence, in such cases, a past founded on traditional loyalty and hierarchy: in this sense, 'historical' memory was royal by definition, even for peasants who were in a state of revolt. (Burke 1978: 150–5, 169–76; Bercé 1987: 3–33.) Nor, after all, was this always unreasonable; kings, and their laws, could sometimes genuinely protect peasants from their oppressors, however seldom this actually took place.) The only alternative founding memory for those who wished to reject the whole social order was the pre-hierarchical world of Eden, as with John Ball's famous invocation of Adam delving and Eve spinning, in the England of 1381, and with the religious imagery of the millenarian groups.[9] Less religious-minded peasants who were unhappy about recalling kings may, on the other hand, simply have forgotten them; but this sort of radical forgetfulness would be peculiarly difficult to test.

One place where Golden Age memories had a particular structure was medieval England, for, while popular stories attached to not a few kings (not least the Richard I of the Robin Hood legends), the time of justice and legality seems to have been put back to a specific period, before the Norman Conquest of 1066, which was a collectively traumatic event for every social group in the country. In 1381, the rebels of St Albans demanded their rights as they were supposedly written in a charter of the eighth-century King Offa. The inhabitants of St Albans were not exactly peasants, and this Anglo-Saxon image for the time of just law has other medieval urban parallels, which would surface again in seven-teenth-century intellectual pamphleteering as the myth of the Norman yoke; only after that would the image be reclaimed by the radical traditions of the Levellers and of Tom Paine (Faith 1981; Hill 1958: 50–122; and compare the image of the 'Frankish yoke' for the French Revolutionaries, e.g. in James 1988: 239–40). But there are authentic peasant memories of the Anglo-Saxons, too, expressed in court cases over disputed rents from the thirteenth and fourteenth centuries, most notably in a set from 1377: peasants frequently claimed that they had lived on royal land before 1066, in order to establish the right not to pay increased dues (Hilton 1985: 129–30; Faith 1984). This highly technical recourse to Anglo-Saxon precedent did not, in practice, safeguard peasants as much as they hoped, but the Domesday Book or, sometimes, still earlier documents show that in their specific claims they were often right; the memory of lost royal association had, in other words, lasted for over three centuries. This consciousness of the national past as a broken tradition – pre- and post-1066, that is to say – would repeat itself in the early modern period, when a nostalgia for the lost Catholic

---

[9] The secular version of this is, of course, the 'primitive communism' that even Marx and Engels, the least backward-looking of theorists, felt they had to put at the beginning of their genealogy of historical time (e.g. Marx 1973: 472; Engels 1891/1968; cf. Hobsbawm 1972b: 11). If one wishes to convince people that hierarchy is not innate in human nature, or of anything else for that matter, historical precedent is a more powerful image than 'mere' logic.

England of before the Dissolution of the Monasteries was quite surprisingly widespread, even among the peasantry (Thomas 1983: 9, 14–20). The recurrent theme of the broken past is an interesting counterbalance to the more recent English myth of unbroken historical continuity (see below, p. 130). But this national theme was not the only one available. In the sixteenth century, it went together with a very complex set of commemorations of the more local past that could be found all over the country, focused on local geography and ritual; we know about these thanks to the richness of contemporary antiquarian writing, which for a long time relied heavily on oral accounts (Thomas 1983; Woolf 1988). It may have been these local mythologies, as much as any national consciousness, that gave the English a sense of a continuous identity, before the seventeenth century brought genuine local commemorations of symbolic national events (Cressy 1989).

In this context, we have got away from the past as resistance, or as the locus of justice, and we find ourselves back with local identity. Even the most loyal peasant is unlikely to have spent much of the *veillée* or the *veglia* (the traditional evening gatherings in France and Italy) reminiscing about kings; local traditions were more relevant to everyone. And there was one type of local tradition, which we have so far only mentioned, without discussing it in detail, that was of the greatest importance for all peasant communities: stories about other people in the village. One good example of this is the case of Montaillou in the French Pyrenees, as it emerges from the Inquisition registers of the 1320s (Le Roy Ladurie 1975). People do not often, as we have said, say much to researchers about their neighbours, but in front of the Inquisition, if it wanted to know, they had no choice. Montalionais memory in this respect turns out to have been very dense. People could remember the tiniest detail of what their neighbours said to them, or claimed they could at least, and, although they could seldom give exact dates, they were able to locate these details very accurately in *space*: 'One day, slightly before the general arrest of the people of Montaillou (I do not remember the period more precisely), I went to gather herbs in the area called Alacot; on the way I met Guillaume Maury with his mule ...' (ibid.: 435). This detailed weave of reminiscence, of good and bad deeds, mishaps, or witticisms, extending across an entire social world, the verbalization of which we normally call gossip, is, at least in a stable community, a much firmer basis for a real historical consciousness than is much 'life history'. Not, perhaps, at Montaillou, where Le Roy Ladurie argued that memory was only a generation deep (ibid.: 429–31) – though this must be one of the weakest parts of the book; rather than arguing that the Montalionais had forgotten their parents, one might wonder whether the Inquisition simply did not wish to know about them. Elsewhere, certainly, memories of family rivalries and feuds can structure the past as firmly as they do the present (Levi 1948: 20–8; Black-Michaud 1975: 234–7; Rosaldo 1980; Wilson 1988: 200–1). Such village-based memories of family interrelationships can go back a long way indeed; one illustration of this is Richard Gough's history of his own village of Myddle, written in 1700–2, a remarkable text that will be our last example in this section (Gough 1981; for commentary, see Hey 1974).

Richard Gough was a prosperous yeoman farmer from the Shropshire village of Myddle, who wrote its history while in his late sixties (he was born c.1635). The bulk of his book is structured geographically, by the pews of the church, the local farms to which they were attached, and the families that held them. It is thus, in effect, less a history of the village than of the families living in it, recalled and ordered by the pews, which had all the more power as a memory device in that they themselves represented the local social hierarchy in visible form. Gough followed these families back three, four, sometimes six generations: regularly to 1600, and often into the sixteenth century. The family weave began, that is to say, a century before he wrote, roughly in his grandfather's time, though some more colourful individuals were still remembered from well before that. Gough was educated in law, divinity, and the Latin classics, and used parish registers and land deeds when he thought them relevant, but his basic source material was oral. A common pattern for one of his pew histories is for him to begin with a series of dated births, marriages, or land sales, from the 1580s perhaps, before the time of the weave of memory, but thereafter to launch into a complex recounting of family relationships and anecdotes for each subsequent generation, without any dates thereafter save the odd death, and except for two overriding external historical markers, 'the time of the [Civil] Wars' of 1642–8 and the Restoration of 1660.

Myddle does not seem to have been a heavily divided community; its networks can be distinguished hierarchically (from gentlemen down to labourers), but not, apparently, by factional or class opposition. It supported Charles I in 1642 virtually *en bloc*. Had the Civil Wars washed over the village with barely a ripple in the memory of its inhabitants, one could have easily enough explained away their apparent irrelevance for the village. But the very opposite was in reality the case. Gough put the Wars close to the beginning of his work, as the capital event of the century, and they constantly recur as well: not just as a dating tool, which Gough could have himself superimposed on family memory, but as an essential part of the family narratives themselves. Myddle was a comparatively remote community (though with several close ties to London, and, at least in Gough's case, some awareness of current political events); but its sense of the past was not entirely restricted to its own internal history. The family networks that constituted the structure of its collective memory themselves provided a framework through which the Civil Wars could be understood and brought into village history, as part of its internal development, and not just an interesting external occurrence. This in itself testifies to the dramatic impact of the Wars everywhere in the country as a unifying event, one which had few parallels in English political history. But this event did not supersede the overarching structuring element for Myddle's past, which was essentially family gossip, several generations deep. This type of pattern for the commemoration of the past is normally hidden from us (particularly if we do not ask about it), but it probably characterizes a large part of the social memory of most stable peasant communities. We shall see it again in the next chapter, when we look at medieval Iceland, a whole nation whose memories of itself had virtually no other structure.

What have we, so far, to distinguish the category of peasant memory? There are few reliable cross-cultural markers. One, certainly, is the constantly recurring importance of local geography as a structure for remembrance: hills, caves, farmhouses, and fields all carry their memories for peasants to talk about. This pattern reflects in the most obvious way the structures of everyday routine in the open air; but the geographical space of the community is by this means itself socialized, its past associations giving it a meaning that makes sense for its inhabitants, in contraposition to the more anonymous geographies that lie round it – both space and time thus locking together to construct community identity. A second internal pattern is the one that we have just seen, the way memories are constructed outwards: first, doubtless, from the individual to the family and its life cycle; but then, through the social relationships between families, both amicable and hostile, from the family to the community. This pattern can have variable forms, depending on the sort of memories that are most important for the community: the memory of feud, for example, will posit a role for family history different from the memory of village resistance against the outside world, even though the latter (as in the case of the Camisards) tends to be recounted through family stories as well. Both of these two patterns of commemoration none the less re-create the community, in its internal structure and its relationship to its immediate surroundings. On the other hand, there are also others that represent the community's relationship to the outside world, and these we have also looked at: the imagery of the community of resistance once again, and the various imageries of the Golden Age. These can (as again with the memory of the Camisards) have complex internal roots; but they are also narrative tropes in their own right, and can be borrowed whole from one culture to another (as is most obvious with the Roland legend; but many local brigandage memories are international topoi as well).

These are at least some of the grids of interpretation through which one must operate in order to answer the questions we posed on page 103 about the sorts of aspects of the past peasantries characteristically commemorate. Perhaps the most powerful element we have met is the memory of the community in opposition to the outside world, for this is one of the most effective recourses any social group has to reinforce its own social identity in opposition to that of others, and it is a memory everyone can participate in, through personal memories and family traditions. Its very power means that it is not always authentic: the Camisards may well have represented Protestant Cévenols, and the French Resistance in World War II was widely supported – if less than is often now believed; but Lampião did not, by any stretch of the imagination, represent any real resistance on the part of most Nordestinos. None the less, community defiance does tend to be remembered by peasantries (along with, sometimes, acts of more ortho-dox affirmation, such as the support for the King in Myddle in the 1640s) with more insistence than many other forms of historical event; it is socially relevant, and will be talked about, when other less resonant and less unifying (often more external) past events will remain undis-cussed and will thus be forgotten.

Patterns of this type can be found in peasant societies all over the globe. But not only peasants live in communities. The image of the community of resistance can be found among the working class as well, at least where its members live in stable and self-contained groups; and it may, indeed, partly be true that some of the patterns we have looked at are not particularly specific to peasantries. This we can check as we move on to look at the memories of the working class. We shall, indeed, find some similarities; but there are differences as well.

Working-class memories

Peasant communities are not fully autonomous, either politically, econ-omically, or culturally (see, e.g., Wolf 1966). But they can be relatively coherent at a cultural level: peasant groups may well take on many of the values of the dominant classes (particularly when mediated by local traditional intellectuals), but these are none the less values which come from outside, and tend to be received only in so far as they make sense inside a local ideological framework that depends on local realities. (Radical ideas tend to meet the same difficulties, indeed.) The situation is different in working-class communities. On one level, the interests and identities of working-class groups are much more explicitly opposed to those of employers, with the state at their back, than are those of many peasantries; radicalism and militancy are much more obviously part of most working-class experience, at least in the particular environment of the shop-floor. On another level, however, many working-class communities are weaker, at least in their *overall* social coherence, than most peasant communities. They are newer, and usually more impermanent; workers move about more than peasants, and are constantly exposed to the influx of new groups from the countryside (or, in North and South America – and since World War II in Europe as well – from abroad), who can often be, culturally, very different from the old ones. Working-class communities, which tend to exist in large conurbations – hardly the 'face-to-face' societies of the rural world – split up into different groups fairly easily; common experiences of relative poverty at home or factory discipline at work (which, anyway, vary from sector to sector) will not always unite them very effectively beyond the rather limited experience of, say, all voting for the Labour Party. For these reasons, working-class cultures are often more permeable to outside influences than are those of rural societies. Indeed, they are often a battleground of conflict between the radical culture of the workers' movements and the dominant ideologies of the groups which, for example, control newspapers and TV. Central in this conflict is the arena of social memory; in industrial societies, memories of different events (or different memories of the same event) have obvious and explicit political connotations, which have to be added to the more politically implicit roles of commemoration as constitutive of group identity that we have already explored. This political aspect of memory is an inescapable part of its analysis; we shall come back to it at the end of the section.

Let us begin with the question of community identity in working-class societies. At least some industrial communities are highly cohesive and stable, much like many peasant communities; how do they remember the past, and how similar are the patterns to those we have just seen? Among the best places to look in order to be able to answer these questions are coal-mining communities, for these societies are as cohesive as any in the industrial world, and very often have a markedly historicized tradition of resistance. In Britain, the inhabitants of the coalfields of South Wales and Durham, for example, have a very clear sense of the past as struggle, and it constitutes a memory that goes back at least a century.[10] (One should not expect deeper commemorations than this in most industrial communities: more than a century ago they did not exist.) The General Strike of 1926 is a common touchstone, and for many miners the strikes of 1972, 1974, and 1984–5 simply replayed the experiences of 1926, with the same *dramatis personae* in each: the community, the employers, and the police. The imagery of the strike as a defiance of the state, not just the employers, is a constant one (of course, all four great strikes were in reality precisely that), and it validates the experience as belonging to the mining community as a whole, rather than just the front-line (male) workers. The coherence of these societies is, however, itself a major contributing factor to the force of this commemoration – as well as vice versa; for most mining families in 1984–5, it was not just their predecessors, but their grandparents, who had fought in 1926, something that one could not say for many working-class societies. Here, the transmission of memory is quite clear; it is made possible by family continuity and a continuity of employment (however much in decline), as well as by the specific nature of that employment (pit culture is a very precise one, which creates rhythms of work quite unlike those of the factory), and, not least, by the institutional role of the trade union. What has resulted is a highly militant commemoration, which has as one of its basic themes the intervention of the police on the employers' side, something that in South Wales is remembered not only for the major strikes, but also for, among others, those of 1910–11, 1921, and 1934.

A good illustration of the pattern is the first of these three, the Cambrian strike in the Rhondda Valley, which has become a *locus classicus* for competing historical memories in Britain, for it was in the context of the Tonypandy riots of November 1910 that Winston Churchill, as Home Secretary, called in the army.[11] Popular memory in the Rhondda is reputed to have claimed ever since that Churchill's

---

[10] For Durham, see, for example, Douglass 1981. For South Wales, Smith 1984: 55–97 and Francis 1985 are good introductions. French miners can have a similar genealogy of struggle: see Dubar et al. 1982: 378–81, for the mines of the Pas-de-Calais; so do the slate quarrymen of north-west Wales (C. Lloyd-Morgan, pers. comm.). People in Pennine semi-urban mining and textile centres, such as Todmorden, can have equally long memories, going in one case back through 1926, the cotton famine of 1863, and the Chartists, to the Luddites (R.J. Holt, pers. comm.); here, the guiding structure is less the industry than a collective geographical identity, for Todmorden, in a relatively remote valley, maintained itself across the period of industrialization as a single community.

[11] For what follows, see Smith 1984: 55–97; Smith 1983; McEwen 1971; Page Arnot 1967: 174–273; Tey 1951: 93–4. The imagery of the strike did not at the time spread very far in space: it was seen as alien and dangerous as near as Cardiff (Paynter 1972: 13).

troops fired on the strikers; Churchill, for his part, was, as late as 1950, still on the defensive, stating that he had kept the troops in reserve, and employed only unarmed London police as reinforcements for the local police to hold down the riot. Churchill was certainly not locally believed, and, anyway, even setting aside the riot of 1910, his role in putting down the strike of 1926 made him into a general hate figure in the coalfields, an image which has lasted (cf. Douglass 1981: 63). Nationally, however, his version was more widely accepted: it surfaced, for example, in a well-known novel by Josephine Tey, *The Daughter of Time*, published in 1951, with Churchill's version portrayed as *the* objective truth, the 'actual facts', as opposed to those of blinded myth-making Welsh miners. In fact, neither version is true, for Churchill's troops had been armed, and had acted as an essential logistic and coercive backup to the local police in the putting down of the strike (not just the quelling of the local riots), as they also did a year later in Llanelli, where they did shoot two strikers. Rhondda memory has conflated this latter event with another death, this time at the hands of the police, at Tonypandy in 1910, and has turned Tonypandy itself into an icon of the miners' struggle against the state. This is not at all surprising, for only minor alterations were necessary to create the image, which itself belongs to an international iconography of unarmed crowds fired on by soldiers or police. It can easily be argued that popular memory is closer to the 'truth' of 1910 than was Churchill's disingenuous self-defence. More significant for us, however, is the evident importance to the miners (as also to Churchill himself) of the exact level of violence of state repression, which has privileged the commemoration of the intervention in 1910 of not only the police but also the army. This sort of imagery of repression can indeed be seen as one of the founding ('mythological') elements in miners' identity. And conversely, one may add, the curt rejection of the Rhondda version of the story by 'national' intellectuals is a good example of the normally contemptuous attitude of national middle-class culture towards the local cultures of the working classes.

British mining communities are classic examples of working-class groups who use the heroic imagery of the strike, whether won or lost, as a representation of community identity in opposition to the outside world (cf. Debouzy 1986: 268). The privileging in such narratives of resistance to the state parallels that in the memories of peasant communities, though in working-class societies the continuous genealogy of strikes often makes the resultant commemorations rather more complex. It may look like a tradition that privileges political militancy, but similar sorts of memories can exist in much less militant communities, expressed in less heroic ways. One such is Calumet, a copper-mining town in northern Michigan, where a hard-fought strike in 1913 dissolved after an entirely contingent disaster, a panic after a false fire-alarm, at a Christmas party given by the union running the strike, that killed seventy-four people (Ivey 1970). This fire was still remembered by everyone in Calumet, including schoolchildren, in the late 1960s, and was used by them as a peg on which to hang an entire imagery of community failure in the wake of the unsuccessful strike (not entirely accurately, in fact: the real turning-point was the Depression of the 1930s). Unheroic failure is by no means always remembered by people, as we shall see; but here the resonance of the lost strike reverberated around a whole community, which indeed it continued to define – the strike had involved almost all the local inhabitants, and the disaster mostly killed women and children, thus reinforcing its relevance in the minds of non-workers. Calumet was evidently a depressing place to be in 1967, but it was clearly a town still united by a shared sense of the past as struggle.

Our final example of community memory in this context is equally cohesive, but is almost entirely devoid of class consciousness: the Italian fishermen of Marseille. This community lived in the Saint-Jean area of the Old Port of Marseille until the Germans destroyed the *quartier* in 1943, only a minority returning there thereafter, and their historical memories are those of a geographical area, an occupational group, and an ethnic group combined (Joutard 1982: 180–1; 1983: 191–3, 239–44; cf. Sportiello 1981). These memories, apart from the trauma of 1943, are not particularly based on real events; like many ethnic minorities, the members of the community have removed from their minds any reference to anti-immigrant agitations (cf. Raphaël 1980: 133–4), and in this case they have substituted a series of legends of evidently written origin, such as the preaching of St Lazare in the first century AD, or the local privileges that King René of Provence bestowed on the fishermen in the fifteenth. These legends have a precise function, that of locating the fishing community in the distant past, not as immigrants, but as long-standing Marseillais: the first group, indeed, to be converted by St Lazare. This instance, with its complex interlinking of written and oral, recalls the learned origin-legends of early modern urban communities rather more than it does the imagery of the strike, but it has the same function as the latter: it identifies the community with relation to the outside world, although this time insisting not on an opposition to the world, but on social continuities, at least with the rest of Marseille. On the other hand, it shows that working-class community identities can, like those of peasantries, be structured at least as much by a geographically based sense of belonging as by an explicit awareness of class: there is certainly no sharp line to be drawn between the rural and the urban world in this respect.

Class awareness of one type or another can, all the same, be taken as the norm in working-class communities; what cannot be taken for granted is the construction of the community. We have begun with social groups that constitute both whole towns (or quarters of towns) and occupational groups, for ease of analysis. But working-class groups can be constituted in very various ways: by geographical area, by employment in a single factory or a single industrial sector, by political or religious alignment, by ethnic origin, and so on, and each of these can have separate, and overlapping, memories. One well-studied factory-based group is the metalworkers of Givors, near Lyon (Lequin and Métral 1980). The metalworkers of Givors were certainly militant; they saw history very clearly as consisting of workers' struggles, culminating in the strikes of 1936 in the context of the Popular Front, which, for some people there, even eclipsed the Liberation of 1944 as a memory. Here, though, unlike that of mining societies, this history was very much a workplace rather than a community history: the imagery of the past focused on apprenticeship and on a pride in being a competent worker, and excluded from this sort of commemoration not only women but also workers in the glass factories in the same town. Strikes were, furthermore, seen much more as local defiances of employers, and in much less of a national political context, than they are in South Wales, even though the Communist administration of Givors was at the same time actively promoting municipal commemorations of a more 'official' working-class history. It is clear that individual metalworkers, and the informal social groups that they made up, structured their memory above all through the experience of working, and with reference to the factory where they worked.

There are parallels for this in other factory studies. In Borgo S. Paolo, one of the parts of Turin that furnishes the workforce for the Fiat factories, Luisa Passerini found a memorialization of the work experience in the 1930s that has often turned the cars into the real subjects of commemoration, rather than the worker – a memorialization which, as well as representing pride in competence, is a real internalization of the alienation of factory labour (Passerini 1987: 42–5, 53–5; cf. Marx 1867/1976: 544–53; 711–24). And in Sesto S. Giovanni, a left-wing metal-working town just outside Milan, some of whose factory workers were interviewed about their lives by Pietro Crespi in the 1970s, we find analogous patterns (Crespi 1979). Time and again in the Sesto interviews, historical events were seen exclusively through workplace experience, including the whole period of the Resistance in 1943–5, which tended to be presented above all as consisting of strikes and factory-based defiance of the Germans, although in fact the whole town was also a Resistance centre, with partisans in the nearby hills, and clandestine publications, community activity, and sabotage inside Sesto itself (cf. Bell 1986: 191–2). These are, that is to say, the social memories not of the working class as a whole, but of factory workers as factory workers; the fragmentation of experience that is possible inside the complex social structures of an industrial culture has created not one working-class Sesto but many, divided not by politics (Communists and Christian Democrats had very similar memories, in fact) but by factory, and, even inside families, divided between workers and non-workers. In this environment, community consciousness is constructed more or less from the outside. Sesto is remembered as, in effect, a collection of factories (in the Crespi interviews, people tended to be identified only by the factory where they worked: 'I remember a certain Maggioni from the Magneti Marelli who denounced many people [to the Gestapo]', Crespi 1979: 111). Givors is constructed as a community above all by the efforts of the municipality, rather than by its inhabitants themselves (Lequin and Métral 1980: 153; Debouzy 1986: 270–1). The social identity of Borgo S. Paolo, too, though certainly greater (it was, in effect, a company town), seems to be remembered principally through the symbolism of its geographical relationships, as much as as an active community (Levi et al. 1977: 444–6; cf. Gribaudi 1987).

Maurice Halbwachs predicted this factory-based patterning of memory for the working classes, and later empirical work indicates that he was entirely right (Halbwachs 1925: 333). Some of its major characteristics need further discussion, however. (Its converse, the memory of non-working women, we shall come back to at the end of the chapter.) One is the way historical time is portrayed. One would expect that factory work would lead to a more complex conception of the division of time during the day than peasants tend to have, and so it does; but it also brings with it a greater awareness of chronology. This awareness is essentially created by characteristically precise memories of the dates of entry into and exit from a given occupation, which often specify the day as well: 'I was at Elettromeccanica from '28 to '31; I can be exact about the dates because they remain indelible in the mind: from 4 August 1928 to 14 March 1931. Indelible dates, because they are part of one's life' (Crespi 1979: 57). These markers can often serve to locate historical events more clearly in time than those we have seen for peasant communities: workers in Sesto could regularly distinguish between, for example, the anti-Fascist strikes of 1943 and the anti-

German ones of 1944, just as Ecléa Bosi's informants in São Paulo in Brazil in the 1970s could distinguish between the uprisings of 1922 and 1924 (Bosi 1979: 377–84). As usual, this greater temporal precision does not guarantee accuracy; in Terni, an industrial city in central Italy, Alessandro Portelli's sources, when discussing the shooting of a worker in 1949, very frequently redated it to 1953, when it could be seen as being avenged by a period of street fighting after mass layoffs (Portelli 1981b: 172–4; 1985: 307–9). But it does at least guarantee a certain linearity of recollection that can make more concrete the perception of historical change and development.

This perception of time as created by the temporalities of employment is matched by a factory-based perception of space. People in towns locate their memories in space, as peasants do, with streets and squares replacing fields and hills; they characteristically have, in addition, an entire symbolic geography of street patterns around the family home, which represents the slow learning of the outside world during child-hood and adolescence (Halbwachs 1980: 131–6; Bosi 1979; 356–71; Bertaux-Wiame 1985: 16–18), and can also represent the contraposi-tion between different social groups, as, for example, working-class Borgo S. Paolo as against middle-class central Turin (Levi et al. 1977: 445). But for factory workers the sharpest distinction is characteris-tically that between the memories of the space of work and those of the spaces of non-work, whether in the city or at home: the types of memor-ies in each case are different, and clearly demarcated. In Crespi's Sesto interviews, *coming into* the factory and reacting to a specific political situation recurred as a symbolic moment: 'so I went to the factory in the morning, and ...'. Daily life, on the other hand, tended to be relegated to the non-factory world, and was often very little discussed; the world of the public, of events which deserved commemoration, was constituted by the world of work.[12]

The workers' memories we have been looking at are, although vari-ously structured, at least extremely articulated, and generally demon-strate a complex political consciousness. One could counterpose to these memories, however, a considerable number of examples of forgetfulness,

[12]One wonders in the case of these Sesto interviews, which are published as monologues, exactly what questions were asked, since the informants say so little, for example, about childhood. But the tendency of male workers to talk only about their work experiences rather than their private lives has been noted elsewhere; for example, in Bertaux-Wiame's work on Sèvres (1985: 20–3), or in the Nantes studies referred to by Perrot and by Debouzy (*Bulletin* 1982: 47; Debouzy 1986: 267). Some of the public *versus* private imagery of the workplace–home contrast, itself largely a product of the Industrial Revolution, is unpicked in Forty 1986: 99–119.

either of individual events, or of the meaning of particular events, or of entire swathes of past experience: there are working-class groups whose sense of their relationship to the past, or of the validity of their experience (individual or collective) as part of history itself, is very weak indeed. The Popular Front may be remembered at Givors, as also at Bobigny in the 'red belt' of Paris suburbs (Fourcaut 1987), but it has largely been forgotten in parts of the Marseille-Aix area (Joutard 1983: 174–8; cf. Aschieri 1985: 116); nor is the General Strike of 1926 universally recalled in Britain, except in occasional anecdotes (*History Workshop* VIII, 1979: ii). Such absences usually derive, as in many of our peasant examples, simply from the different criteria of importance that working-class informants have for determining the personally and collectively relevant past, criteria which do not have to be those of academics. But sometimes the past entirely slips away. The retired farm labourers of the Vexin, west of Paris, a real agrarian proletariat, in about 1980 could remember their first jobs, and the names of their bosses (a workplace memory again), but nothing about the development of their working lives – even the great strikes of 1936, which they actually won (Bozon and Thiesse 1986). They lacked any sense of group identity; it was not altogether surprising, therefore, that they did not have much social memory as a group; but even personal memories were remarkably incoherent, with people confusing, for example, 1914 with 1940. Bozon and Thiesse argued that this amnesia derived from a sense of unstructured failure: of lives steadily deprived of meaning by agrarian mechanization. One could add that the personal isolation of individual informants deprived them of a social context for speaking about memory, a context that was normal, for example, in Givors; it is likely, too, that the instability of their work had deprived them of much of the geographical and social grid of *aides-mémoire* that a stable industrial environment might have given them. Not only a sense of meaning, then, but even a context for the transmission of memory was lacking among Vexin labourers.

There are, too, larger-scale examples of forgetfulness, at least on the level of the participation of individuals in wider social processes. Several people working in North America have made this point. Studs Terkel has argued, on the basis of his oral-historical work on the Depression in the United States (in particular, in Chicago), that people have been 'conditioned not to have a sense of history': experiences are perceived as individual, almost chance, not collective; unemployment is seen as being personal bad luck, or personal failure, rather than a shared experience with outside causes (Terkel in Grele 1985: 43; Terkel 1970; cf. Frisch 1972). Nicole Gagnon found a similar absence in Quebec, and argued that a 'historical consciousness' was restricted to the professional classes and to labour militants, who have a clearer sense of participation in a society's history; other informants could have very clear personal memories, and a rough awareness of social change, but the content of this awareness could remain very implicit in their narrative accounts (Gagnon 1981: 53–7). And Isabelle Bertaux-Wiame and Daniel Bertaux, who have worked on the Parisian baking trade, would generalize this to working-class memory as a whole, which they portray as focused on cyclic events (the factory siren, the evening meal, the weekly holiday, child raising), and not on a linear political consciousness at all; this is restricted to the ruling classes and to workers' leaders (1980: 113–16).

These arguments have several levels of implication. We saw analogous points made earlier about the cyclic nature of peasant memory, and we might feel suspicious of these arguments for the same reason: that they counterpose 'us', that is, those who have a historical consciousness, and 'them', that is, those who do not. The authors we have cited here, however, are all sophisticated and sympathetic analysts who are capable of asking the right sort of questions: we can assume the accuracy of their empirical analyses, and we must take their interpretations seriously. On one level, they are making an important point: the labour movement, particularly in Europe, has made a major contribution to giving the working classes a sense of the meaning of change perceived across linear time, in effect as an alternative 'national' memory to that of the upper middle classes, and often deliberately constructed as such (cf. below, p. 135). One might counterpose this to the relative weakness of the same movement in North America, where the dominance of alternative models, above all that of individual progress, often makes those who do not succeed (i.e. most people) feel personally responsible for their own misfortune, rather than aware of the relationship between this and a collective experience, seen historically. In Europe, a highly atomized sector such as the Paris baking trade, with a very traditional structure of apprenticeship, and no union organization at all, would certainly be capable of forming a microsociety almost impervious to the linear time of the socialist movement.

But one cannot conclude from this that a non-linear consciousness of the past is *normal* in working-class culture; that the memory of the workers' movement is imposed on this experience from outside, 'distorting' collective memory and 'contaminating' individual memory (cf. Debouzy 1986: 272–3). For a start, there is no impermeable membrane between the non-militant and the militant in most working-class societies. Workers participate *en masse* in strikes and other trades union and party activities, and, whatever they really think about what is going on, they can recognize – and, sometimes, recall – their role in historical developments; and, not least important, they talk to each other about it afterwards, militant and non-militant alike. In Givors, workers remembered strikes in ways quite different from the formal commemorations of their political organizations, but they remembered them all the same. Welsh miners' memories are certainly related to the institutions of the union, but are in no sense dependent upon them: here, it is the community that has constructed its own linear memory. Even the most politically innocent of Bosi's informants in São Paulo remembered the Vargas labour laws of the 1930s as the great historical watershed of the century in Brazil, and they were by no means wrong in that (Bosi 1979: 372–5). That is to say, some working-class societies do remember and commemorate the historical past, even if others do not. Any characterizations of working-class memory must be able to subsume this genuine empirical contrast.

One solution to the problem is suggested by the work of Luisa Passerini and her associates on Turin in the Fascist period, focusing on inconsistencies and silences in informants' descriptions of life under Fascism, which, in effect, they had often virtually wiped from their memories. This elision was not only a rejection of an unacceptable period of history (as opposed to the years of militancy in the early 1920s, or of the Resistance in 1943–5), but also a real victory of Fascism in restricting people's consciousness to their private lives or to the work ethic. Nevertheless, inside these silences, an awareness of the nature of the regime could be reconstructed through a reading of the subtexts of, for example, accounts of illegal birth control or abortion, which could be seen by people as images of day-to-day political resistance. (Levi et al. 1977: 440–1; Passerini 1979; Passerini 1987: 67–133, 150–82.) Such analysis is extremely subtle and difficult, and it may not be surprising that it has not often been carried out; in any event, it is likely that the most atomized of working-class cultures would not show any collectivity of memory even by these procedures. But it points us to two conclusions: that traces of historical consciousness can lie very deep, and have to be sought out before it can be asserted that they do not exist; and that the absence of such a consciousness may be, rather than innate to a working-class society, a pointer to its defeat.

Marxists used to talk about 'false consciousness', which meant, essentially, the failure of the working class to realize it was exploited by capitalism. The phrase was never a happy one, for it assumed a 'correct' consciousness that was the special preserve of the right sort of activist. But it did at least serve as an indicator of a very real conflict, that between a social identity based on the reality of working-class experience and one imposed from above, more or less deliberately, by the ruling classes, who have always had their own versions of truth, as we can see in the national media at any time we choose. It is not the case, for example, that Parisian bakers do not remember the past at all. They certainly remember World War II, even if not the Popular Front. But they are most likely to think in terms of national (i.e. middle-class) rather than local (potentially working-class) structures of signification; to remember school and media versions of history, and to downgrade or perhaps not recognize at all any local collective experience. This tells us about the collective identity of Parisian bakers, which is genuinely very weak; but it also tells us about the ideological hegemony of ruling-class culture (see, for example, Johnson et al. 1982; Gramsci 1971). The stakes are high in industrial society: when a dominant culture loses hegemony in a working-class community (as, say, among South Welsh miners), the latter will typically be highly radicalized and difficult to 'control'; conversely, when such a society is effectively controlled by external cultural influences, local senses of belonging, local memories, and the very concept of class identity may cease to exist. Some working-class groups are better able to withstand the dominant historical discourses of the ruling classes than are others; and different elements of hegemonic discourses affect different groups in different ways. One example is the notable work discipline of many Communist industrial communities in postwar France or Italy, a discipline which demonstrates a respect for one crucial aspect of the hierarchical relationship between workers and employers, despite the rejection of other aspects of that relationship by community culture at large. Another example is, quite simply, silence: the perceived irrelevance of personal experience to outsiders (the amazement of some informants that anyone might be interested in hearing about and recording their lives has been recounted by countless oral historians), or the lack of any social meaning attributed to that experience, either now or in the past. These are not absolutes, of course. The strength or weakness of a social, historical memory in a given working-class group is a result of the ways in which several variables interact: the strength of the group's identity vis-à-vis employers or the outside world; the occupational and locational stability of the group and the trust its members have in each other; the precise role that spoken commemoration of the past has in constructing that identity; the faith that group members have in their own version of the past (and the present) rather than in that of employers or the state; and so on. These variables relate to both the relationship between local and hegemonic discourses and the extent to which the local group exists at all as a society with its own version of the past. Both of these have to be recognized, however, if we want to understand how collective memory works, whether to define a class, as in this section, or any other social group.

The complexity of working-class culture is far greater than that of most peasant communities. The family and the village impose themselves as the principal frameworks for understanding peasant culture, though one should not forget the importance of different patterns of land tenure, as well as the varying role of traditional intellectuals. Working-class societies are far more complicated, with workplace, family, and geographical community, the only networks we have even touched on, set against religious and ethnic identity, political activism (which imposes, as Portelli and Passerini have commented, not just a particular form of historical consciousness, but also its own narrative discourse – more obviously text-based, more deliberately argued, and more often in the national language than in dialect: Portelli 1981a: 99; Passerini 1987: 39–42) and the often very clearly defined cultures of the clubhouse and the bar. Many current discussions of working-class cultures, in the oral-historical tradition or elsewhere, fail to do justice to this kaleidoscope of difference, and still less to the complex relationship between each element and the rival analytical frameworks of dominant cultures. It is easy to see why: the task is almost impossible. But one can generalize less easily as a result, and one is forced more into a simple listing of possible analyses than a fully synthesized discussion of actual ones. Nevertheless, one point emerges very clearly: that the way memories of the past are generated and understood by given social groups is a direct guide to how they understand their position in the present; that one can, in fact, barely separate social memory from an analysis of the social at all, and that, conversely, any analysis of social identity and consciousness could become, if the researcher wished, an analysis of perceptions of the past. If Welsh miners remember past struggle so clearly, it is because they define themselves through it; they have, and have long had, a clear perception of an essential antagonism between themselves (and their communities) and their employers (and the state), which is worth commemorating. If Québecois textile workers really see the past entirely in terms of individual experience, it is because they have almost no class or group identity at all. If Sesto metalworkers remember everything through the optic of workplace activity, it is because they are more prepared than some others to restrict their view of themselves to their status as (militant) employees and 'good workers'. Analyses of social identity of all kinds could well give more attention to memory as one of its major constituent elements, and as one of the clearest guides to its configuration.

National memories in the modern period

We have begun to use the concept of a 'national' memory, and this, too, needs a certain amount of definition. Nations do not remember spontaneously and collectively any more than smaller groups do. Essentially, the bearers of national memory since the arrival of capitalism in each country are the upper middle classes and the intelligentsia, who have inherited the mantle from the aristocracies, lawyers, and clergy of previous epochs. Memory on this level can be spontaneous or manipulated; it can involve rhetorical discourses directed at internal or at external opponents; it can be internally divided and fought over. Its articulation belongs essentially to political elites, however, and is relatively rarely contested by other social groups – and very rarely with success. It is on this level that the role of schoolteaching and the media is most important. So, indeed, is that of professional historians, whose function, whether conscious or unconscious, is, more often than they realize, less to analyse the 'pastness' of the past than to give an objective veneer to the preoccupations and self-legitimizations of national bourgeoisies. Examples of this process include the English obsession with the nation-state and the Industrial Revolution; the Italian obsession with the autonomous city, the Renaissance, and the Risorgimento; the US obsession with the frontier, the freedom of the individual, and the self-made man; and so on: all of them not only major building blocks of national self-identity, but also permanent objects of analysis and re-analysis among historians. In this section we intend to look, at least briefly, at some of the ways national culture constructs itself on such memories.

One way is expressed as well as anyone by Marx in *The Eighteenth Brumaire of Louis Bonaparte*:

Men make their own history, but not of their own free will; not under circumstances they themselves have chosen but under the given and inherited circumstances with which they are directly confronted. The tradition of the dead generations weighs like a nightmare on the minds of the living. And, just when they appear to be engaged in the revolutionary transformation of themselves and their material surroundings, in the creation of something which does not yet exist, precisely in such epochs of revolutionary crisis they timidly conjure up the spirits of the past to help them; they borrow their names, slogans, and costumes so as to stage the new world-historical scene in this venerable disguise and borrowed language. Luther put on the mask of the apostle Paul; the Revolution of 1789–1814 draped itself alternately as the Roman republic and the Roman empire; and the Revolution of 1848 knew no better than to parody at some points 1789 and at others the revolutionary traditions of 1793–5. In the same way, the beginner who has learned a new language always re-translates it into his mother tongue: he can only be said to have appropri-ated the spirit of the new language and to be able to express himself in it freely when he can manipulate it without reference to the old, and when he forgets his original language while using the new one. (Marx 1852/1973: 146–7)

Almost all political rhetoric depends on the past as a legitimation device. The French Revolutionaries had to go back to the Roman repub-lic to find a legitimation for political action that did not depend on kings (it was convenient in other ways, as well, for Roman law gave an altogether appropriate attention to the centrality of private property, which was very important for the theorists of the 1790s). It had been easier for tax rebels in previous years in France, who, as we have seen, could simply revolt in the name of the juster kingship of the past. It would be easier, too, in the future, for any revolutionary or republican would need only to go back to the French Revolution itself, either (for real radicals) to the Sans-culottes and the execution of the king, or (for conservative progressives) to the Girondins and the Directoire, or (for the more autocratically-minded) to Napoleon: the Revolutionary period, that is to say, offered an entire gallery of models for future activists to choose from.

Learning entirely new historical languages, as Marx put it, has seldom been an entirely spontaneous process, and once the new language is in place, it, too, comes to condition future activity; unavoidably, as Marx himself saw. The French Revolution thus became a founding moment for the historical imagery of France (and not only France) for a long time in the future, in effect as an origin myth, the time of *history*, since which there have been only events (cf. Cunnison 1951: 12 for a classic African parallel). Similarly, in Ireland, the equivalent moment is 1916–23; there is virtually no political position or party in subsequent years that does not take its legitimacy from the remembered divisions of that time. In Italy, the current moment is 1943–8, which has, for nearly every political group from the extraparliamentary Left to the Fascists, entirely submerged the previous founding period, 1859–70. In Turkey, the period is that of the political career of Atatürk (1915–36); in Brazil, that of Getúlio Vargas (1930–54). And these differences have political consequences in themselves: the traditional incoherence of the Brazilian Left and the impermanence of its political groupings is, in substantial part, a product of the lack of meaning in Latin America of the traditional points of reference for socialist and Communist views of the past, such as the Russian Revolution, in a continent whose history was differently constructed and which was barely affected even by the World Wars. The same event can carry different resonances in different countries, as with the French Revolution again, an image of liberation in Germany but of national oppression in Spain, and of unbridled licence in England; or with World War II, a powerful image of national affirmation against huge odds in Britain or the Soviet Union, but one of defeat and division in France or Germany, and in Italy one of distanced humiliation, almost entirely replaced by the positive image of the Resistance.

These kinds of social memories are very widely shared. They constitute discourses that are available to everybody, not just elites, and most people think and speak in terms of them. They make up the substructure of national historical consciousness, a largely uncontrollable rhetorical field inside which all political actors themselves have to operate; even though elements of this consciousness can be deliberately invented, emphasized, or popularized, as we shall see, the overall interpretative framework of what in the United States is called the 'usable past' (e.g. Commager 1967) is generally based on much less consciously perceived foundations. Take, for example, England, which was a highly atypical country, for it seems to have been the first place where a genuine national memory developed at the popular level, as can be seen in the local commemorations in the seventeenth century of such moments of Protestant state affirmation as the defence against the Spanish Armada and the Gunpowder Plot (Cressy 1989). A memory as long as this – it may well date a good way back into the medieval period – has come to exist in a variety of different images. The imagery of the 'island race', for example, which dates at least to the Tudor period, setting 'free-born Englishmen' against all manner of dreadful, idolatrous, dictatorial Continentals (and equally dreadful – and also ungrateful – Celts) is one of the underlying structures on which many an organically developing or consciously created memory has subsequently been based (cf. Hilton, Furtado in Samuel 1989, I; Samuel, Surel, Dresser, Stallybrass in Samuel 1989, III). The 'Dunkirk spirit', though enthusiastically furthered by the wartime government, would probably have become a central mythic image even without government backing, thanks to the generalized popular experience that lay behind the Dunkirk evacuation, the Blitz, and the whole war economy. But its power was also due to the fact that it replicated perfectly the island-race image, which had itself been continually reconstituted through the centuries by similar representations, as, most recently, during World

War I, and, even more exactly, during the Napoleonic period: each replication superimposing itself over (and, as usual, largely blotting out) the one preceding. This recurring structure could be exploited by governments (hence, too, the easy success of the manufactured hysterias of the Falklands War), but was not created by them.

Much the same can be said of another basic myth of English national identity, which goes back to the eighteenth century, though probably not earlier: that of constitutional and democratic advance based on pragmatism rather than ideology. This myth was berated decades ago by Herbert Butterfield as part of the 'Whig interpretation of history' (Butterfield 1931), but it is located deep in national consciousness. It becomes apparent in, among other things, the widespread and complacent belief in the unbroken nature of the English past (parliaments, the monarchy, etc. – in contrast, see above, p. 111); the lack of interest in socialist ideas of most of the English (as opposed, sometimes, to the Welsh and Scots) labour movement; and the tendency among many English historians, past and present, to privilege political negotiations rather than political ideas and institutions in their writings, in a way that seems inexplicably mysterious to writers in, for example, Germany (Rohe 1987). None the less, though these elements of a national identity may be subconscious, and widely accepted – often with enthusiasm – among all classes, they are essentially bourgeois (and, before that, aristocratic or at least 'gentle') in *origin*, and expressed most emblematically by the various strata of the national bourgeoisie. This follows simply from the fact that England industrialized early; as a result, its dominant elites and political image-makers, however divided, have been middle class, generally upper middle class, for a long time. (That 'patriotism', one of their expressions, is normally right-wing in England, a fact generally lamented by the English Left, essentially derives from the fact that the middle classes in England, unlike those in France or Italy – or Wales and Scotland – have tended *en bloc* to support the Right.)

The relationship between national memories and the middle class is most visible when we can see them actually being created or changed, in the context of the construction or reconstruction of nations themselves – for we must not forget that all nations have to be invented; none, whether old or young, are 'innate' or self-evident to all their members. Often, this process is entirely conscious. One example is the sanitized reinvention of the French Revolution after 1871 by the Third Republic (a more sophisticated system than that of 1848), as an ideological rallying call for all but the monarchist Right, through ceremonies (Bastille Day, the Centennial of 1889), innumerable monuments, the adoption of the Marseillaise, and the careful historical reconstructions of the public education system (Gérard 1970; Hobsbawm 1983: 269–78; Ory 1984). Hobsbawm has remarked that this was a past entirely devoid of heroes, for none of the revolutionary leaders were unambiguously acceptable to enough of the population to be unifying rather than divisive images; in France, whose history was already long, the Revolution could only be reinvented, not entirely invented from nothing and superimposed on a national memory based on a completely different past. Such commemorations in France were unlike the very personalized history-making of Imperial Germany in the same period, with its genealogy of leaders from Arminius through Barbarossa to Wilhelm I; but they also contrast interestingly with the experience of the United States, whose historical past had to be created *ex novo*, largely by early nineteenth-century writers, but whose revolutionary leaders were considered more suitable cases for hero-making; for example, Washington, Jefferson, and an array of other figures up to Lincoln (Commager 1967: 3–27).[13]

This contrast is not entirely surprising, none the less. France was an old nation, and any new national commemorations had to take into account what people already remembered about their country. The United States was the first 'new' nation, and national memory, for it and all its successors, had to mark a clear break with the past. One of the commonest ways of doing this was to commemorate anti-colonial leaders themselves; and there is no doubt that in the United States the moment of founding self-affirmation after colonial oppression was sufficiently universally accepted to allow for an unambiguous mythological commemoration of its leaders, which indeed still exists (Frisch 1990: 29–54). Washington has been subsequently joined in his empyrean by figures such as Bolívar, Cavour and Garibaldi, Atatürk, Gandhi, Jinnah, and a host of probably more ephemeral postwar figures. Atatürk may belong more with Lenin and Mao as a mythologized leader of an internal rather than an anti-colonial revolution; in all three cases, however, the *revolutionary* imagery that they convey has been all but subsumed into the same sort of *national* myth of the Liberator that one finds for Washington or Bolívar.

These images are often recent enough to be obviously crafted, as

---

[13] Lincoln is an interesting example, for he was commemorated in two opposed traditions inside the USA: one from the East, portraying him as a mythological hero, risen from nothing to win victories and emancipate slaves, and killed at the height of his powers; and the other, from the West; presenting him as a Western, frontier hero, a strong, lazy practical joker. This reflects the early complexity and heterogeneity of American literary culture, but also its interrelationship with an array of popular stories based on folk motifs that circulated orally at quite different social levels. (Donald 1961: 144–67.)

personality cults of the dead, complete with a mausoleum, an air of respectful silence in it, and – as first and most emblematically with Lenin – a visible embalmed body; the rituals they replaced, those of previous dynastic royalties, lie very clearly at their back, thus making the process of invention still more explicit. (Dynastic royalties, of course, had developed ritual just as consciously, especially after 1870 or so: Hobsbawm and Ranger 1983.) Such images will last only as long as, and in so far as, they have or acquire a real and permanent place in popular memory which itself, therefore, has often been fairly carefully manipulated. Hence, for example, some of the most obvious examples of ideological engineering this century, such as Atatürk's inauguration of the Roman alphabet to replace the Arabic alphabet in writing the Turkish language. This change was largely associated with an entirely different project, a literacy drive; but an important subtext of the language reform was that it would henceforth prevent people from reading the (largely religious) books published before his revolution, and thus encourage them to forget what was there before. (It was accompanied by a systematic removal of words of Arabic and Persian origin from the Turkish language; pre-1930s Turkish is thus, even when transliterated, almost incomprehensible to modern Turks.) However, such operations were themselves, by definition, aimed at the literate members of society; that is to say, in Atatürk's case, at the new national Turkish bourgeoisie that itself had to be created to fill the gaps caused by the ethnic massacres and the migrations of World War I and its aftermath. The bourgeoisie were the first subjects of this, and other 'new' national popular cultures; other social groups would follow subsequently, although preferably soon. (Heyd 1954; cf. Berktay 1990.)

These processes of conscious and semi-conscious creation can be associated with state building, and are the responsibility of politicians (and the intellectuals in their following). The same processes can be found, however, in national groups which had (or have) not yet achieved the self-determination that allowed them to be backed by the state. The intellectual spokesmen for Wales were doing it in the late eighteenth and early nineteenth century, through the revival or outright forgery of a whole array of national traditions: either rituals (such as the Eisteddfod), or literature (much medieval Welsh literature was not only rediscovered but also, sometimes, written from scratch by one of the leaders of the revival, Iolo Morganwg), or emblematic figures from the Welsh past, such as the legendary prince Madoc, twelfth-century discoverer of North America. Even Owain Glyndŵr (d. 1415?) owes his national fame principally to this time, his original historical commemoration in the fifteenth century as the last fighter against the

English (and as a 'hidden king') having, in the meantime, fallen victim to the transient Welsh triumphalism of the early Tudor period. (Morgan 1983; 1981; Williams 1979; Williams 1974.) What Iolo and his contemporaries did for Wales, romantic intellectuals all over Europe were doing in their own ways for their peoples, including Sándor Petőfi in Hungary; Elias Lönnrot, transcriber/author of the *Kalevala*, in Finland; the 'restorers' of the Jocs Florals, the supposed medieval national cultural festival, in Catalonia; and, in the preunification period, Herder and the Grimms in Germany (Burke 1978: 3–22; Pi de Cabanyes 1979). The past they created is still, in many of its most crucial elements, a dominant image for their compatriots and, not surprisingly, they themselves have often remained in national memory as cultural liberators, preceding, even in subsequently independent nations, the (sometimes more controversial) political leaders who actually presided over the independence process.

The word 'cultural' is important here; for, in nations without statehood, and thus without a recent historical past that held any legitimate national points of reference that seemed worth commemorating (as in Wales since 1282, in Hungary since 1526 or maybe 1681, or in Finland perhaps always), national culture came to be mythologized in its place, whether through writing literature, forging past literature, or writing *down* a previously oral literature. (The Grimms themselves, it has been argued, did the second of these as much as the third: see, e.g., Ellis 1983.) These movements, and the nationalisms that produced them, were all part of the romantic tradition, of course, which privileged popular culture for its own reasons, not all of them historicist. But national traditions needed the discourse of the past as a constitutive element for their identities, for the same reasons as any other social groups we have looked at; and thus the romanticization of peasant culture and oral literature that was a feature of most places in nineteenth-century Europe came to have, as a major aim, the establishment of an 'authentic' historical memory for a given people (see, e.g., Herzfeld 1982, for Greece). On the other hand, the visions of the past that they produced, however populist, were once again almost always those of a national bourgeoisie; or else, in places where a bourgeoisie had not yet sufficiently developed, such as parts of south-eastern Europe, those of the traditional intellectuals (lawyers or clerics) that preceded it.

These visions were produced for their own consumption first and then, in intention at least, imposed on the rest of the population from above. Oral literature, to become part of this world, had to be legitimized (i.e., written down) and purified (put into 'proper' literary form, and often bowdlerized); if it got back to the peasantry at all, as

Grimms' folk-tales or the *Kalevala* certainly did, it did so from the top. When these literary cultures became part of nation-*states*, as in Germany after 1870 or Eastern Europe after 1918, they could thus fit seamlessly into the national images of the past that each state strove to create as quickly as possible. Perhaps the only nation in Europe whose image of the past was not predominantly mediated through this intellectual and bourgeois culture was Iceland, where the thirteenth-century written historical narratives known as sagas, which commemorated the independent Iceland of before 1262 (see below, pp. 163ff.), were known to the peasantry in all subsequent centuries, whether in oral or in written form – for Iceland had mass literacy by the eighteenth century (Hastrup 1990: 184–200). It may be in part because the saga literature was already linked to the peasantry that the emergent intellectual bourgeoisie of the independence period in Iceland (1918–44) was hostile to any idea that sagas had an oral base, claiming, rather, that they were literary and (sometimes) clerical creations, i.e. not only that they did not belong to the peasant world, but also that they had no status as *historical* texts, that is to say, as guides to any 'genuine' commemoration of the past, at all. (Cf. Byock 1988: 38–48.)

In the dialectic between a 'popular' social memory of the past, and the conscious creations and manipulations of it in the national development of the last two centuries, we are emphasizing the middle-class elements in the process: national memory as articulated or created by the bourgeoisie, or for the bourgeoisie, or for the bourgeoisie *first*. These discourses about the past are dominant, imposed on other classes from above, by public and private means: schooling, newspapers, books, and radio and TV programmes. They are linear in their conception of time, and indeed teleological: very explicitly, all of them lead up to and legitimize the present situation. They are mythological charters for the whole national community, of course, and are intended to define that community; but this definition will include a legitimation of its structures of political and economic dominance, by which the elite justifies itself as an elite. They are thus hegemonic, and totalizing: alternative memories are to be regarded as irrelevant, inaccurate, and even illegitimate, though the harshness of this delegitimization will vary according to the intolerance of the national culture and the degree to which it has, on any given occasion, been challenged. But national memory can also be oppositional. This is clear in the cases of the minority nationalities that we have just seen, the Czechs and the Finns of the nineteenth century, or the Welsh and the Catalans now, as also in the case of cohesive populations ruled by governments that are regarded as wholly illegitimate, such as, among others, the Czechs and Slovaks

of the years 1968–89: peoples in this situation have historical consciousnesses that totally exclude the reference points of the state, and
that are fashioned by an intellectual culture equally separate from and
subversive of that state. A more obviously class-based national memory
of opposition is, however, that created in each country by the labour
movement, either by parties or trade unions, as an alternative point of
reference to the social memory of the bourgeoisie. Such memories have
different foci: the genealogy of strikes that we saw in the last section, or
the teleology of growing working-class self-awareness, both national and
international, that ran (to take the French example) from the Sans-
culottes of 1792, through the Paris Commune of 1870–1, to the emer-
gence of the mass socialist movement at the end of the century, and
then, via the Revolution of 1917 (for part of the movement) and the
Popular Front, to the Maquis.

Even this memory, however, despite its proletarian base, has tended
to be articulated at the national level by intellectuals. Gramsci
counterposed to his traditional intellectuals, who, whether conservative
or radical, represented the culture of the middle classes (from which
they stemmed, or to which they attached themselves: see above, p. 103),
the concept of the 'organic' intellectual, who maintained organic links
with the 'subaltern' classes (proletariat or peasantry) and faithfully
represented and structured *their* values, rather than those of universities,
professions, or the state (Gramsci 1971: 5–23). Indeed, whether using
this terminology or not, radical movements since the late nineteenth
century have sought to establish, as part of the conditions for political
victory, not only an oppositional memory, but also an organic (especially
working-class and trade union) intelligentsia to match and eventually
replace the traditional one that was there before. If this ever happened,
then it might be possible to discuss a national culture and historical
memory that was not bourgeois. It does not seem to us that it ever has.
Tribesmen, peasants, and industrial workers, often with very localized
or class-specific perspectives and memories, have won revolutions, but
their interpreters from then on have been intellectuals of the old style;
even Gramsci's own party, the Italian Communist Party, the only Western Communist party to have had and held onto a real hegemony over at
least some parts of national culture, has always been run by such
intellectuals. This, in the 1990s, does not seem to be something that will
soon change: the interpretation and structuring of national historical
memory remains for the foreseeable future in their hands.

Even opposition movements tend to have as their most effective
points of reference nationally *shared* memories, which can, however,
be commemorated with slightly different political valencies. Thus, for

example, we have in Italy the privileging by the Left of Garibaldi over Cavour in the mythology of the Risorgimento, or the different symbolisms of the Resistance of 1943–5, which has a resonance for all Italians as a moment of purging from Fascism (and from responsibility for the War). The Italian Resistance is generally seen as an affirmation of opposition against external and internal oppression, but it has always been most powerful as a touchstone for the Left, whose imagery most recalls that of the Resistance itself.

The dialectic between such interpretations can, however, be best seen in France, by now perhaps the most successful of all modern national re-creations, and the country, therefore, where (in national matters at least) Left and Right most visibly understand each other's languages., The French Right has for decades accepted and drawn heavily from the Republican and Revolutionary tradition of 1789, which is still a distinctly divisive inheritance in many countries. Conversely, the French Left can use not only the language of the movement that we have just cited, but also some very traditional national historical discourses. In the 1940s, the national Resistance rhetoric of the histori-cal past can be followed for both Gaullists and Communists through their official propaganda: it was strikingly similar. Vercingetorix, St Louis, Joan of Arc, and the battles of Valmy, Sedan, and Verdun were the reference points for the Gaullists; Joan of Arc and Valmy again for the Communists, and then, instead of Sedan, the guerrillas of 1870 and the Paris Commune; instead of Verdun, the *poilus* (infantry) of World War I – a popular, rather than an elite nationalism, but with the same rhetoric at root (Michel 1962: 25, 49, 132, 136, 246, 601–3). It is interesting, on the other hand, that both of these imageries can be set against the historical imagery used by the French Resistance on the ground, which was not at all similar, and which varied considerably from place to place: the Camisards in the Cévennes; the 1851 resistances against Napoleon III, the Commune, and Dreyfus in Languedoc; 1851 at Valence; Dreyfus at Marseille; French Revolutionary rhetoric and a nineteenth-century silk-workers' strike at Lyon (the list is from a recent study of the early Vichy regime: Kedward 1978: 59, 151–9). These images were generated by local not national groups, and they remained local; they were images, too, of internal resistance (linked, indeed, to the oppositional 'national history', though not dependent on it), rather than of the wars, however defensive, commemorated at the national level. 'Organic' intellectual commemorations of the linear historical past do, then, exist; but in order to find them, rather than concentrating on the national workers' movement, one should perhaps return to *local* class commemorations, such as those we discussed in previous sections of this chapter.

In 1981 François Mitterrand, at his presidential inauguration, instituted a 'cérémonie à la mémoire' at the Panthéon. Here he laid red roses on the tombs of Jean Moulin, the Resistance hero; Victor Schoelcher, who abolished slavery in 1848; and Jean Jaurès, the founder of French socialism, before going to the Hôtel de Ville to be received by Jacques Chirac, the mayor of Paris (who was also a leader of the defeated coalition in the election), who was surrounded by images of St Geneviève, Joan of Arc, Henri IV, and de Gaulle (Ozouf 1984: 139–41). Mitterrand was, effectively, signalling his victory as one of the French Republic over the French Nation, almost as if it were the 1889 Centennial again, and, by so doing, claiming Republican symbolism as the property of the contemporary Left, despite the fact that Chirac would have recognized most of the same touchstones. French historical discourses are, perhaps, sufficiently ideological and explicit to allow an effective operator to pull a trick like this off (it would have been harder in Britain: one would barely know where to start).[14] But Mitterrand's success also derived, precisely, from a certain consensus about much of the national past that has for a long time extended to nearly everyone in the country – including the local Maquisard groups mentioned above. French national consciousness, perhaps, reaches parts that other national consciousnesses cannot reach.

Women's memories

We have moved from the very specific to the very generalized in this chapter, and it is therefore fitting that we should conclude with the speculative. As we have said, the memories and traditions used in this chapter, and indeed elsewhere in the book, are almost all those of men. Can a women's historical consciousness be identified as distinct from this? There are, as in our other cases, problems of method that are involved here. One is the objective diversity of women's experience in different societies: societies constituted by different family structures, different levels of male tolerance of female points of view or of female articulacy, different economic roles for women, different levels of sexual exclusion and difference, and different levels of women's mutual cooperation or 'complicity' with men. Another is the as yet unresolved issue

---

[14] For the background to this sort of symbolism of commemoration, stretching back to the rivalries of Gaullists and Communists in 1944–5, see Namer 1983. Mitterrand's style changed somewhat during his first term, one should note; he ended up looking more like Henri IV. In his 1988 inauguration he did not repeat the gesture.

of how far women's separate consciousness depends on a diversity of experience different from men's rather than on something innate in gender. A third is the fact that, despite all the work in the field of women's studies in recent years, very little has yet been done on the specific nature of female perceptions of the past; we shall be posing questions that can be asked, rather than, in most cases, reporting on those that have been answered. Here, however, even more than in other parts of this book, we are describing a field that is in rapid development. And at least one basis for future work has already been clearly established, that is, some sophisticated analysis of life histories by scholars such as Isabelle Bertaux-Wiame, Luisa Passerini, and Anna Bravo; it is on their insights that we shall be principally relying.

The essential problem for anyone wishing to identify a distinctively female view of the past is hegemony: that of a dominant ideology and a dominance over narration, as expressed through the male–female relationship. This is much as in the relationship between working-class and ruling-class memories, in fact, but, this time, the dominance is not from outside the social group but within it. This dominance is near total for the surviving records of societies in the past, for most written genres are constructed by men, even when the texts themselves are composed by women; such texts need close reading to pick out any authentic female discourses. But among the living, too, rare are the families and social groups in which male voices, values, and images are not those that are principally heard and discussed. In most societies, women have little or no entirely autonomous space outside informal friendships (though these can be of crucial importance), or the particular but transient relationships between female relatives at various moments in the life cycle; and even the latter are not always easily restricted to single-sex groups (mothers certainly give different sorts of social and moral information to daughters than they do to sons, but, at least some of the time, in situations when both are present).

These are not iron rules, and there are exceptions. When women actually do form conscious collectivities, they use social memory in the same way that all groups do. One example is the women's movement itself, which has produced, particularly in the last two decades, a whole host of specific accounts of past female contributions to different professions, or different academic or cultural fields: these works, whether scholarly or not, are classic examples of commemorations which help to constitute the social identity of each women's professional group. Outside the Western professional classes, however, such a group consciousness seems less common. Societies with a great deal of sexual segregation could certainly produce, as an unintended by-product, all-women subgroups that could establish autonomous views of the past (and, of course, of the present); and there have been special cases even in other societies of all-women institutions – in Europe, the most obvious example is the nunnery. In the case of segregated societies, however, the dominance of men tends to be very determinedly and explicitly maintained, at least over the public arenas of the past. And this goes for nunneries, too: the literature that emanates from them in, for example, the medieval West, however original, shows little conscious sense of a past that differed from that of men (see, e.g., Dronke 1984). This is largely a matter of genre again; but, as institutions, nunneries remained a part of the very male world of the medieval church, and this fact seems to have dominated their formal, public, collective personae, including nuns' descriptions of past history: even their past female role-models tended either to behave like men or to do what men expected women to do. Resistance to male ideology in this environment seems to have been individual rather than social, just as in the lay world outside it; and such individual resistance was marginalized in both the religious and the lay environment of the Middle Ages (as in other periods) as hysterical, deviant, or even heretical – only a few such 'deviants' achieved saint-hood.[15]

In this book we are minimizing the difference between 'oral tradition' and 'life histories', on the grounds that both of them, in the very process of retelling, encapsulate the same sorts of group commemoration of the past. But, if one is dealing with a social category that is not often constituted into autonomous social groups, then group retelling is not, in practice, a useful object of study; separate women's commemorations may, in many cases, simply not exist.[16] The only sort of social memory

[15] Suggestive examples can be found in Bynum 1987; and, for nunneries and memory, see, for example, Cabré 1990. Bynum 1984 argues that women constructed sanctity differently from men; they lacked the male capacity to become liminal and to return with renewed spiritual power, because they were, at least to men, liminal already. As a result, women's religiosity was much more continuous and undramatic than that of men; their stories lacked the same sort of turning-points. This has some parallels in modern life-history analysis, as we shall see.

[16] Among women, friendship is certainly constructed through conversation, often on a more intimate and personal level than is normal among many men (see, as an emblematic example, Tannen 1990); such conversation can indeed include shared narratives of past experiences, although not necessarily always the construction of *group* versions of the recounted past. It would be interesting to find out if women's commemorations existed in West Africa of some of the women-only political disturbances that are a feature of the area (cf. Ifeka-Moller 1975 on the Igbo 'Women's War' of 1929): historical events of this kind are among the few that women might be able (or wish) to inherit autonomously.

that one can study in this environment is the unconscious or semi-conscious patterning found in autobiographies: hence the importance of the women's life histories mentioned above. But, when trying to capture women's memory, there are other problems too. Even the spoken narrative process is gendered. On a practical level, it is notoriously difficult even to tape-record women remembering in the presence of their husbands: most men interrupt, devalue their wives' memories, take over the interview, tell their own stories instead, or even, most bizarrely, themselves recount their wives' life stories (e.g., *Bulletin* 1982: 9; Revelli 1985: xviii–xix; Keesing 1985: 30). And even when women find their own voice, too often they find themselves caught by the fact that the principal narrative *styles* that they know for commemorating the past are about male activities. Public activities, for instance, even everyday ones (not to speak of 'Great Events' history) have easily accessible genres by which they can be narrated, but they tend to be performed by men; the more private experiences that women have may not have any established narrative format by which they can be systematically described, at least to strangers (for inside their own friendship circuit they might well be able to do so), thus forcing them to use a male perspective in their depiction (Ardener 1975; *Bulletin* 1982: 26; Young 1983; cf. Bravo and Scaraffia 1979). In one Tunisian town, for example, there are two storytelling styles: 'true stories', told by men, and 'fantasy stories', told by women. In recent years, with more public experience, women have begun to tell 'true stories'; but it is a male genre none the less, even if women can sometimes begin to subvert it (Webber 1985). Even the relatively articulate women of Malaita, the Melanesian island studied by Keesing, who were keen to relate their experiences, were following a male project of recounting customs to the anthropologist; and Keesing has suggested that women in Malaita owed their capacity to describe themselves and their society not only to their real role in the transmission of local culture, but also to the more explicit self-representations derived from essentially male reactions to the colonial experience (Keesing 1985). These sorts of complexities make it unsurprising that anthropologists have often called women's discourses 'muted'; and such mutedness is an obvious feature of Western societies too.

It is, none the less, possible to set out a few tentative generalizations, especially if we restrict ourselves to the smaller range of societies of modern Western Europe. In life histories, there do seem to be some consistencies in women's choices about what is important to relate, or to emphasize. Some patterns are obvious. Women's life stories give less, or different, space to 'public' history than men's do, for the simple reason that women were less involved in it, or involved in ways that created different sorts of perspectives. For a start, even when they were involved, they were often, at least traditionally, more so when they were single than when they were married: Claire Auzias in France and Ecléa Bosi in Brazil have both described cases of female left-wing militants, whose memories of militancy – and even their private recollections – stopped abruptly when they got married (*Bulletin* 1982: 7; Bosi 1979: 172). Some of the most totalizing events of the century, such as the Depression and the two World Wars, cannot fail to be remembered by women as well as men, however, and here some gender divergencies can be pinned down. War itself is less often remembered with nostalgia by women; few have any ideological stake in the (male) self-image of the fighter, and they can feel marginalized by the standard run of war stories. Anna Bravo's peasant informants in the Langhe, the hills of southern Piemonte in Italy, remembered World War I with hostility; they had supported and fed the deserters hiding in their area. That war was, however, also a period that gave them considerable independence and 'public' experience, often leaving them with a greater familiarity with confronting local bureaucracy than their husbands had when they returned from the front; the experience brought with it, therefore, a pride and a social identity that lasted long after, and is still recalled. War as a period of independence in the absence of men, and war as *more work*, for much the same reasons, are common themes in female recollections of both World Wars, in fact; the 'national' and ideological dimensions are often left to men. (Bravo 1982a; Bravo and Scaraffia 1979: 41–5, 53; cf. Filippini Cappelletto 1983: 25–6; *Bulletin* 1982: 53.) And this sort of gendered recollection can even be extended to activists: male resistance workers against the Nazis in the Ruhr in the 1930s were found by Detlev Peukert to recall the details of political activity and individual heroism; women resisters tended, rather, to recall the everyday aspect of resistance, the small-scale defiances of daily life (Peukert 1980: 118).

Women in their life histories give more stress to home life. Indeed, in some societies they are unchallenged here, for men sometimes do not spontaneously recount their home lives at all, as we have seen (p. 121). But they also tend to be more exact about home and family events than are men – Isabelle Bertaux-Wiame, working in Paris, discovered that women often know more dates of past family history than do men, and could correct them on detail; the commemoration of the home, like its day-to-day organization, remained under their control (Bertaux-Wiame 1982: 191–3; *Bulletin* 1982: 6, 9; cf. also Bertaux-Wiame 1985: 23–7, for a family-based female memory of a collective geography).

Women in most societies run many or most of the key moments of the life cycle (most characteristically, birth and death); it is not only because they often have little experience outside the family environment that they structure their recollections around such moments, but also because such moments are in their hands, rather than those of men. Moreover, in most Western societies, women, rather than men, have the responsibility of encapsulating (sanitizing, moralizing) accounts of the experienced past for young children, as part of the process of socialization: images of 'the way we were', recounted by a line of female narrators, can stretch back for generations. (See, e.g., Straw and Elliott 1986, for Scotland.) This type of commemoration of experience is separated in genre from the male personal autobiography. It is identifiable by its tenses (more imperfect, fewer past or perfect), and, as Bertaux-Wiame has noted, by its pronouns (among her female informants, 'nous' or 'on' predominated over the 'je' of males). It is also identifiable by an analogous absence of specific events, of life cruxes, resoluble by choices and discontinuities with the past. Indeed, relationships and situations tend to be privileged over events in female narratives of all kinds. Bertaux-Wiame even found that her male informants, portraying their lives as a series of self-conscious acts, found these acts relativized and reinserted into a web of social relationships by their listening and commenting wives (compare Tannen 1990: 74–95, 176–8). For the women, memory was of ongoing experience, rather than of personal choice.

It is this absence of emphasis on choice, perhaps, that constitutes the most recurrent characteristics of women's memories of the past. Women, however powerful, have tended to live their lives in environments whose public, external power structures have been under the control of men; political activism, for example, is often determined in the memories of older informants by brothers or fathers ('we were always a socialist household'). Passerini has argued that it is for this reason that her female informants about life between the Wars in working-class Turin use a certain rhetoric of rebellion and irreverence, including sometimes the imagery of carnival, when describing their lives: laughter, and the (reversible) inversions of the carnival world, which could even be used to recount, for example, the Fascist breakup of a demonstration in 1920, reflect an individuality of the margin, for women were genuinely marginal to such events, and knew it (Passerini 1987: 19–31; Bravo et al. 1982; cf. Davis 1975: 124–51; Bynum 1984). This imagery of rebellion, the naughty girl or the self-willed adolescent, an urban image in all probability (it does not recur nearly so often in the countryside: Bravo in Bravo et al. 1982: 103–5), could well be an image of mother-to-daughter discourse, reinforcing, at least this once, a female complicity against the outside world.[17] But it remained a discourse; rarely among Passerini's female informants was concrete rebellion actually recounted.

In Turin, the only context where female choice was talked about was that of entering the factory: the world of paid work outside the family was perceived as giving women a certain independent social role and therefore a certain (however limited) autonomous identity. One could say that women were enabled to exercise these 'male prerogatives' of choice and identity simply by imitating men, by taking on positions in the outside world. But they carried their 'rebellious' narratives into the factory with them; women were much more irreverent than men in recounting their factory experiences (Passerini 1987: 48–51, 60; Bravo et al. 1982: 102–3). Working has often been a double-edged experience for women, of guilt at leaving children, fatigue from having to work in the day and then having to run the house as well at night, and frustration at the discovery of their powerlessness in the face of men even in the factory or office, all set against the money and the 'public' role that even the most gruelling and unqualified job can bring. It is perhaps not surprising, then, that outside work, too, can be commemorated by women through a narrative genre of ironic detachment. But the point is none the less important. The factory is one environment in which men and women alike can exercise choice (which job, which factory, etc.) and have a certain degree of public identity as a result; but in the Turin case, at least, it was remembered differently by each gender: men emphasizing the enthusiasm of (however alienated) creation and a certain pride in (however basic) skills, set against women emphasizing the irony of factory-floor powerlessness. Here, for all the reasons sketched out above, similar (though certainly not identical) experiences produced social memories that were genuinely divergent in *type*. This sort of analysis seems to us one of the most productive that could be followed in the future.

---

[17] Such complicity certainly broke down over sex, however: traditional mothers in many parts of Europe by their very silence barred knowledge about menstruation and intercourse from the arena of the spoken, and thus of the social: see, e.g., Bravo 1982b: 86–90; Revelli 1985: lxv–vi; Straw and Elliott 1986: 40.

4
Medieval Memories

If one wishes to understand the social framework of memory, written sources are not, in principle, any different from spoken ones. When they are written by historians, however, the issue is more complex. Historians have their own, more or less consciously formulated, interpretations of the past that they use to structure their material: as re-elaborators of the past, they are, so to speak, already competing with us, in compiling and analysing their material (both oral and written) to express particular points of view. When our informants are all dead, we can scarcely do without written sources; and when one gets back beyond the discursive complexities of the millions of texts and dozens of genres of the modern period to the sparser writings of the Middle Ages (especially before 1300 or so) and the ancient world before that, we find ourselves unable to avoid their historians – political history, in particular, from the time of Herodotus to that of Froissart, is hard to write without them.

The ways in which modern historians have dealt with such writers are various, but one can, in general, separate them into two ideal types. For the positivist tradition of the nineteenth and twentieth centuries, it was enough to work out the sources and the 'bias' of ancient and medieval writers, and to discount 'obvious' errors and superstitions, in order to draw reasonably firm conclusions about the 'truth content' of their writings. Such procedures were often naive, and, indeed, particularly in periods where the writers so analysed were the only sources, logically circular. Even the best of them, however, can be subjected to the same sort of criticisms as we have given to the writings of Vansina (see above, pp. 76–86): they are self-defeating, because the 'facts' that result are decontextualized, deprived of the meaning that they had in the original narratives, and often appear as just a jumble of data, which are hard to put together except in banal or speculative ways. (A classic example of the product may be found in the narrative sections of the *Cambridge Medieval History*.) At the other extreme, particularly in the last two decades, we find a more textual approach, which, through literary analysis of structure, style, or the network of meanings inside a work, aims at restoring an understanding of the internal context of what a writer intended. The problem of this approach is that it sometimes tends to assume that it is pointless to use historians as sources for anything but themselves; it argues that Livy or Bede were so far from the events they described, and intervened in their material so much (whether for literary or ideological reasons), that we can analyse only their world-view, rather than their world. Analyses of this kind decontextualize in a different way: historians themselves, rather than what they wrote about, are removed from their environment and their audience. And one assumption is shared by most historians at the first extreme, and some even at the second: that there is an opposition between a historical text and a literary text, sources that are (potentially) 'true' descriptions of the past and those that are not. Such a distinction is essentially artificial; only by regarding the 'objective' and the 'subjective' as indissoluble can we understand the relationship between the world as it empirically was, and the world as it was represented by writers. This is the way that we ourselves all deal with the present, after all, through our analyses of daily conversations and the media, as we manoeuvre between the innocence of people who think they can believe 'at least' the BBC, and the nihilism of people who assume that the papers are all lies. For that matter, indeed, very many modern historians deal with the historians of the past like this too. But only by confronting the problem explicitly shall we be able to avoid the methodological traps that await the unwary. One way of doing this is by concentrating on the analysis of social memory.

This does not make the process easy, nevertheless. As at other times, historical writers in the medieval period wrote in clearly demarcated genres, which (even in relatively non-literate ages) tended to have more affinities with other textual styles than with oral genres of commemoration, even when their direct sources were oral. They may have been dependent on social memories (and, at times, they certainly created their own, as later societies used them as sources); but they tended to transform the patterns and even the content of these memories in ways we cannot always identify. They also had more commonly studied orientations: specific patrons, specific political programmes or political/moral assumptions, or (in the case of the more educated) specific theologies of the historical process itself, all of which would further contribute to distance what they wrote from what they heard – and that is when they were directly dealing with oral material, rather than with one or more levels of written sources. Nevertheless, one can sometimes infer, from their own narrative styles, some of their principles of selection; and, from their metamorphoses of their material, something of the material itself and its own styles. Whatever they did with the past, they were writing in – and usually for – worlds that had their own ideas about the nature of the usable past, the current, functionally relevant past, and the collectively remembered past, just like any of the twentieth-century informants that we discussed in the previous chapter. What aspects of the past seemed relevant to historians to play around with for their own purposes is perhaps the key question: and when it is put in this form one can see that the question can cover oral and written commemorations, just as it can cover 'true' and 'false' pasts. The usable pasts thus uncovered will be those of historians and their audiences only, the former almost always, in the medieval period, churchmen, and both the former and the latter almost always of aristocratic extraction or aspiration: a tiny proportion of the population, but the only part of society before 1300 or so whose voice can normally be heard. The potential material for such analyses is none the less vast: every historian of the Middle Ages could be so discussed.[1] Our intention being only introductory, we shall restrict ourselves to three examples which show some of the ways such analyses can be done: Gregory of Tours, one of the most detailed of medieval historians; the memory of Charlemagne, taken through a number of different accounts in different genres (important for the relationship between narrative style and the content of the material commemorated); and the thirteenth-century Icelandic prose narratives of the past (sagas), which, unlike other medieval texts, tell us something about non-aristocratic sensibilities. These three, however briefly discussed, may serve as models for other discussions.

Gregory, bishop of Tours (539–94), wrote, besides several works on miracles, a long book of *Histories*, which occupied him for the last two decades of his life, amid his political and pastoral duties as bishop.[2]

---

[1] Useful and critical guides to the bibliography are Ray 1974 and Guenée 1980. Examples of our approach include Folz 1950; Clanchy 1970; Autrand 1977; Wickham 1985; Bordone 1988; and the classic Bloch 1961: 88–102. For genre and modern authors, see, as a key example, White 1973.

[2] Basic guides to Gregory include Wallace-Hadrill 1962: 49–70; Brown 1977; Pietri 1983: 247–334 (for his career); Van Dam 1985; Goffart 1988: 112–234. The text of the *Histories* is edited in Krusch and Levison 1951; it will be cited in the text as *LH*. A translation of it is Thorpe 1974.

Two-thirds of the latter text is a roughly contemporary account of the events that took place in the Frankish kingdoms which replaced the Roman Empire in sixth-century Gaul, seen from a privileged vantage point, for Gregory was a leading Roman aristocrat, and the confidant (and opponent) of kings; the rest is an account of the past, that begins with Adam, though very quickly reaches fifth-century Gaul. Gregory is almost our sole source for the Frankish kingdoms of his lifetime; and his is by far the most detailed account of any of the Germanic kingdoms that succeeded the Roman state.

Gregory was certainly not a classical figure. His education was entirely clerical, something which would have been very rare a century earlier, and his Latin is notoriously untraditional; he is the first major writer to give us a 'medieval' rather than an 'ancient' view of the world. This contrast between two worlds cannot, however, be deduced from Gregory's own writings; he seems to have been totally uninterested in that famous event, the fall of the Roman Empire in the West, and he gives us no signs that he was aware that something identifiable as the 'ancient world' had passed away, or even existed. This apparent lacuna in Gregory's interests has always made historians uneasy. Earlier writers in the late Roman West certainly thought of their world as in decline, and sometimes planned their writings as, in effect, survival packages. Gregory, on the other hand, regarded his *Histories* as themselves the solution to the literary decline he saw around him, and, for all his pro-testations of linguistic inadequacy (taken too seriously by subsequent scholars), writes in a very self-confident way about his society. This is not entirely surprising; Gregory was proud of his environment, and could not have known that sixth-century Gaul would be regarded by many modern historians, largely as a result of his own writings, as one of the most dreadful periods in human history. But it is interesting none the less that he could move from fourth- and fifth-century sources, writ-ten in a classical environment, to his own very different world, without giving any indication that he noticed the contrast. Indeed, even when his written sources dry up in the mid-fifth century, and are replaced by oral ones, one sees little change in Gregory's style of writing, or in the principles by which he organized his evidence. It may well be that one aspect of antique historiography that was quite simply lost by Gregory's time was the awareness of patterns of wide-ranging social and political change. One of the first phrases in the *Histories* is the startling banality, 'Many things happen, both good and bad'; and this is a fairly accurate guide to the book. Gregory fragments his material. Much of his account is anecdotal, with the evildoing of kings, the virtue of saints (usually bishops), and the colourful and generally malign goings-on in the neighbourhood of Tours and Clermont, the two cities he knows best, constantly and deliberately interlaced. It is indeed very difficult to work out firm and certain political narratives from Gregory's accounts of his kings; he barely bothers to give one any sequential lead from one story to the next (his chapters tend to begin 'meanwhile', 'some time after', 'once again', or 'in the same year').

Gregory has sometimes, as a result of all this, been depicted as a credulous automaton, simply regurgitating all the gossip that reached him, and injecting only a strong dose of moralism, a series of sharp likes and dislikes, and a considerable element of the miraculous. There is no doubt that this estimate of him is untrue. Much of his writing is highly structured; if he had wanted to write a political narrative with a secular causal thread he could certainly have done so. His *Histories* are, at least in part, moral tales – Walter Goffart has recently called them satire (Goffart 1988: 199–203); they presuppose, in effect, a theological claim that the only real causal thread that a Christian can properly accept is the providence of God, which, indeed, figures very largely in the work. This may help to explain, too, why most of his contemporaries seem so frightful; Gregory is concerned to point up their wickedness for specific pastoral reasons. But that Gregory was not very theoretically minded is nevertheless likely; his stories often have an inner logic to them that seems to belong to one of the less elaborated genres of oral storytelling (cf. Auerbach 1953: 77–95). He chose them for his own purposes, which could often be quite complex, but then retold them relatively little changed, trusting to their content, or sometimes their juxtaposition, to point up the moral conclusions he intended.

Precisely Gregory's lack of awareness of, or interest in, the past's difference from the present – his total lack of nostalgia for the Roman or even the heroic Frankish past (though he admired Clovis, who, for all his savagery, had founded the Frankish kingdom in the years around 500), and his lack of any preoccupation about processes of historical change and development – makes him useful for our purposes; however he was manipulating his material, it was not in order to *invent* a past, either to legitimate or to condemn the present. (Bede, the great historian of early medieval England, by contrast, constructed the past in precisely this way; he would be much less useful for our analyses here.) The density of Gregory's incidental and anecdotal detail makes it possible to say quite a lot about the sort of material he was working with, including the memories of the past of himself and his informants. Indeed, given that Gregory does not confront past and present, one could use his accounts of the present as easily as those of the past to illustrate our points about memory: this is how the world was being commemorated

in the late sixth century, at least by an aristocratic bishop; however much he left out, whether consciously or not, it was these sorts of things that it seemed relevant to him to recount. But, in order to match more precisely the subject-matter of the rest of the book, we shall restrict ourselves here to the parts of the *Histories* that are based on longer-term memories, coming through people who had to remember or recount the past rather than simply describe the immediate present.

Gregory's idea about historical images was simple: they were kings and bishops. He worried greatly that his written sources did not record the names of kings of the Franks before the early fifth century, and part of his relief at reaching Clovis was that the lineaments of the political system he was describing became more straightforward, for Clovis had killed off all his rivals in Gaul – Roman, Frankish, or Visigoth – and created a polity whose rulers were restricted to his own Merovingian family (*LH* 2.9, 27–43). Gregory's interest was in kings rather than kingship (still less government), and so the details of royal activities, mostly wars and sex, comes through with greater insistency than anything else. In his contemporary sections, these two are considerably fleshed out by court gossip, the machinations of this duke or the evil end of that official; when, however, he is discussing his father's and grandfather's generations (essentially the era of the reigns of Clovis's sons, 511–61), there is relatively little such gossip, and hence the basic structures of the transmitted memories come through with greater clarity. It would seem that Clovis's sons were essentially remembered through whom they fought and whom they went to bed with; and that these patterns had a greater chance of being remembered, while the figures of courtiers were for the most part forgotten.

Take, for example, King Theudebert (ruling 534–48), a king whom Gregory approved of, but knew little about (Collins 1983). The memory of Theudebert probably largely reached Gregory via his elder relatives (who frequently were or became political bishops like himself: see Wood 1980: 120); it included a brief but articulated story about a woman called Deuteria (*LH* 3.22–3, 26–7). Deuteria's career was meteoric: she sent to Theudebert to ask him to occupy her city in southern Gaul, became his mistress (or wife: Merovingian kings did not greatly distinguish, although bishops did), came to the north with her daughter when Theudebert became king, and supplanted his affianced bride; but murdered the daughter when she became adult, for fear that Theudebert would sleep with her, and was eventually put aside by the king for other wives. Why remember Deuteria, among all the salacious stories of the 530s? Presumably because it was only she, out of all Theudebert's consorts, who produced a male heir, an heir who, indeed, succeeded him

briefly: she and other women like her were retrospectively legitimated as worthy of commemoration (however hostile) because she was a king's mother.

Once again, one should not regard these stories as necessarily 'true'. When Deuteria has her daughter driven into the river Meuse in a bull cart, one may be forgiven for finding the tale slightly odd; and when one finds the story paralleled in the 580s by another queen trying – though for different reasons – to kill her daughter, this time by slamming a chest lid down on her head (*LH* 9.34), one realizes where one is: back with 'The Juniper Tree' (see above, p. 64), and the *Motif-Index of Folk-Literature*. This latter story purports to be contemporary, though it was about a queen Gregory particularly hated, and might, perhaps, have believed anything of. Before his own time, on the other hand, the folk motifs were often quite dense. Deuteria's initial invitation of Theudebert to her city is certainly another topos, for it is related to several early medieval (and indeed ancient) stories in which the wife or daughter of the defender of the city lusts after the besieging general and lets his army in. And some of the other royal anecdotes about Clovis's sons have taken on other very evident popular tale motifs: when, in 524, two kings personally murder their brother's children in cold blood, with one king remorseful and the other callous (*LH* 3.18), the story begins to sound like 'The Babes in the Wood'.[3]

The important issue for us is not the reliability of the stories, however, but rather their structural position in Gregory's narrative. Deuteria, and for that matter the royal murders, are remembered because they fit into a *genealogical* framework of commemoration. Even taking into consideration Gregory's personal preference for patterns of anecdotes rather than explicit analysis, it looks as if the role of the kings themselves was essentially to provide a dynastic narrative, with the genealogical cruxes acting as the pegs on which to hang more specific accounts. Indeed, the kings of the early sixth century tended simply to turn into shadow representations of royal qualities (good and bad); it was irrelevant, when remembering them, to attribute to them more personality to act as the basis for narrative structures than could be found in the always available treasury of folk motifs. Nevertheless, the Merovingian dynasty itself evidently remained at the centre of attention. For Gregory, 'national' political history was structured, defined, by kings and nothing else.

---

[3] For the besieged city, see Paul the Deacon, *Historia Langobardorum* 4.37 (ed. in Bethmann and Waitz 1878); *Chronicon Novaliciense* 3.14 (ed. in Alessio 1982); it is K 781 in the *Motif-Index* (Thompson 1955–8). See also S 121, K 512, for the other stories cited.

But kings were not his only interest: they were counterposed to bishops. Gregory evidently intended to make a real point about the nature of the past – and the present – here, for, as a churchman, he was very concerned about spiritual hierarchies, and saw any spiritual authority not looking to bishops as illegitimate: bishops were, when they were moral (which was not always), the most proper bearers of a principled Christian life, to set against the more typically wicked lives of secular powers. They were also the proper guardians of the most directly available sources of spiritual power, the relics of saints; such relics, particularly in episcopal churches, figure very largely in Gregory's narrative as the immediate agents of supernatural events (Brown 1977; 1981). Gregory is not exaggerating in these characterizations; bishops did have this sort of spiritual authority in his time. They also had a genuine political role, as city leaders, for bishops had very considerable local power in the cities of later Roman and post-Roman Gaul (Van Dam 1985). In this respect, kings are counterposed to bishops not only as secular vs. ecclesiastical power, but as central vs. local power. Gregory thought this highly important; he was, of course, a bishop himself, and, indeed, Tours' relics of St Martin were those of one of the most powerful saints in Gaul.

Gregory knew a good deal about bishops everywhere in his own time, through his wide ecclesiastical connections. It is significant, however, that the bishoprics he tells us about in his sections on the past are almost entirely restricted to those in which his family had important interests, most notably Clermont and Tours. The episcopal successions of these two sees are recounted to us in considerable detail, in fact, from the fifth century onwards (Wood 1983). This brings us to Gregory's other source of memories, which was his own family history. Family history was not restricted to the succession of bishops. Although Gregory often neglects to make the point explicit, many of the more detailed anecdotes from the courts of the early sixth-century kings, or from other cities, also relate to members of his own or of other Clermont families (*LH* 3.15, 36; 4.36, 39). Both the lay and the episcopal stories, however, had been told to Gregory as part of a different structure of commemoration from that of the kings. This was not at all unusual, of course; as we have seen in the previous chapter, families commemorate themselves in this way everywhere, and, indeed, can construct whole local histories out of the weave of memories of rival families. But they created an organizational problem for Gregory, one that he did not manage fully to resolve. He had two sets of historical foci, kings and bishops; and two sets of memories at his disposition, dynastic and family/local memories. These two categories did not entirely match up.

Gregory put some of his family material into his royal stories (particularly when kings came anywhere near Clermont), but regarded the rest as essentially about bishops, even if many of his local stories are notably secular. He did attempt some reordering of his material: he tells us, for example, about bishops of Clermont and Tours who were not his relatives; in Tours, episcopal successions seem indeed to have functioned as an independent mnemonic device, in part written down (*LH* 10.31). But this reordering was incomplete; Gregory's image of episcopal history, even when derived from written texts, is restricted almost entirely to his family's fields of interest. A full ecclesiastical history of Gaul was not, in any event, easily available to a writer in the late sixth century; it would have required very conscious and specific research. The only alternative to memories of the kings normally available was memories of the writer's own family and city. Gregory's family was unusually widespread and rich; hence, in their case, it was two cities (cf. Van Dam 1985: 205–21). And this was enough: it did not seem important to him to research the deeds of past bishops even of neighbouring dioceses, such as Bourges or Poitiers.

It is in this sort of way that it is possible to reconstruct the memories available to Gregory, against the grain of his own writing. His conscious structuring of his material is, of course, important for understanding his own world-view; but the divergent origins of this material are important as well. In reality, the memories of kings and those of families and cities did not necessarily have much to do with one another. Central-southern Gaul was a honeycomb of individual cities, all with their own warring elites, who had long been defined against each other by struggles about who was to be bishop, and, sometimes, count as well, and who were much more conscious of this world than any wider one (Wood 1983). Royal memories sometimes intersected with this, when family members went to court, or kings came to Clermont and Tours; but there was no organic meeting between the two sets of memory. This intense local consciousness (at least in the more urbanized areas of Gaul) may have been a reality that kings tried to make an impact on, but, if so, it was a very external one. Clearly, they did fit into at least one framework for social memory, that of folk-tale, for this must be the source of many of Gregory's royal stories, as we have seen; that is to say, people did talk about kings. But it is quite possible that only a family as elevated as Gregory's would know enough about them to have access to the dynastic narrative framework that structured the folk motifs in Gregory's *Histories*; other people outside the court would remember more disembodied stories about isolated rulers. However many stories were recounted about anything else, for most people in sixth-century Gaul the only overarching narrative structure for memory was likely to be local: kings must have just seemed like outside forces, who at most would sometimes have arrived, incomprehensibly, in one's locality (and thus into real history) and then left again, without sacking the town, if one was lucky. This is, indeed, how even Gregory depicts kings when he is writing from the standpoint of Clermont.

The overwhelming relevance of local rather than 'national' memory, even to aristocrats, is something that would recur very often in the Middle Ages, and not least in France. We find it in the comital histories of the eleventh and twelfth centuries in France, as also, in different environments, in the city histories of twelfth- and thirteenth-century Italy or of late medieval Germany. (See, for example, Duby 1973: 267–98; du Boulay 1981; Dunbabin 1991; Wickham 1991.) All these local historiographies gained ground at the expense of the king-centred histories that came out of royal courts, and which were always dominant in, for example, England. These were real contrasts at the level of the organization of political power, and not just at that of memory; and so was the king-bishop/city opposition in sixth-century central and southern Gaul. But that does not make the focusing on memory less important. It was, precisely, a weakness of sixth-century kings that they did not seem central enough to be able to replace a city-based structuring of political memories. They may well have lost legitimacy as a result, for their relatively recent origin was all the more apparent: the kings went back only three generations, to Clovis; Gregory's family, and those of his rivals, were far older, going back into the heyday of the later Roman Empire. Gregory respected his kings and was proud of their political system, but he knew they were parvenus, not with respect to their Roman imperial predecessors, who had justly been defeated in battle, but with respect to himself. His lack of nostalgia for the Roman past, though partly derived from that same pride in the present, was also due to the fact that, looking at himself, he could not see that it had stopped. His lack of ethnic prejudice, which has often been remarked on (Romans and Franks were all one to him), may well derive from the predominance of a family or local identity and consciousness, over any 'national' preoccupations, that would not necessarily bode at all well for the permanence of Merovingian hegemony. And it was, indeed, at least in central-southern Gaul, precisely into city units of the Clermont type that Merovingian hegemony would disintegrate in the following century.

Gregory of Tours can serve as a clear example of how one historical source can be used to get at independent sets of social memories:

Gregory manipulated his materials, like all writers, but he did not manage to hide their disparate origins, and some of their original structures. This relationship can be pursued further through a second example, the way one person was remembered in different ways and in different styles, by groups themselves differentiated by place, time, and social status. Charlemagne, king of the Franks from 768 to 814, is an obvious candidate for this, for he was then, and probably still is, incomparably the best-known figure of the medieval world, rivalled only by King Arthur; indeed, we have already seen his shadow fall over the collective memories of many social groups in more recent times. And Charlemagne, unlike Arthur, certainly existed and is, in fact, very well documented: we have a much clearer idea of how his memory developed than we have for any other single individual. It was a highly complex process, but a short discussion of it should be enough to set out some points of comparison with other developments we have discussed.

The first full-length narrative account of Charlemagne, by his own courtier Einhard, written less than two decades after his death, was also the most influential text about the emperor until at least the twelfth century, and maybe thereafter as well. Einhard was, in fact, a lay aristocrat rather than a cleric, although his legal status was less important than his considerable Christian education. Despite this, his model for his biography was an utterly secular text, Suetonius' *Lives of the Caesars*, particularly the life of Augustus. Charlemagne emerges as a pious figure, certainly, keen on learning, but also as a man of the world, a just judge and statesman, and an organizer of wars, rather than an epic hero. This relatively secular, indeed relatively human, picture dominated the written imagery of Charlemagne for 300 years, and recurs in dozens of texts; it evidently formed a crucial part of his commemoration at the oral as well as the written level. It derives, however, from the part of the *Life* in which Einhard drew most heavily on Suetonius. It may well be a true picture in large part; but its very existence was owing to Einhard's reading of an earlier text – certainly no early medieval written model was available for a portrait of this kind. One of the core elements of the social memory of Charlemagne, one of the most fervently and closely commemorated of kings from well before his death onwards, thus derives directly from a work written more than 600 years before his birth: the intertextuality of writing and memory is very clear here.[4]

---

[4] Einhard, *Vita Karoli*, ed. in Holder-Egger 1911; for commentary, see Ganshof 1971: 1–16 and Beumann 1951, who stresses the religious elements in Einhard's intent. The basic analysis of the Einhardian tradition is Folz 1950. A translation of both Einhard and Notker (see n. 5) is Thorpe 1969.

If Charlemagne was larger than life in Einhard, his stature grew still more in the next couple of generations, and when in the 880s Notker of St Gallen, a royal monastery in the foothills of the Swiss Alps, wrote an account of Charlemagne's life for the latter's great-grandson, the German king Charles the Fat, it was already enmeshed with a complex tradition of oral anecdotal material from what are apparently both lay and ecclesiastical sources. Charlemagne was already, in fact, taking on the characteristics of the cultural archetype of the just king in popular memory. Notker did not have direct access to classical models for his portrait, apart from what was already in Einhard, and the most obvious alternative genre available to him was the saint's life; as a result, Charlemagne appears in his text as the hero of what, in effect, are a series of quasi-hagiographical moral tales about kingship, with the wise king showing up bishops, nobles, or luxurious foreign ambassadors for their foolishness. But the sensible, just, and ascetic king, however bedecked with superlatives, is still that of Einhard: evidently the oral stories Notker was reworking themselves presupposed such a character. The occasions in which Charlemagne is rewritten by Notker on an epic scale, as, for example, in his conquest of Italy with an army entirely clad in iron, so terrifying that the defenders faint dead away, are rare, and are atypical of the tone of the rest.[5]

After the ninth century, direct narrative material about Charlemagne becomes sparser for two centuries. The reason is simple: historians in this period tended to write contemporary history rather than accounts that were focused further back in time; when Charlemagne figures in their sketchy accounts of the past, the detail about him is generally taken straight from a fuller, Carolingian period text. But he is ever-present, for all that: the image of Charlemagne as an archetypically just ruler was present in nearly every area historically connected to him. Very often he appeared in a more clerical guise, as the Christian emperor, the patron and saviour of the pope; and this image was most of all marked in Saxony, where he appeared as the apostle of the pagan Saxons, the patron of their entry into the brotherhood of civilized Christian peoples. (This account is particularly interesting for its distance from and supersession of the original eighth-century picture of Charlemagne the systematic and ruthless conqueror of the Saxons, who forced them to convert or die; see Folz 1950: 28–37, 110–19; Leyser 1979: 5–7.) But the force of Charlemagne's reputation was not just as an ecclesiastical patron; the tenth- and eleventh-century emperors of Germany, from Otto I (936–72) onwards, often clearly modelled their

---

[5] Notker, *Gesta Karoli*, ed. in Häfele 1962; 2.17 for Italy. Commentary: Löwe 1970.

actions on what they identified as Charlemagne's tradition, very much on the Einhard pattern, and they presumably did so to impress secular as well as ecclesiastical aristocrats. Emperors came routinely to be compared to Charlemagne, as the major paragon of royal virtues; if they were particularly ambitious or highly praised, they could be seen as Charlemagne returned to life. Otto III (983–1002) went so far as to open his tomb in Aachen, in the perhaps not arbitrarily chosen year 1000, and, it was soon recounted, found an awesome figure, still undecomposed and sweet-smelling (a familiar topos of sanctity), sitting upright on his throne. Otto removed a few symbolic articles and organized a fitting reburial; he had achieved his object, the most immediate association with Charlemagne that could be imagined (Folz 1950: 47–105, 191–202).

Germany was one of the major heirs, along with France, of the Frankish political system, and its kings could quite naturally link themselves to the prowess of their great predecessor. (Indeed, the kings of France did the same, although less systematically, at least after the end of the Carolingian dynasty in 987; but kings were far weaker there until after 1200.) But Charlemagne appears as a major figure even in more regional chronicles, including some of those that are relatively uninterested in contemporary kings. In the early eleventh century, Adémar of Chabannes, a southern French writer based in Limoges, wrote a largely contemporary history, focused on Poitou and the Limousin: but Charlemagne is a central figure in the text, the focus of the work's whole structure, and the symbolic centre of its chronological pattern.[6] At the other end of the Frankish world, too, as has already been noted, Saxon chroniclers had adopted Charlemagne's conquest as the mythological charter for their local identity, and the Saxons maintained him as a focus even when they were in revolt against the German emperor.

In these texts, Charlemagne is not only just; he stands in some sense as the originator and legitimator of the contemporary world. At one level, this should not be surprising; Charlemagne had indeed left his stamp on nearly the whole of Latin Christian Europe, and these genealogies of legitimacy were in a strict sense authentic. But they were genealogies that left other people out: Charlemagne replaced much of

---

[6] Adémar is ed. in Chavanon 1897. The chronicle is in three books; Charlemagne's reign makes up the whole of book 2. For the kings of France, see, among others, Schneidmüller 1979; Poly and Bournazel 1980: 287–97; Spiegel 1971; Guenée 1978. The great period of the political use of the Charlemagne legend in France began with Philip Augustus in the 1180s, but Capetian royal ideology had never abandoned the Carolingian connection, even when it was fairly vaguely expressed.

the commemoration of his grandfather and father, Charles Martel and Pipin, founders of the Carolingian dynasty, not to speak of Clovis, who had founded the Frankish world itself. Indeed, Charlemagne was the only major legendary figure in the medieval world to postdate the 'Heroic Age' of the Germanic invasions of the Roman Empire, presumably by direct replacement and maybe takeover of the legends of his Merovingian predecessors. (Paris 1865: 437–46; Chadwick 1912; Bloch 1961: 99–101.) And no one took over *from* Charlemagne, either. In Germany Otto I was revered, as was the saintly Henry II, and, as were, later, Frederick Barbarossa (1152–90) and Frederick II, who gained their own legends; but Charlemagne dominated them all. When Barbarossa needed an imperial saint, in 1165, he did not develop the cult of the already sanctified Henry II, but instead canonized Charlemagne, the 'apostle of the Saxons' (as well as, by now, the Frisians, the Spanish, and the Vandals). The pious but very secular warrior will have thus found himself in heavenly company he would hardly have expected during his lifetime (Folz 1950: 203–34).

Evidently, the crucial point is not so much the fact that Charlemagne was one of several people who determined the major political and religious structures of the central medieval period, but rather that he came to be remembered, in much of France and Germany at least (rather less so in Italy: Fasoli 1967; Wickham 1985), as the fount of *all* of them. Charlemagne was a safe point of reference: his activities were so geographically and politically universal that everyone, however divided, could draw some legitimacy from him. Who controlled this commemoration? This is more of a problem, for, with the notable exception of Einhard himself, almost all the people who wrote about Charlemagne were clerics and monks, writing inside a classic ecclesiastical framework of history, and very often simply copying their information from one text to another. We have seen, furthermore, that significant aspects of his legend became distinctly more clerical – indeed, he ended up as a saint; one must ask, then, how much the memory of Charlemagne developed solely within an ecclesiastical environment, and how much it reflected evolving traditions among the laity as well. On one level, however, this is a false dichotomy, for clerics lived in the world as well; it was as a secular ruler that they commemorated Charlemagne before any other, and even as a saint he lost none of his regal qualities. And it is also important that many of the recipients of these writings were kings and princes, who must have been able to identify with Charlemagne, and his particular (still Einhardian) brand of muscular piety. When kings themselves commemorated or imitated him, they were aiming at a still wider secular audience, this time one of nobles, who must themselves have seen some sense in Carolingian ritual or claims to Carolingian legitimacy; indeed, when aristocrats moved towards independence or autonomy, they would sometimes claim Carolingian origins for themselves.[7]

Even if we restrict ourselves to ecclesiastical writings, then, we can see that Charlemagne was a crucial historical figure for clerics, lay aristocrats and kings alike: the particular narrative genres associated with clerical texts do not prevent us from recognizing the existence of an essentially secular social memory of Charlemagne as well. But we can discover the existence of such a memory more directly, too; for, at least in France, the legend of Charlemagne also flourished in a much more secular environment, through a much more secular genre, that of the *chansons de geste*, from the eleventh century at the latest. (It did not reach Germany in this form until after 1150.) This legend developed largely independently of the Einhardian tradition, and barely reached written form until 1100; the earliest complete texts of *chansons* that we have do not predate 1130 or so. When it did, however, it would have a considerable impact on the commemorations we have been discussing.

What *chansons de geste* are like we have already shown, in our discussion of the narrative patterns of the *Chanson de Roland* in chapter 2. In that context we treated the text as an example of oral-formulaic narrative, of which, indeed, it exhibits many obvious features. This whole issue is, however, very hotly debated by people who see the surviving texts of *chansons* as direct records of oral tradition and those who see them as the entirely literary compositions of clerics (for it was certainly clerics who wrote them down).[8] We would at least maintain a minimum oral position, which is all we need for our arguments: that

---

[7] One clear example is the chronicle of the counts of Anjou written by a count himself, Fulk le Réchin, in 1096 (ed. in Halphen-Poupardin 1913: 232–8): he carefully ascribes the origin of the countship to the patronage of 'the offspring of Charles the Bald, son of Louis, son of Charlemagne', as opposed to the 'kin of the impious [King] Philip', his Capetian contemporary. The counts of Boulogne and Flanders claimed Carolingian descent, too, the former falsely, the latter rightly (see e.g., Spiegel 1986: 215–16; Dunbabin 1991).

[8] The main *Roland* text is ed. and trans. in many editions; we have used Whitehead 1946, Jonin 1979, and Robertson 1972. For guides to the debates, with bibliography, see Vance 1970, a sensible introductory summary, updated by Victorio 1988. The interested reader can choose between, at the extremes, the claim that epic songs stretched back in an unbroken oral tradition to the minstrels of Roncevaux in 778, and the suggestion that *chansons* were all first written down by clerics around 1100 on the model of Virgil; the texts have also been argued to be the virtual stenographic records of minstrels in full flow (Rychner 1955), or else fixed and written ballad texts that singers actually sang from (Tyssens in Victorio 1988: 244–8). The debates are exactly analogous to those about Icelandic sagas (see below, p. 164) or Homer (see above, p. 42).

however reworked our texts are, they reflect an oral milieu and could have been sung more or less in the form in which they survive; and that singers did sing long and complex (oral-formulaic) songs about Charlemagne and his dependants by at least the eleventh century, as doubtless (even if quite conceivably with fundamentally different contents) before. And, any way the material is argued, there is no doubt that Charlemagne, Roland and Oliver, Guillaume d'Orange, Ogier the Dane, and many other heroes from the epic tradition were widely remembered and talked about in eleventh- and twelfth-century France, as also sometimes in Norman England: indeed, two twelfth-century accounts of the Battle of Hastings state that the Normans attacked while a singer sang about Roland.[9]

These texts show a different Charlemagne from the wise judge and warrior-missionary we have already discussed: at the same time both more and less than these roles. This Charlemagne is still justice personified; and all his major wars are legitimized by being waged against pagans. But, in addition, he is lord of all Christendom, and a fighter on an epic scale – in some texts he is actually a giant; if he lets his warriors gain the glory, it is only because he is immensely old (200 years old in *Roland*). In the latter context, on the other hand, he is also a relatively passive figure, who sometimes lets his vassals browbeat him, even though he is ruler of every Christian land the poets have ever heard of. This contradiction is a relatively easy one to explain: it derives in part from the logic of the genre, as we shall see, but also very largely from the contradiction between the memory of an all-powerful king and the reality, in the France of 1100 or so, of substantial royal weakness: correct royal behaviour, to the mind of any French aristocrat of 1100 except the king himself, was virtually confined to taking the advice of vassals. This points up very clearly the close relationship of the *chanson* texts to a real situation: that of aristocratic audiences faced with a contradiction between memory and experience. It is interesting, none the less, that our epic narratives, however respectful of the problems of contemporary royal power, hardly ever, until very late, put Charlemagne in the wrong; the part of the inept king who causes trouble by his weakness and wilfulness is played in the Guillaume cycle or in *Raoul de Cambrai* by Charlemagne's son Louis the Pious.[10] In one sense they did not need to cut Charlemagne down to size, for royal weakness in 1100

[9] The accounts are William of Malmesbury (in Latin prose) and Wace (in French verse): see Douglas 1960.

[10] The *Couronnement de Louis*, ed. Langlois 1920, is the clearest example in the Guillaume cycle; *Raoul* is ed. Meyer and Longnon 1882.

could easily be legitimated by the kings' failure to be as just as Charlemagne: comparisons with a glorious past were not always advantageous to kings. But the French kings themselves, during their slow, twelfth-century return to a more central political position, undoubtedly used Charlemagne's example for all they were worth (Spiegel 1971; Guenée 1978): it was an image of kingship, after all, and therefore in the end useful, above all, to them.

We thus find two principal sets of narratives of Charlemagne that were available to the inhabitants of post-Carolingian Europe from 1000 or so onwards: the largely Latin and largely clerical tradition derived eventually from Einhard, and the vernacular tradition of the *chansons de geste* (the latter until the late twelfth century restricted to France and the areas influenced by French culture). These two traditions barely met for a long time. Roland and Guillaume do not appear in Latin texts before the late eleventh century, even in casual references, apart from one or two fragments. (See, for example, Wilsdorf 1962, for a list.[11]) The audiences for each must have been rather similar – both clergy and lay aristocrats could appreciate vernacular literature, just as both responded to the Einhardian tradition; but, nevertheless, history and epic were two distinct narrative genres, with different frames of reference and different authorial traditions, which did not have to influence each other. It was not until *Roland* became transformed into a Latin text, the *Historia Karoli Magni et Rotholandi* (ed. Meredith-Jones 1936), supposedly recounted by Roland's archiepiscopal comrade-in-arms, Turpin, which reached its present form around 1140, that *chanson* material made much impact on Latin history-writing; but then it did so, very fast. The 'pseudo-Turpin' has still more medieval manuscripts than Einhard, even though it is so much later. Already in 1165 it was perhaps underpinning part of the ceremony of Barbarossa's canonization of Charlemagne, and the Barbarossan saint's life, the *Vita S. Karoli* of the 1170s, certainly borrowed whole sections from it; by 1200 it was in historical compilations all over France and Germany, and was beginning itself to be translated into vernaculars (Folz 1950: 214–25; Spiegel 1986). Its success was surpassed only by that of Geoffrey of Monmouth's telling of

---

[11] Adémar (see n. 6) is one example of a writer who could well have known the epic cycles; but in his portrait of Charlemagne there is nothing of significance that he did not derive from ninth-century Latin texts. The only possible exception is his claim that Charles ruled Spain as far as Córdoba, which has a Rolandian ring to it: 2. 1, Chavanon 1897: 68. Historians of the eleventh and twelfth centuries very often were quite explicitly hostile to oral sources that were not 'reliable' – i.e., not clerical. See, for example, Stock 1983: 76, for the views of Orderic Vitalis on this theme in *c*.1130.

the Arthur legend in the 1130s; and the parallel is indeed very instruc-
tive, for both are Latin histories, based on vernacular texts (Geoffrey
certainly invented his main 'source' himself, but he must have had
access to vernacular material), which in this form and only in this form
were in the right genre to take over other literary traditions in both
Latin and vernacular.[12] Audiences were evidently very receptive to these
Latin versions; one could conclude that people in Europe were beginning to get a little tired of Einhard, and wanted a king and a heroic
imagery which were more recognizable in twelfth-century terms. From
this point onwards, however, these two Charlemagne traditions became
relatively unified, at least in the sense that authors could draw from
both.

The legend of Charlemagne points up a number of different themes
that are relevant to us. One is that as society and politics changed, the
social memory of Charlemagne changed to fit: the slayer of Saxons
becomes their saviour; the Frankish king becomes a French lord of the
whole of the Christian world, both separated from the weakness of
French kings and enveloped in it. Charlemagne was a generalized
symbol of legitimacy that anyone could claim an association with, and
who would benefit anyone who succeeded in getting such a claim
(however outlandish) believed; he and he alone managed to achieve
legendary status while remaining firmly in his chronological place in
the histories and memories of the past, and this gave added force to such
symbolism. And not only oral but also written traditions altered as time
went on. Even Einhard had presumably been read in different ways by
different generations looking for different things in him, for people do
this to literature in all periods; and in the end writers went beyond him,
and invented new characterizations. The changing social memory of
Charlemagne was more powerful in each successive society than any
mere written text.

However, if we look less at specific writings than at genres, the situation is different. No matter how much the Charlemagne legend
changed or was manipulated, it was carried by narratives, both written
and oral, in specific genres, each of which had its own narrative logic,
which would tend to depict him in specific ways. That is to say, the
changing content of the memory of Charlemagne was inescapably
structured by its different forms. Einhard's portrait was itself structured,
and partially created, by the Suetonian model he took, which led him to

---

[12] For Geoffrey and his effect, see, for example, Hanning 1966: 121–76; Brooke 1976;
Flint 1979; Cingolani 1991.

emphasize certain aspects of Charlemagne's character and to ignore others; he in turn created a secular biographical genre that was a more powerful paradigm than any other in the Latin tradition, even when it was partially undermined by new commemorations, until pseudo-Turpin introduced the possibility of epic Latin narrative. Similarly, in the vernacular epics, the most typical dissonance, the conflict between a king with limitless power and his aggressive adviser, a hero who himself has limitless strength and moral valour (Roland, say, or the Guillaume of the *Couronnement de Louis*), had, as we have seen, a resonance in the political realities of the period; but the dissonance also depended closely on the logic of the genre itself, for both king and hero, if portrayed positively, had to be depicted as the ultimate moral authority, and this led inevitably to at least implicit contradiction between the two (except, at least, when Charlemagne was himself the central hero; but this tended to be in conflict with his venerability). The rules of genre may work just as well as the fact that the socially irrelevant gets forgotten, to explain what Charlemagne was not remembered for, too: no Carolingian Renaissance to speak of, and no administrative reforms; even law, at least before the twelfth century, came in only as the logical consequence of Charlemagne as the epitome of justice, and most texts gave it little space.[13] The fixity of a given written text may not have contained the changing image of Charlemagne for long – written texts do not even have that power now, never mind in a less literate age. But the rules of narrative had and have a greater power of containment; it is not possible to avoid them, for they were and are intrinsic to all genres in which Charlemagne, or anyone else, could be spoken or written about at all.

This emphasis on the containing power of genre is not intended to undermine the historical reliability of texts: far from it. As we have stated, literary and historical analysis are not in conflict; rather, any understanding of the historical value of a written text – i.e. its capacity to represent matters that predate the text in time – must proceed from an understanding of the rules of narrative through which that text was written, whether it is a document, a chronicle, a vernacular epic, an oral

[13] Law was not necessarily forgotten; we may simply not have the genres in which Charlemagne as lawgiver was initially recounted. It appears as a strong theme, though, in the first major German vernacular text about him, the mid-twelfth-century *Kaiserchronik*, and this tradition in the German world may have been older. The legal tradition of Charlemagne would, also, of course, develop further in the intellectual environment of the revival of law in the same century. See, for all this, Folz 1950: 169–70, 371–5.

account, or, indeed, a modern historical monograph. These rules are part of the structuring of social memory. When people wish to remember the past socially, through verbal or written communication, they do so through narrative conventions that are remarkably stable inside each culture, and that, as a result, are implicitly recognized by everyone. But, inside this continuity of form, content can vary greatly. And, of course, new genres can appear; it is just that, as they crystallize, they will develop their own rules. Such an observation is relevant for our last example in this chapter, medieval Iceland. Here, we are dealing with a society substantially different from others in Europe; and, when writing came in from England, France, and Norway around 1100, there developed new written genres restricted to Iceland, which were essentially unlike the available literary models of the countries from which the Icelanders got their written traditions.

Icelanders, unlike almost all other Europeans, did not have a view of the past that focused on rulers, for they had none. They had no kings to provide an institutional focus for memory or a genealogy of legitimacy in historical time. They did not even have institutions, except an annual formal law court and legal gathering, the Althing, whose lawspeaker had only a ceremonial role; the succession of lawspeakers was known, but was not much used to structure the past. They had forty-odd hereditary chieftains (goðar), who were also pagan priests before the conversion to Christianity around the year 1000, but these, too, were no more than local notables with as much personal power as their wealth, their friends, and their political skill could get them – and only the first of these was automatically heritable. The same can be said for the bishops, whose succession began on the island in 1055. In effect, the Icelanders were a nation of free peasants and their slaves. They varied considerably in prosperity and influence, but only a tiny handful (at least before the thirteenth century) were so rich that they did not have personally to work on the land at least some of the time. The hierarchies in this society were neither stable enough, nor sufficiently defined institutionally, to be in themselves objects of commemoration. But this does not mean that Icelandic memory was weak; far from it. The vision of the past Icelanders held was essentially a peasant memory, and, indeed, very consciously so, for one of their founding myths was that they had come to the island in the first place to escape the 'tyranny' of King Harald of Norway, in the late ninth century – rulers, that is, not only did not exist but also were held to be, by definition, illegitimate. As often happens in peasant societies where institutions (which both control and simplify ideas) are lacking, Icelandic social memory needed to develop genres which preserved the complexity of their social topography.[14]

We have seen that peasants commonly recall the past through the memory of their own families, and of the struggles between their families and those of others. This is certainly what happened in Iceland. A high percentage of our narrative texts (sagas) about the Icelandic past, although written in the thirteenth century, deal with the period before 1030; they talk about almost nothing but family rivalries. The Icelandic 'history of events', in effect, consisted of only two elements: the settlement, in c.880–930, and the conversion of the island in c.1000. Both tend to appear in nearly every 'saga of Icelanders' – this is, indeed, one of the reasons why such sagas focus on the generations around the year 1000; but the texts are about individuals and their families, not these two founding historical moments. Icelanders were very conscious of being part of an Icelandic polity; but, from the time their ancestors had left Harald's Norway, their perception of the past consisted essentially of what these ancestors did after they arrived – the memory of the polity was constructed through the memory of the family, and not the other way round.

We know about this memory, of course, only through the texts. There has been a fierce argument since the 1920s about how 'reliable' the sagas are, an argument which closely parallels that about the historical origins of *chansons de geste* (see above, pp. 134, 158), with scholars divided between those who see the sagas as being based on oral narrative patterns, probably old, and those who argue that they were all composed as written literature, and are therefore literary rather than historical works.[15] As usual, the details of this argument are not our concern here; not only

[14] A good basic introduction with good bibliography is Byock 1988; a convenient literary survey is Kristjánsson 1988, which covers all saga types, those of kings, bishops, and legendary heroes, as well as the 'sagas of Icelanders', which are the only sagas discussed here. The social pattern broke down somewhat in the thirteenth century, a time of political instability, stronger hierarchies, and more stable links of dependence (see, e.g., Sveinsson 1953, with Byock 1986), leading up to the Norwegian takeover of 1262. It is not chance that most of the Icelandic literature about the past dates from then (cf., e.g., Hastrup 1984). But even the thirteenth century did not see any real equivalent to the aristocratic society of the rest of Europe. Exactly who wrote the sagas is not at all clear; writing in the Middle Ages is held to be clerically dominated, but many of Iceland's principal named writers were certainly laymen, and often influential ones. One might assume the writers to be 'traditional intellectuals', a bit like *cordel* poets in Brazil (see above, p. 104), although Icelandic society was certainly much less divided than the Brazilian north-east.

[15] See, for a guide, Andersson 1964. Our position is similar to those of Andersson, Byock (1982; 1988), Miller (1983a; 1983b), and Andersson and Miller (1989).

has it become a somewhat sterile debate, but also, in its present form, it has little bearing on the questions about memory that we are concerned here to explore. In fact, the 'sagas of Icelanders' resemble continental European genres so little that it seems unreasonable not to assume that the texts we have are essentially the written successors of previous oral narratives – although that in itself does not, of course, make them any truer. (Once they were written down, there were some changes, perhaps speeded up by the change in medium; some influence of the French prose romances can, for example, be detected in later sagas. But the overall effect was relatively minor.) They were certainly, on the other hand, accepted already in the thirteenth century as authentic accounts of the past: right from their original recording on parchment, at the latest, they constituted the commemorated past for Icelanders, and can be analysed as such. Indeed, for understanding the social memory of the community as a whole, they may be more useful than the sometimes more empirically reliable ecclesiastical chronicles of the rest of Europe.

This is very clear if we look at the whole range of Icelandic literature. Many early Icelandic written texts were rather more similar than were sagas to Continental models (they included translations of saints' lives, for example, and the first versions of the law code); and the first narrative of the history of the island, Ari Thorgilsson's *Íslendingabók*, written in the 1120s, is evidently an attempt to construct an Icelandic history based on a linear chronology, to set against those to be found for the rest of Europe, explicitly on the basis of the oldest and most reliable informants, who are named. It is, however, very short: it consists of little more than the settlement; the conversion; the principal steps in the development of Iceland's legal institutions; the lawspeakers; and the establishment and succession of the bishops. There was, apparently, nothing else to say; and it is significant that though Ari was widely known of, and, indeed, venerated as 'the Learned', the father of Icelandic history, no one else in the medieval period ever attempted to write another chronological history of Iceland from its beginnings – although Icelanders wrote a considerable number of histories of Norway in the thirteenth century, all duly focused on Norway's rulers, and some of them extremely lengthy. Ari's successors, even when they were trying to model themselves on him, instead developed another pattern, which allowed a much greater flexibility: the *Landnámabók*, or *Book of Settlements*, whose various versions (all of which postdate 1250) seem to stem from a common, early twelfth-century original. This text essentially consists of a list of the first settlers of Iceland, over 400 of them, arranged geographically around the island in clockwise order, with greater or lesser genealogical material attached and a few brief anecdotes.[16] It is not much more generous in its information than is the *Íslendingabók*, but it is much longer, and capable of considerable expansion: it was, indeed, substantially added to and altered in its thirteenth-century redactions. From the simple fact that the text was subject to continual alteration and updating, it can be inferred that it was of greater immediate relevance to the Icelanders than was Ari's more conventional linear history. It contained the information they needed about the past: about who their ancestors were and where they lived. Rafnsson has convincingly argued (1974) that they needed this in order to be able to contest land claims against each other; and this would also explain many of the later alterations. But a glance at the text shows that by no means all the information in the *Landnámabók* is related to such needs; it is structured instead by the geography of the island itself, which must have served as an essential *aide mémoire* for the genealogical material that makes up its body.

These patterns of remembering are characteristic of peasant societies, and other relatively egalitarian societies too. The use of geography we met in modern southern Italy and southern France (see above, pp. 87, 93). The structuring of the networks of the past through the genealogies of all the families in a community we have also seen (p. 112), and it has been explored in more detail for several societies in Africa, notably the Tiv in Nigeria (Bohannan 1952) and the BaKongo in Zaïre (MacGaffey 1970). MacGaffey found that each family in the village he studied had a set of land claims, and a genealogy to back it up, that was, at least in recent generations, irreconcilable with that of other families. Talking about the more distant past was thus less contentious, easier, than talking about the recent past. This parallel might indeed help to explain the relative shortage of Icelandic narratives about the generations immediately preceding the thirteenth century. But the crucial importance of even simple genealogical lists as constructions for the past in these societies is clear. In effect, where a society does not have a dominant set of institutions or a single ruling family whose own history – that is, whose institutional or lineage memory – dominates the political unit, and the bounds of whose rule constructs its geographical space, then the

---

[16] These two texts are edited by Benediktsson (1986) in the *Íslenzk fornrit* series, which also includes most of the sagas. They are translated in, respectively, Hermannsson 1930, and Pálsson and Edwards 1972; the principal sagas all have easily available translations, usually in Penguin Classics or Everyman. The *Íslendingabók* survives only in a second, shortened version, which excludes some discussion of the kings of Norway and some genealogies – these last, judging by those that survive in it, were similar to those in the *Landnámabók*.

society itself can be constituted only by the family histories of all its members, and, presumably, the geography it itself chooses to claim.[17] In Iceland, who and what constituted the polity was not contentious, at least among free members of society, for it was an island, but these structures mattered all the same; they were themselves the legitimating past. As one version of the *Landnámabók* says: 'We think we can better meet the criticism of foreigners when they accuse us [Icelanders] of being descended from slaves or scoundrels, if we know the truth about our ancestry' (Pálsson and Edwards 1972: 6).

It is against this background that we must see the saga narratives about Iceland. They are patterned throughout by geographical and genealogical awareness. Genealogy serves as an essential guide to the whole social location of each principal saga character, and sometimes (through wicked ancestors, or else high-status forebears in Norway) his or her moral nature as well. They are also, frequently, structured by verses, attributed to the characters at crucial moments, which are themselves part of a highly structured poetic genre, and some of which may be very old (see, for guides, Turville-Petre 1976, Frank 1978, Dronke 1981, Lindow 1982, Faulkes 1987); the verses seem sometimes to have been sources for the plot of the saga, and were probably regarded as proofs of its authenticity. But sagas as we have them are evidently 'literary' works, in the sense that they are artistically constructed for the purpose of giving pleasure; their narrative lines were, as a result, generally more complex than could be generated by these fairly static formal elements. They were, essentially, about feud, usually violent feud, among the various families depicted in the texts. The disputes so described could be very complicated indeed, and the strands of the feuds very long-lasting – feuds could last two or three generations before they ran out. The logic of feud, in effect, constituted a narrative form in itself, which could underpin texts several hundred pages long (Byock 1982; Miller 1983b).

Let us look briefly at the structure of one saga, *Gísla Saga*, in order to see how this works. This is the story of Gísli, his brother, his sister Thórdis and her husband Thorgrímr, and Gísli's wife and her brother, all of them living in the mid-tenth century. To put the story very simply, Gísli's brother suspected Gísli's wife's brother of sleeping with

---

[17] These statements work only for patrilineal societies; matrilineal ones tend to be less preoccupied with descent (although there are certainly exceptions: Price 1983). But they are not restricted to peasant societies, as we saw for Gregory's Tours and Clermont; for other urban histories constituted partially or wholly by family memories, see further Thomas 1989, for classical Athens, and Dakhlia 1990, for the Jerid in modern Tunisia.

his wife, and, together with Thorgrímr, killed him; Gísli, to avenge his wife's brother, killed Thorgrímr, his sister's husband, and was outlawed and eventually (after many years) killed. The whole business was very wretched, for kin-killing was very unlucky, and, besides, both men were killed in secret, which was a frightful crime in Iceland (open killing, which was common enough, could be compensated for; secret murder could not). In fact, Gísli's crime was uncovered and reported by his own sister Thórdis, who heard him speak a particularly obscure verse about it (a narrative crux in the text) and puzzled it out. The saga manages to be sympathetic to nearly all the parties, however (except for Gísli's brother, who is weak and arrogant, and will not work on the farm); it implies that what brings people down is words spoken out of turn; unlucky, rather than wicked, people who talk too much. A text such as this is so highly structured that it reduces feud almost to mathematics: a man kills his brother-in-law and is avenged by another man killing his brother-in-law, and so on. This was a structure that made sense to people, as a way that both they or their ancestors might in unlucky circumstances behave; but it was a structure that was very easy to remember as a story, because, given the family situation, the choices facing Gísli and then Thórdis posed themselves with a continuous logic. Once the verse was composed (which is thought to have been in the later twelfth century, i.e. much later than the events, but in a still oral milieu), the psychological aspects of the narrative would have fleshed out the skeleton of the feud structure, and the saga would have virtually existed in its present form (Johnston and Foote 1963).

Many sagas are roughly like Gísli's: tight feud narratives fleshed out by verse. Once the feud had happened (or been invented) or the verse composed, either or both could have existed, separately or together, in an oral environment, perhaps retold slightly differently each time but maintaining the same structure (almost as oral-formulaic poetry is, though the parallel is not exact), until they were finally recorded and perhaps reworked by the saga writer. Here, the guiding lines are the rules of the genre: it is like this that narratives were recognized to develop. But why remember Gísli himself? Here, there is no doubt about the answer: he was part of one of the great families of north-west Iceland. The son of Thórdis and Thorgrímr was no less than Snorri goði, the central political figure of the area in the early eleventh century and ancestor of half the thirteenth-century Icelandic elite: Gísli's eventual killer, Eyvindr, was, too, an ancestor of Ari the historian. The tension between Thórdis and Gísli's killer also underlies one of the key moments in the landowning history of one of Iceland's most important political and religious centres, Helgafell, as we discover in another text,

Eyrbyggja Saga. There was every reason for an audience to be interested in hearing about precisely these people, as well as precisely this tragic sequence of events. And nearly every saga has analogous roots: in the memory of the ancestors of prominent men of the thirteenth century.

Iceland's medieval literature is interesting to us as another example of an essentially peasant (although often, as we now see, rich peasant) social memory, that can be reconstructed for a period as far back as the thirteenth century – if not, indeed, sometimes the tenth, for those feuds that were accurately recalled in their main lines (those, probably, with most successive genealogical resonance) had presumably been commemorated orally in the intervening period as well. But it is also interesting, like our previous medieval examples, as an instance of the relationship between the social relevance of memory and genre. The social memory of Charlemagne changed as society changed, but it was continually constricted by the requirements of different narrative styles. Icelandic society did not, in fact, change very much between 900 and 1250 in its basic social presuppositions, even if powerful men were more powerful at the end than at the beginning, at least if we accept what the sagas tell us; as a result, the meaning of memory and the genre in which it was recorded would continue to fit like a glove. Icelanders in the thirteenth century prided themselves on being tough and laconic, their worth being shown in their actions rather than their words, except for the telling phrases that they appear to have held ready for the most crucial moments (such as death) so as to be remembered well. Sagas about the past were full of such models – they provided, indeed, a whole process of socialization, into every aspect of proper behaviour, and have materially influenced the behaviour and character of Icelanders to the present day. But the whole narrative style of sagas fits this image too: men and women are described physically, but not characterized or judged, apart from occasional phrases such as, 'people thought that Gunnar had come out of that well'. Even the syntax fits it, with the minimum of adjectives and subordinate clauses (at least in the prose), and the maximum of conjunctions and other paratactic elements. The role of syntactic complexity, one could say, as well as the conceptual patterning that renders the story memorable (see above, p. 59), is instead played by the underlying logic of the feud relationships at each point in the narrative. Feud, then, constitutes the basic form of the text (Byock 1982). But it is also the content; indeed, in a totally stateless society, feud in the widest sense is the only means of dealing with political issues at all, and disputes, whether violent or not, constitute 'political' history.

In this sense, the disputes of the past were both continuously relevant to commemorate (as the deeds of ancestors and as morally resonant stories) and easy to commemorate (as etched into the dramatic structure of the principal secular narrative prose genre of medieval Iceland). It is scarcely surprising, then, that they were so important a literary form; indeed, thanks also to the lasting literary quality of the best of them, they have dominated the culture of the island even in the present century.

Icelandic social memory is not only interesting in its own right; it also helps to put in perspective the two other examples cited in this chapter. Gregory of Tours and the historians writing in Latin about Charlemagne in the ninth to twelfth centuries were writing for explicitly ideological reasons, as historians tend to do, patterning their material in order to make sense of it and make it serve some purpose. Indeed, the memory of Charlemagne was very evidently used as part of the political justifications of all sorts of people in the leading ranks of continental European society. Icelandic saga writers, precisely because they were writing to entertain, did not have to reshape their material so much. They did, of course, pattern it artistically, and doubtless they did indeed invent some of it as well – and they certainly made moral points in their narratives. But there was no overt ideological programme in the average saga; it seems to have been enough that it should be able to entertain. (Much the same can be said of the *chanson de geste* tradition in France, although this does not mean that all 'literary' genres are like this; many later medieval romances are highly programmatic texts.)

In the case of Gregory of Tours, it is relatively easy to read past the historian's restructuring to the oral material that was his primary source. Gregory's deliberately simple style, and his lack of interest in historical change or systematic historical explanation – indeed, his deliberate fragmentation of his material – all allow us to see the joins in his evidence, as he counterposed stories about the kings (told, often, as part of the genre of folk-tale, though reconstructed into a chronological narrative by Gregory) against stories with a local basis, about his family, his cities, and their bishops. It looks as though we can postulate the existence of local chronological narratives, family- or bishop-centred, as being the dominant interpretive framework for memory in sixth-century urban societies in Gaul, underneath the more king-centred reorganization of the past that Gregory presents to us on the surface. And each of these had its own narrative logic, as is clear in Gregory's text, as he moves from folklore to family or court anecdote to miracle story and back again. In so far as Gregory was trying to set it all in a different genre altogether, that of history, the forms of the narrative kept slipping out of his control. But it is likely that what interested Gregory more was the overall structure of events as the exemplification of the providence of God; the detail could look after itself.

In the case of the legend of Charlemagne, we ranged over rather more sources, using the content of the memory of Charlemagne as our guide rather than individual texts. As a result, the ideological manipulation of that memory is very obvious; in France and Germany, Charlemagne soon became a symbol, a legitimation device for all sorts of subsequent activities. He represented an image of just kingship that was used as a prop for, and as a critique of, subsequent kings. He represented, too, an origin legend, a point of reference for claims of legitimate rule by a wide variety of later kings and princes; not surprisingly, many churches and monasteries would claim to be founded by him as well. Charlemagne the converter of the Saxons, Charlemagne the crusader, and (rather later) Charlemagne the lawgiver were other justifications of subsequent activity that we can easily find in the sources. But such devices only made any sense, only had any efficacy, in an environment which really did remember Charlemagne in this way or something like it. As with the official commemorations of the French Revolution (see above, p. 130), they show us a past that could be only manipulated, not invented; it was not only possible, but, more important, also necessary to place one's actions in the framework of a political past that, as often as not, really was thought to stretch back to Charlemagne, as the vernacular epics make very clear for aristocratic society in France. It is in this way that one can, as with Gregory, get past the conscious purposes of the texts to the changing memories that lay behind them; here again, however, we find in each case that the retellings of the memories we have, the social commemorations of Charlemagne, were patterned by the narrative genres through which they were retold – most obviously in the texts of the *chansons de geste*, which must be pretty close to one of the ways the past was actually recounted by people in the early twelfth century.

In Iceland, all the texts that we have looked at are likely to be similar to the way people remembered and talked about the past, and that goes for both the 'sagas of Icelanders' and the *Landnámabók*. The relationship between the content of what was remembered and its form, the narrative structure of saga, remained particularly close in Iceland, too, for laconic descriptions of family feuds not only are a feature of the sagas about the tenth and eleventh centuries, but dominate the contemporary accounts of thirteenth-century events as well. There are folk motifs in these sagas, but the dominant narrative pattern remained the feud, together with, as a result, a whole array of social relationships and obligations that make sagas look to us much more 'naturalistic' than most medieval texts. Icelanders had access to the folk-tale tradition, as also to king-centred history, hagiography, what was left of Scandinavian pagan mythology, and, later, romance, for they wrote other prose narratives about all of these. But they did not situate them in Iceland; the kings and the legendary heroes belonged, for the most part, to Norway. One could conclude that Iceland's past was conceived of in opposition to that of Norway; Icelanders knew what standard European historical memories were like in their time, both legendary and royal, and even wrote about them (almost all Norwegian history was in fact written by Icelanders), but rejected them as models for their own past – much as they had, as they believed, rejected King Harald's hegemony by coming to the island in the first place. In this sense, narrating feuds and genealogies and so little else was actually part of the self-representation of being Icelandic, even and especially in a period of increasing Norwegian control (cf. Hastrup 1984). Recounting the family-centred past proved that one was not Norwegian, at the same time as it allowed Icelanders to define themselves through memories of ancestors who had, for the most part, come from Norway itself. This is how the saga texts have since been used by Icelanders in their social memories of Iceland at the national level, and indeed they are still so used.

The medieval world was as heterogeneous as that of today, or indeed more so, and it would be improper to attempt to generalize too precisely about any aspect of it, least of all its social memory, in the space of one chapter. Instead, we have, in effect, used some examples of its historical literature as guides to memory as if they were modern oral texts, in order to see how one can relate the social function of the past to its narrative structures; for Einhard, for all his self-conscious literariness, was, in his intertextuality, his moralistic intent, or his use of genre, not very different from anybody today reminiscing about World War II. We need not give up the attempt to analyse memory just because our sources are dead; and, armed with that realization, we could look at any part of the past in a similar way. To conclude this book, we shall look at nineteenth- and twentieth-century Sicily in just this manner, as a final case study of the relationship between memory and social identity.

5

The *Mafia* and the Myth of Sicilian National Identity

I think it is fair to say that the ideal of the so-called Nietzschean super-man [in nineteenth-century political culture] has as its origin and doctrinal model not Zarathustra but Dumas *père*'s *Count of Monte Cristo*. (Gramsci 1991: 145)

According to Gino Doria, a Neapolitan historian writing in the 1930s, the *camorra*, or criminal underworld of Naples, was not, as legend had it, a Spanish import, but was rather a form of resistance organized by the poor of Naples 'to avenge insults or affronts to family honour' offered by the Spanish rulers (Doria 1935; cf. Seward 1984). As regards the Spanish origin, Doria is certainly right. In the nineteenth century, nationalist historians in Italy had tended to trace the origin of any defect they perceived in Italian culture or society to the period of Spanish domin-ance, and this was particularly true in the south. The *camorra* is, broadly, an organized extortion ring. It resembles criminal underworlds in large cities throughout the world. Local *amour propre* notwithstanding, there is no reason to suppose that the Neapolitan variant is anything but indigenous. In relating the *camorra* instead to themes such as family honour, and to the tradition of the vendetta, Doria puts the discussion on firmer ground. These are background themes, characterizing a wider social milieu from which extortion rings arise and in which they oper-ate. Any treatment of organized crime in southern Italy, whatever its conclusions, cannot fail to acknowledge this.

Thus, family honour and the tradition of the vendetta are both themes that form part of the social history of crime in Italy. Yet these themes play another role as well; they provide a set of images or topoi through which organized crime could be imagined and remembered.

Doria continues his discussion of the *camorra* by observing that 'the bodies of Spanish soldiers were frequently found at crossroads, knifed in the back.' The image of corpses left at crossroads by a sect of silent avengers is, in fact, a recurrent motif in south Italian literature; and we might wonder whether, in using the theme in his demystification of the legend of Spanish origin, Doria is doing anything more than sliding from one topos to another.

The vendetta is a powerful image, and, unsurprisingly, one which recurs in Sicilian *mafia* stories as well. It appears, for example, in G. Gabriele Amico's 1972 description of the *mafia*'s role in the Allied invasion of Sicily in 1943:

> The Sicilian, who, under Arab domination, had acquired the gravity of that people as well as its jealousy in regard to women, would not – in that hour of the Vespers in 1282 – lightly permit a French soldier to rummage between the breasts of his woman. But instead of denouncing him to the competent foreign authority (for Sicily then was under French rule), the Sicilian pulled out his knife and plunged it into the belly of the hapless trooper.
>
> And so it was, at the distance of centuries, that in 1943 during the days which immediately followed the Anglo-American landings in Sicily, many Moroccan soldiers were found at crossroads, their bellies slit open with a knife. These poor fools had formed the advance party of the Allied troops landing on their island, and they imagined that they could grab anything they liked, just like the ancient invaders had done. But some of them stretched their paws just a little too far in the direction of the ample graces of Sicilian womanhood – and paid for it with their hides. (Amico 1972: 41–2)

The author, a native Sicilian, worked as a journalist in Palermo in the early 1950s. He was thus well placed to gain accurate, firsthand information about events in Palermo in 1943. This makes his account very surprising, for it is total nonsense.

To begin with, Moroccan troops, though used by the French during the invasion of the Italian mainland in 1944, were not used in Sicily by the Anglo-Americans in 1943 (Kogan 1956). Yet in Sicily, it was – and still is – widely believed that they were (Rigoli 1978). A partial explanation may be that the Allies arrived from North Africa, and that the United States forces included black troops. These latter evoked a certain amount of consternation among the local population, many of whom were quite unprepared for anything of the sort (Rigoli, ibid.; cf. also Dolci 1963). In southern Italy, the term *marocchini* is applied generically to all North Africans, and, by extension, was probably applied to any dark-skinned foreigner, as the use of the word by Rigoli's informants shows.

Yet, substituting black United States troops for Moroccans does not really resolve the confusion. The problem is not only the identity of the victims, but also that the alleged event seems never to have taken place at all. There is no mention in contemporary sources of bodies of Allied soldiers of any description being dumped at crossroads, like the victims of some primal apotropaic ritual. The 'insult' to Sicilian womanhood mentioned in the sources was of a quite different sort. In Palermo and other Sicilian cities, the Allied command cordonned off supposed red-light districts, treating them as in quarantine, and posted notices graphically warning soldiers of the dangers of venereal diseases (Dolci 1963; Giarizzo 1970; Attanasio 1976: 247ff). A number of Sicilians were profoundly insulted by this. We might suspect that the topos of avenging family honour is here a fantasy which serves to cover a memory, which, to many Sicilians, was far more distasteful.

Still, even this explanation is insufficient; for it does not explain the specific reference. The 'Moroccan' soldiers of 1943 were not just any black troops; they were the descendants of the 'ancient invaders' – presumably the North African Muslims who had conquered and ruled Sicily in the early Middle Ages. This historical reference, however, is as confused as the first. There is no connection between the North African occupation of Sicily and the Sicilian Vespers of 1282, when Sicilians rose up and expelled their French (more properly, Angevin) rulers. The French in 1282 were even less likely to have been using 'Moroccan' soldiers than were the Anglo-American invaders in 1943. The author is amalgamating two different legends: first, the legend of the Sicilian Vespers, an event which, in the most widely spread version, was indeed set off by a soldier who, pretending to search for contraband, put his hand into the blouse of a Palermitan woman; and, second, a large body of stories and popular entertainments about knights and Saracens in Sicily (Mazzamuto 1970; Pitrè 1913, ch. 19).

On strict empirical grounds, we would be right to dismiss Amico's account entirely. It has no 'historical' value. Yet, as the wayward reference to the Sicilian Vespers helps make clear, the account should not be read as strictly factual at all. What the account is commemorating is not history, but a myth of Sicilian national identity. We shall attempt to unravel certain elements of this myth.

In one way or another, the Vespers of 1282 casts a long shadow in Sicilian history. Nineteenth-century Sicilians proudly claimed it as the first uprising for national unity in Italian history. This is pure anachronism: the issue of Italian unity had no meaning in thirteenth-century

Sicily. Especially in the south, the unity of Italy was a nineteenth-century theme, not a medieval one. The claim, of course, is not really historical; it is rather what Alberto Asor-Rosa calls a 'rhetorical myth', an ideological image (Asor-Rosa 1966: 8ff.). The 'rhetorical myth' that the Vespers of 1282 was a prefiguration of the nineteenth-century Risorgimento uprisings was an interpretation first elaborated in the nineteenth century itself by early Sicilian 'patriots'. After the unification of Italy in 1860, the theme became part of the standard baggage of political oratory in Sicily.

This 'rhetorical myth', however, was not wholly the invention of nineteenth-century liberal ideologues in Sicily. It was also an adaptation and ideological elaboration of popular traditions that had long existed in Sicily itself. Sicily possessed a venerable and deeprooted storytelling tradition. It is probable – though we do not know for sure – that the story of the Vespers had always been part of this tradition. In whatever case, it is a story which virtually all contemporary Sicilians would have known.

Thanks to the work of the nineteenth-century Sicilian folklorist, Giuseppe Pitrè, we have the story as it existed in a large number of purely oral versions (Pitrè 1882). The story could be found throughout Sicily, both in the towns and in the countryside: in this sense, it represented a genuinely 'national' tradition. Although the oral versions of the story vary considerably in detail, they all have certain points in common. In all cases, the historical context has been largely effaced. Although the story is told as a true event, it is an event that happened 'a long time ago', when the 'king of France' ruled Sicily. The plot of the story itself is invariably built around folk-tale motifs. It concerns an exchange of sexual insults in which Sicilians avenge themselves upon the French and expel them from the island. It is thus a story which, in oral versions, already contains two of the motifs that will be central to the rhetorical myth: honourable vengeance, and the expulsion of foreign oppressors from Sicily.[1]

---

[1] In his 1882 study of popular stories of the Vespers, Pitrè points out that much of the information remembered about the Vespers was preserved in proverbial form. This is an important observation; indeed, folklorists have frequently observed how themes and motifs are fixed in popular memory through proverbs. Pitrè also alludes, rather obscurely, to the connection in collective memory between Charles of Anjou and the droit de seigneur (cf. also above, p. 96). This seems to contain a reference to another extremely widespread Sicilian folk-tale concerning the king who decreed that all cuckolded Sicilians were to appear in public with horns on their heads. Charles of Anjou and his French soldiers were proverbially associated with the cuckolding of Sicilian husbands. Thus, one

There are, of course, also a number of differences between the oral version and the subsequent myth. In the first place, the myth elaborates a simple story of the sexual affront avenged, enlarging, ennobling, and giving it a political significance. In this version, the Vespers exemplifies the virile determination of a freedom-loving people not to bear the tyrant's yoke. Yet this difference is more apparent than real. Not only do the two themes – sexual and libertarian – prove compatible, but the sexual motif is also, almost invariably, retained in the myth. The myth thus incorporates the story in its folkloric form: it elaborates the form by giving it a new meaning in context; it does not, however, change the story itself.

In this way, the rhetorical myth of Sicilian national identity took shape as an old story which, in a specific external context, was elaborated and given an extended meaning. The retention of a tale from oral tradition at the heart of the myth ensured that it would be immediately clear and memorable to the people of Sicily. Its inclusion also helped give the myth its sense of popular legitimacy.

The first authoritative reinterpretation of the Vespers along these lines was Michele Amari's *Storia della guerra del Vespro*, published in 1842. Amari was already a distinguished historian of medieval Arab Sicily. Yet it was as a Sicilian patriot, as well as a historian, that Amari described the Vespers as a popular and nationalistic uprising. The authorities in Naples (Sicily was ruled by a Neapolitan branch of the Bourbons until 1860) well understood this, and, judging Amari's book to be inflammatory, endeavoured to suppress it, forcing the author to flee to France.

---

point of reference for Sicilian social memory of the Angevins is probably the sort of ribald and salacious tales that Pitrè does not include.

The memory of the Vespers as a specific event seems to have been best preserved in Palermo and the surrounding region. Typically, the story in this zone starts with the rapacity and lechery of the French soldiers. Thus, the version from Ficarazzi starts: 'It is said that once the French came to the city of Palermo. These French took everything in sight, and, whenever anyone got married, the bride had to spend the first night with a Frenchman.' The story goes on to tell of how the people decided to rise up one day and throw the French out. Typically, these stories include the motif that anyone who could not pronounce '*ciciri*' (chick-peas) correctly was put to the sword.

Interestingly enough, none of the oral accounts represent the Vespers as a spontaneous uprising. It is popular in the sense that it is always the people who decide to take revenge; but, in most of the versions, the date of the uprising is decided beforehand. This is probably why the oral accounts attach comparatively little importance to the image of the French soldier thrusting his hand under the Palermitan woman's blouse. In popular versions, this is just another example of the lecherous and insulting behaviour of the French; it is not conceived as a cause of the uprising itself.

Amari's study was – and, to a large extent, still is – the definitive account of the Vespers. He continued to work at it throughout his long career, the work eventually going through eleven revised editions. In 1882, on the 600th anniversary of the Vespers, the by now elderly Amari was persuaded to write a popular synopsis entitled *Racconto popolare del Vespro siciliano*. Even here, Amari remains a historian: he is factual, careful of details, and critical of his sources. This does not prevent him, however, from emphasizing his ideological message. Allusions to the popular struggle against foreign usurpers appear on virtually every page.

One way that Amari links the two levels – that of the facts, and that of the significance he wishes to give them – is precisely through the folk-tale motif. When the narrative reaches the point of the outbreak of violence, Amari stops the flow to focus on the incident as a separate, dramatized scene. The stage is set, the characters described: Amari tells the story of the French guard who thrusts his hand under the chemise of a Palermitan woman, and of her Sicilian husband who responds by plunging his sword in the guard's belly, shouting '*Muoiano i francesi!*' ('Let the French die!').

Amari has not, of course, invented this particular motif; he is drawing on Sicilian social memory, which has consistently preserved the incident in the story of the Vespers. Indeed, there is no reason to assume that the motif itself is factually incorrect at all. This is not really the point, however. Amari's intention in embedding the folk motif in the middle of the account was, no doubt, in part literary: the placement of the motif at this point renders the narrative lively and memorable. Yet Amari uses the incident not simply as added folkloric colouring; it is also cited as a cause. The problem is to determine what sort of cause – real or rhetorical.

In the final paragraphs of his 1842 account (reprinted in the 1882 synopsis) Amari returns to the folk-tale motif. Historical tradition, he remarks, remembers the 1282 Vespers as a feudal conspiracy. This is false: the Vespers was instead a popular, nationalistic, and explicitly republican uprising (we shall see the importance of the 'republican' aspect later). The conspiratorial explanation, he continues, is no more than a slander. Conspiracies there were, yet they would have all proved vain had not the Sicilian people themselves decided to throw off the tyrant's yoke. For all the feudal plots, for all the discontent of the barons, for all the general dissatisfaction, Amari insists, no uprising would have occurred had not the sexual insult 'filled to the brim the cup of vendetta, which the murder of the aggressor overturned' (1882: 98–9).

In this way, the motif comes to exemplify the whole story – the humiliations and abuses to which the Sicilian nation had for so long been subjected, until, finally, the nation exploded in an act of virile and honourable violence against its tormentor. This gives us a clue to the sense in which Amari regards the motif as the cause of the Sicilian Vespers. As a conscientious historian, Amari describes the rebellion as arising from a complex range of causes and prior conditions. Within this set, the avenging of the sexual insult simply acts as the immediate cause – the spark that ignites the powder-keg. At the same time, however, the motif plays a far wider causal role, for it exemplifies what, for Amari, was the underlying, and historically most significant cause – the character of the Sicilian people.

More than anything else, Amari's reinterpretation of the Vespers takes off from a new notion of the 'people' in regard to the 'nation'. For an older tradition, the 'nation' could stand for the aristocracy, higher clergy, and higher civil servants in Sicily. The 'people', however, were not part of the 'nation'; they were its 'subjects'. These subjects had no claim to sovereignty, nor certainly any right to take up arms against authority on their own account.

In Amari's history, however, the common people of Palermo who rose up against their feudal rulers in 1282 were not the 'vile populace' or 'rascal multitude', but the 'nation' in the act of asserting its sovereign will in the face of unjust tyranny. As an expression of the Sicilian 'nation', the Palermo mob had a legitimate right to resist oppression by taking the law into their own hands, for sovereignty belonged to them, not to their foreign overlords. Thus, Amari's conception of the people also implied a new definition of the 'nation' and a new conception of 'popular sovereignty'. These were all ideas that derived from the French Revolution.

By any standard the French Revolution had a tremendous impact upon Sicily, as it did upon the rest of Europe. In Sicily, however, this effect was delayed. In the eighteenth century, the Enlightenment had spread to Naples, and its influence was further strengthened in the Napoleonic period, when Naples came under French rule. The result was an indigenous movement for cultural and political reform. Yet, only weak echoes of these currents were felt in Sicily, which remained isolated from the intellectual developments on the Continent, and cut off from the political ferment until the early decades of the nineteenth century.

An intellectual movement aimed at political and social reforms was thus slow to develop in Sicily itself. It materialized more as a consequence of the Sicilian struggle for independence than as its cause. Independence for Sicily was a traditional issue, and, in its earliest stage, the British-supported bid for Sicilian independence in the decade after the Napoleonic wars represented little more than a transfer of power to the island's aristocracy. None the less, the intellectual climate of early nineteenth-century Italy was such that the movement soon took on radical and populist overtones. Rather than a struggle for insular separatism and baronial control, it evolved into a 'national' struggle, first for Sicilian independence, and, only at a later date, for Italian unity (Alatri 1954; Ganci 1968; Mack Smith 1968).

Sicily experienced major uprisings in 1820, 1848, and 1860. In between, there were local risings, riots, and conspiracies. From the 1830s onwards, Sicily was a hive of popular discontent and clandestine plots. After unification with Italy in 1860, this entire story of social unrest and political resistance came to be commemorated as a single national resistance movement. Urban riots, especially those in Palermo in 1848 and 1860, were treated as the Sicilian version of the *Journées* of the French Revolution. Neapolitan Bourbon authorities had insisted that the rioters were brigands, criminals, and plebeian 'scum' (*freccia*). After the success of the revolution, however, these rioters were commemorated as '*il popolo alla riscossa*' ('the people redeeming and revenging themselves'). They were the Sicilian Sans-culottes – the Sicilian counterpart of the *peuple* in Michelet's account of the French Revolution.

History records few of the rioters' names. Nevertheless, and especially in the Palermo area, contemporaries recognized them as generically '*mafiusi*'. This can be seen in both police files and in newspaper reports (Scichilone 1952). Nor is this surprising: '*mafiusu*' was Palermo slang for a young tough (cf. the definition in Pagano 1867). A Palermo *mafiusu* was hot-blooded and aggressive; he was vain, violent, and had an exaggerated sense of personal honour – just the type, in short, to declare a vendetta against constituted authority, and to take to the streets for independence. The identification of the rioters in 1848 and 1860 as '*mafiusi*' was, given the meaning of the term, perfectly natural. By the mid-1860s – like the nearly contemporary London epithet, 'hooligan' – it had become a quasi-official term, common in both pro-government and anti-government sources.

At first, there was no attempt to attach a political significance to the term: *mafiusi* were troublemakers; whether they made trouble for good or for ill depended on one's political preferences. Still, a connection was there to be made. It was hard to assert that the *mafiusi* had played a leading role in the struggle for liberty without also representing them as patriotic Sicilian freedom fighters.

Turning the *mafiusu* into a Sicilian nationalist was thus an unintended consequence of the nationalist and populist reinterpretation of Sicilian history. Nor was the reinterpretation of the *mafiusu* as a freedom fighter limited to political rhetoric. In 1866 there was a new uprising in Palermo – seven days of barricades and anti-government rioting. Later, in 1877, the police chief of Palermo, in his report to the government on 'public spirit', wrote: 'The mournful events of 1866 are for the masses a comforting historical memory. They take pride in it, and associate it with those bombastic aphorisms about the initiative of the people, almost as if it were a precursor of the Commune of Paris' (cited in Brancato 1972). The common people, at least in Palermo, seem to have assimilated much of the Jacobin rhetoric, including the 'bombastic aphorisms' about popular sovereignty. These *mafiusi*, the common people argued, were not mere 'hooligans'; they were *communards*.

Once the identification between the *mafiusu* and the Sicilian freedom fighter had become fixed, it was easy to project it back into history. Could there be any doubt that the patriot who first plunged his sword into the belly of the wretched French guard was not a *mafiusu*, perhaps even the first *mafiusu* of Sicilian history? The temptation was irresistible, and thus there arose a popular tradition that the 1282 Vespers was not only the origin of Sicily's independence movement, but also the origin of the *mafia*.

To support this legend, there evolved a piece of folk etymology. Amari has the common people of Palermo rise up to the rallying cry, '*Muoiano i francesi!*' With a bit of alteration, this cry becomes, '*Morte ai francesi, Italia anela!*' ('Death to the French, Italy is yearning!'). In this altered form, the cry is an acronym – MAFIA. According to this tradition, the *mafia* arose as a sect of avengers in 1282, taking the acronym as both its title and its war cry.

Like so much of the Sicilian national myth, this explanation is wholly implausible. Even if we accept that the term '*mafia*' is an acronym (and there is no reason why we should), thirteenth-century Sicilians would surely have formed it in thirteenth-century Sicilian dialect, not nineteenth-century Italian, a language which, needless to say, did not exist at the time. None the less, this origin is still asserted and widely believed in both Sicily and the United States (it is accepted, for example, in Reid 1952 and in Sondern 1959). The origin of this tradition is, however, not hard to guess. The language, as well as the sentiments, could come only from the late nineteenth century. The same can be said for the 'countermyth' of the *mafia*'s origins, probably originating in right-wing and pro-government groups. According to this, '*mafia*' is indeed an acronym, but one with a quite different message: '*Mazzini autorizza furti incendi abigeati*' ('Mazzini authorizes thefts, arson, cattlestealing'). The two competing etymologies were probably invented sometime in the 1870s.

By the late nineteenth century, Sicily had therefore developed a typical myth of national identity. Sicily was a 'nation', and the Sicilians were a 'people' – combative, honourable, freedom-loving, and republican. What complicated this myth – but what also made it particularly Sicilian – was the traditional motif incorporated within it. This associated Sicilian national identity with the tradition of the vendetta. A vendetta stood at the opening of Sicilian national history, and the the vendetta expressed the hot-blooded nature of the Sicilian people, who would not allow a slight upon their honour to go unavenged. The personification of this tradition of the vendetta was the *mafiusu*; thus, it was appropriate that, in the popular account of the Sicilian struggle for freedom, the *mafiusu* should also play a central role.

This myth, however, was largely just a myth; it was not history. In terms of the Sicilian perception of the 1282 Vespers, this hardly mattered. Sicilians might commemorate the Vespers in any way they pleased; no practical consequences, no claims for legitimacy, hung on the rhetorical claim that an unknown *mafiusu* had begun the Risorgimento in 1282. In terms of the Sicilian perception of the situation after 1860, however, it did matter, for the myth incorporated claims about popular sovereignty and the legitimacy of rebellion that were contradicted by political realities. The myth represented the struggles for independence of the early nineteenth century in terms of spontaneous, popular uprisings. In fact, popular uprisings had been only one aspect of a more complex political situation. In this, the network of conspiratorial societies had played a role; so had Garibaldi and his followers, and so had the Piemontese government under Cavour. The political synthesis that emerged after 1860 was far more a consequence of these last three aspects than of popular uprisings. Sicily had not won its independence; it was, rather, incorporated into the new Italian state, and this, in the years immediately following 1860, meant rule from Turin.

Despite the popular struggle, the new political elite that rose into prominence during and after the Risorgimento were not *mafiusi*, for they were not from the common people. They came instead from a tiny minority of the well off and well educated. They were sons of landowners and professionals. Many had participated in the struggle for freedom as members of clandestine, revolutionary conspiracies. This new elite might well accept the populist myth of the struggle for independence, at least for purposes of commemoration. Yet even when they accepted the Jacobin notion of popular sovereignty, they interpreted it in the sense of ruling in the name of the people, rather than in terms of direct democracy.

Thus, although the new ruling elite in Sicily continued to commemorate the history and populist ideals of the struggle for independence, they did so in a way that did not bring their legitimacy and authority as a governing class into question. From their perspective, the people had had a legitimate right to rise up against authority in 1848 and 1860. In 1848 and 1860, they had been fighting against tyranny; the uprisings were legitimate expressions of popular sovereignty. The year 1860 was, however, a watershed date. Any uprisings thereafter were no longer expressions of the sovereign will of the people, but rebellions against the people's legitimate government.

This change in perspective, as the new ruling elite settled into power, set off, in its turn, a series of changes in the Sicilian perception of the *mafia*. From the perspective of the new rulers, resistance to authority was no longer patriotic but criminal. *Mafiusi* were violent troublemakers, and it was no longer opportune for any member or ally of the new government to claim any connection with this element. Yet the *mafiusi* could not simply be eliminated from the legend of the struggle for independence, for their role was enshrined in the commemorative myth. Public opinion continued to remember the *mafiusi* as playing a leading role in both 1848 and 1860. The myth itself needed to be 'rewritten'.

One way of adjusting the myth was to argue that the *mafiusi* had been patriotic before 1860, but that afterwards they had changed character and become criminal (Colajanni 1900 is a classic example). This supposed character change, however, required an explanation. In the original version, the behaviour of the *mafiusi* was spontaneous. There was nothing in this version to suggest that the *mafiusi* were in any way organized. If they were capable of suddenly changing course, however, and opposing the authority of the revolution, this would suggest that they were in some sort of organization. The rhetorical image of the *mafia* that had emerged as a by-product of the commemorative myth of the Sicilian struggle for independence had to be adjusted in this direction.

Interestingly, this reconsideration was first hinted at in the theatre. In 1862 there appeared in Palermo a dialect play entitled *Li Mafiusi di la Vicaria* (Rizzotto 1962).[2] The Vicaria was the name of Palermo's central

---

[2] Although the author of the play is usually given as Giuseppe Rizzotto, it was, in fact, co-authored by Gaspare Mosca. Mosca had been involved in the 1846 uprising, and, in

prison, and the play described how, in the days preceding the 1860 revolt, two underworld figures incarcerated there helped a young intellectual who had been imprisoned on account of his revolutionary activities.

The novelty in the 1862 play was not the idea of revolutionaries befriended by the underworld. Such cloak-and-dagger scenes were the standard fare of popular literature in nineteenth-century Sicily, and similar stories had been told of the 1848 uprising (D'Asdia 1980). What was new in this case was the decision of the playwright to call the members of the underworld '*mafiusi*'. The title was an afterthought; the term '*mafiusu*' is not mentioned in the play itself. Both the term itself, and the identification of the 'unknown' political prisoner with Francesco Crispi, a leading revolutionary and, subsequently, parliamentary leader, were added by the author to give the play a greater sense of contemporary realism (Ciuni 1979; Loschiavo 1962: 60). Before this time, '*mafiusu*' does not seem to have had any specifically underworld associations. Giuseppe Pitrè later insisted that the *mafiusu* of the 1860s was a rugged individualist. Although '*mafiusu*' implied an aggressive troublemaker, it did not imply a criminal, still less a gangster or racketeer. Nothing in the term '*mafia*' connoted an organization, much less a secret society (see, in general, Buttitta in Buttitta 1968).

Like the folk-tale motif incorporated in Amari's account of the Vespers, the idea of contact between the revolutionary sects and the criminal underworld of Palermo in the Vicaria prior to the 1860 uprising is not impossible. A criminal underworld existed in Palermo, and probably ruled the Palermo prison. Bourbon authorities did not separate political prisoners from other categories of inmates. There are cases where political prisoners struck up friendships with underworld figures

---

order to escape the Bourbon police, had later joined a company of travelling actors. After 1860, he returned to Palermo, where he made the acquaintance of Rizzotto, who was the leading actor in Palermo's dialect theatre. Rizzotto and Mosca decided to collaborate on a play which would have the recent uprising as its principal theme. One of Rizzotto's employees, a certain Gioacchino D'Angelo, also called Jachinu Funciazza, had spent a considerable amount of time in the Vicaria, and had been made a member of the prison *camorra*. Rizzotto and Mosca used Funciazza as a source of information, eventually modelling one of the play's major characters on him.

The original title of the play was simply *La Vicaria di Palermo*. Shortly before the play was completed, however, Mosca encountered two men fighting in a Palermo street. One of the men grabbed the other and said, '*Vurrissi fari u' mafiusu cu mia?*' ('So you want to play the *mafioso* with me?') The use of the dialect word '*mafiusu*' struck Mosca, and he decided that it would give the play the sort of contemporary atmosphere he sought. Thus, the play was renamed *Li Mafiusi di la Vicaria*. Its success started a tremendous vogue for *mafia* plays in Sicily. On Rizzotto and Mosca, see Ciuni 1979.

(cf. the career of Angelo Pugliese, in Ajello 1868). Once again, however, what is interesting is less the factual basis of the events recounted than the way in which the recounted event takes on an emblematic significance in the causal structure of the story. That is to say, the motif functions as another causal element.

Amari had used the image of the sexual insult avenged to exemplify the spontaneous and popular character of the Vespers. The dramatized scene in Palermo's central prison in which the leader of a clandestine, revolutionary sect accepts the aid of the leaders of organized crime also provides an encapsulated explanation of the 1860 uprising. The two images lend themselves to diametrically opposed interpretations, however, for the prison scene is an emblem of conspiracy.

Thus, by the mid-1860s, there were two myths of the struggle for independence in Sicily; one telling the story in populist, Jacobin terms; the other in terms of conspiracy. Significantly, the *mafia* was at the centre of both these legends.

The two accounts contradicted each other; yet they did not blot each other out. One reason why they could co-exist lies in the memorable nature of the motifs themselves. Both the image of sexual insult promptly avenged, and that of the secret bargain struck between the revolution and the underworld, stuck in Sicilian social memory. Like Cinderella's glass slipper, the two motifs both became part of the oikotypical version. Neither the story of the national struggle, nor the story of the *mafia*, would seem right without some reference to these two motifs. Another reason why two, implicitly contradictory conceptions of the *mafia* could persist together was that the contradiction itself was fertile. In the acrimonious and often violent political rivalries that developed in Sicily after 1860, it was frequently opportune for political figures, especially on the Left, to argue that there existed a 'good' *mafia* and a 'bad' *mafia*. This was a way of contrasting the true, authentic *mafia* (or '*mafia* spirit'), which was identical to the Sicilian 'national spirit', with an opportunistic, criminal underground which helped the police in their persecution of true Sicilian patriots in return for the government's tacit acquiescence in their criminal misdeeds (cf. Sceusa 1877, for an instance).

This distinction between the noble and patriotic *mafia* and the evil *mafia* could be articulated in such a way that the term '*mafiusu*' retained its original, positive meaning, while letting the term '*mafia*' stand for the criminal underworld. Palermitan dialect seems to have used the two terms in this way until fairly recent times. Thus, for all the sinister connotations that the '*mafia*' was acquiring, '*mafiusu*' continued to mean a swaggering young Palermo tough. Like the *guappo* in Naples or the *bullo* in Rome, the *mafiusu* was too familiar a figure in Palermitan street life to be abruptly excised. Thus, in 1878, the conservative and pro-establishment *Giornale di Sicilia* could still refer to the *mafiusu* as embodying 'the *cavalleresque* side of crime' (cited in D'Asdia 1980: 22).

In one of his books on the *mafia*, the Sicilian police official and criminologist Antonino Cutrera elaborated this same distinction, writing that the young *mafiusu*, though not a criminal, had a propensity for getting into trouble with the law. When this led to his imprisonment, Cutrera added, he was liable to meet members of the underworld and to be inducted into the real *mafia* (1896: 27–8; Pitrè makes a similar observation, 1870: 70–1).

Thus, for Cutrera, Pitrè, and the *Giornale di Sicilia*, *'mafiusi'* continued to stand for a disorganized 'hooligan element' made up of teenage boys and young men. *'Mafia'*, by contrast, referred to an organized criminal underworld composed of older men. *'La mafia'* (or, sometimes, *'la maffia'*) was taken to be the name of an organization of criminal bosses, or patrons of the criminal milieu, capable, on the one hand, of making clandestine deals with local political groups or government agencies, while, on the other, exercising a controlling influence on the restive 'hooligan element' below.

Although this way of defining the terms represented a fresh interpretation, it was one that reflected Sicilian realities. A disorganized and tendentially violent element existed in Palermo and the surrounding regions, and this element had taken part in the chain of nineteenth-century uprisings. It was to this element that the term *'mafiusu'* properly referred. A criminal underworld, centred perhaps in Palermo's main prison, capable of having dealings with both political groups and government agencies, certainly existed as well. Although this underworld did not then, or even subsequently, regard itself as *'la mafia'*, the term was appropriate, and, eventually, it stuck.

This general scheme could be further elaborated in any number of ways. The former revolutionaries could picture themselves as the leaders of the *mafia* – at least of the *mafia* as it existed before 1860. This claim was sometimes made by left-wing Sicilian deputies in the parliamentary debates on Sicily in the 1870s. A variant of this version, still widespread in both Sicily and the United States appears in the autobiography of the Siculo-American underworld leader, Joe Bonanno. He explained that the *mafia* (which he prudently chose to call the 'Tradition') had originated in the Middle Ages, as a sect of noble avengers, who intervened to avenge violation of family honour, and who, in times of political trouble, would rally the common people in defence of their native liberties against the foreign oppressor (Bonanno 1983: 158).

Bonanno's version clearly derives from the original rhetorical myth. Yet, by now, the myth has been adjusted. Originally, the *mafiusu* had exemplified the common people in the act of asserting their popular sovereignty. In this version, it was projected back to the story of the 1282 Vespers. In the revised version, although the *mafiusi* still come from the common people, their leaders, and the founders of the 'Tradition', come from the nobility. Just as the original myth was projected back to the Vespers, the revised myth is now extended back into the Middle Ages as well. A social distinction between the leaders of the *mafia* and the simple followers has, according to this version, existed from the beginning. This is significant not only because it revises the legend of the *mafia*'s origins, but also because it eternalizes the *mafia* in an image of class relationships that are emblematic for Sicily as a whole. The *mafia* stood for the patron class of Sicily; the *mafiusi* stood for their clients and followers. The *mafia* were the bosses, the rulers, the heads of the families. To them was due respect and obedience. The *mafiusi* were the followers and henchmen. They carried out the bosses' orders. In this way, much of Sicily's class and political structure, as well as its family ethos, could be projected into the symbol of the *mafia*.

Representing the *mafia* as the elders or patrons of the criminal world also, of course, linked the two causal themes represented by the two motifs: the popular and spontaneous, and the aristocratic and conspiratorial. Amari had set out to re-evaluate and minimize the aristocratic and conspiratorial element in the 1282 uprising. The popular myth eventually restored the aristocracy to its original place in the story; and this constituted an acknowledgement of the real situation in Sicily. It restored the conspiratorial element in a way, however, that still permitted the term '*mafiusu*' to stand for the anarchic, freedom-loving, and honour-regarding character of the Sicilian nation in general.

In this way, a notion of '*mafiusu*' and '*mafia*' took shape in Sicily out of a variety of historical, folkloric, and political elements. The notion, portrayed in innumerable stories and anecdotes, or represented in songs or dialect plays, came to constitute a mirror of Sicilian culture and politics.[3] It served as a category of cultural reflection as well. *Mafia* became, for better or for worse, inseparable from Sicilianness, a sort of 'ghost in

---

[3] The relations between the *mafia*, as portrayed in the dialect theatre and in popular journalism, and the Sicilian perspective on politics and history, has never, to our knowledge, been thoroughly studied. The best treatment remains Mazzamuto 1970. In any case, there is a good deal of incidental information in Loschiavo 1962, D'Asdia 1980, and Nicastro 1978. Also helpful in this respect are the popular songs collected by Antonio Uccello (Uccello 1974). Finally, there are, of course, the prison songs collected by Pitrè (Pitrè 1870).

the machine' of Sicilian collective identity. Yet, at the same time, the notion was a source of endless confusion. Who, in concrete terms, was the *mafia*? Were all true-born Sicilians *mafiusi*, or only a minority of criminals?

The idea that the *mafia* was an expression of the Sicilian national character was espoused by populist politicians and the writers for the dialect theatre. Not surprisingly, this was an idea with which the Italian police had little sympathy. For them, the *mafia* was a criminal association.

We see this in police reports and journalistic accounts in pro-government sources from the 1860s onwards. Faced with continuing violence and political unrest, it was tempting for the new government to lay the blame at the door of some sinister, secret sect (*Moti* 1981: 117, 175ff.). Calling this sect '*la mafia*' enhanced the sense of mystery. When, in 1865, the prefect of Palermo reported that the breakdown in public confidence had allowed 'the so-called "*maffia*", or criminal association, to grow in audacity', he was picturing the *mafia* as an underground, criminal association which was capable of aiding the extremist revolutionary sects in stirring up public unrest (Alatri 1954: 92–7; Brancato 1972: 36–8).

The police wished to define this *mafia* in as concrete a way as possible. None the less, the conception of the *mafia* that the police accepted already contained much of the myth of national identity, and thus, no matter how hard the police tried to be concrete, the ambiguity inherent in the term continually reasserted itself.

Despite their opposed perspectives, the nationalist version of the *mafia* is quite compatible with the one that the police elaborated for themselves: in fact, they were virtually identical. There was, however, an important difference in practice. Those who claimed that the *mafia* was, at least in part, or at least originally, a brotherhood of Sicilian patriots or social avengers, did not usually specify who these avengers were or how the brotherhood was organized. This is logical; the claim was purely rhetorical. What had existed earlier in the century was a network of secret or semi-secret clubs and Masonic societies working for the goal of Sicilian independence. However, neither their members, nor the Bourbon authorities ever used the term '*mafia*'. If, in the period after 1860, the term was used in connection with these clubs, this represented an attempt to assimilate the activities of the conspiratorial sects to the myth of the national struggle.

The police sometimes seemed to take this literally, and this could mean accepting that there existed a shadowy group or groups which, on the one hand, controlled and directed what the police called the '*bassa criminalità*', while, on the other, forging links with political groups. For the police, penetrating the veil of secrecy and uncovering the workings of these groups was a central concern.

Thus, the police never regarded the *mafia* as an exclusively criminal organization. Their image of the *mafia* was that of something that linked the upper and lower classes in Sicily by bringing the political elite into contact with the criminal world. From the middle of the 1860s, therefore, the police regarded the *mafia* as a criminal organization embedded in local politics. In their reports, they tended to represent the *mafia* as, in concrete terms, a network of politically protected extortion rings: that is, as groups of criminals who terrorized a local community, living off extortion and other illegal gains, and controlling access to jobs and local markets. These groups, however, were always connected to local political parties and factions, whom they supported, and from whom they drew protection.

What was the exact identity and political colouring of the groups in league with organized crime? From the late 1860s onwards, local police delegates submitted lists of 'dangerous' or 'suspect' persons in their jurisdictions. Invariably, such persons were characterized under headings such as: 'republicans', 'anarchists', 'protectors of brigands', and '*mafiosi*' (the Italianization of '*mafiusi*'). This assortment of labels is significant, for the police supposed criminal bosses to be in league with the political enemies of the government, and, throughout the nineteenth century, these political enemies were always on the Left. Even though the true-born Sicilian nationalist of the rhetorical myth may have been a republican, the model citizen of liberal Italy was a monarchist. Republicanism, in the 1870s and '80s, was regarded by the police as political subversion. The republican party was not outlawed, but, especially in unsettled parts of the new state, the police kept it under as much surveillance as they could, and were always ready to see, behind any outbreak of public discontent, the machinations of republican plotters. For the police the republicans and the *mafia* were often the two faces of the same coin.[4]

The 'discovery' by the police of an alliance of *mafia* and republican sects had, of course, already been presupposed in *Li Mafiusi di la Vicaria*. There, the two social forces – the revolutionary party, personified by the incarcerated young lawyer, and the criminal underworld, personified by the prison *cammorra* – are balanced. The play even establishes a sense of analogy between the two parties, for, in the course of the action, the

[4] See, for example, reports in Archivio centrale dello stato di Palermo [ASP], Gabinetto di Prefettura, busta 29, categoria 20, fascicolo 15.

audience learns that the prison underworld has its own organization, with rules and internal ranks – just like a revolutionary sect.

The police conception of the precise nature of the *mafia* was, in its essentials, nothing more than a practical working-out of this original analogy. From their point of view, *mafiusi* and republicans were both troublemakers. The police associated republican groups with the *mafia* – in some cases, representing them as simply the same thing. In other cases, however, they separated them, representing the republicans as the political aspect of the alliance, whereas the *mafia* represented the more purely criminal aspect. In these latter cases, where the *mafia* was assumed to possess a separate identity, the police needed to form some notion of the *mafia* as a separate organization. Given the circumstances, it is hardly surprising that the police assumed that the *mafia* and the republicans were not only similar in nature, but in form as well. The *mafia* was presumed to be a clandestine sect.

Nor was it just any kind of clandestine sect. It was, specifically, a Mazzinian, Masonic sect, complete with internal grades, initiation rites, passwords, and links with brother sects. This was part of the Jacobin-Mazzinian legacy of the French Revolution to Sicilian politics, which, as we have seen, had such an impact upon Sicilian social memory. This had been the organizational form that revolutionary conspiracies had taken in the earlier part of the century, and it was the organizational form frequently adopted by republican, and other far-Left, groups after 1860. This, then, was the organizational form that was projected onto the Sicilian underworld.

Before continuing, we may well ask in what sense the police conception of the *mafia* was, in fact, true. In one sense, it was true; for its general picture of organized crime as politically embedded extortion rings was quite accurate. There were, moreover, numerous towns under the control of local political strongmen who ruled by fiat and through their own network of followers, ignoring procedures and instructions from the prefect in Palermo. These men sometimes committed grossly illegal acts, even allying with brigands to terrorize their enemies. Not all of these local despots had links with the far Left, yet many had; for this provided them with an additional layer of armour against the incursions of constituted authority into their petty kingdoms.[5]

Yet there was nothing new in this. For centuries the landowning families of the Sicilian interior had resisted attempts by the state to stop their feuding and force them to submit to state authority. Feuding

---

[5] See, e.g., reports on Bivona and Naro in AS Agrigento, fascicolo 18; there are many other examples both in the Madonie region and in and around Partinico.

families had always formed parties and sought alliances with other groups. This feuding had never been associated with the *mafia*, nor, indeed, with the underworld in Palermo. If, in the 1860s and '70s, the police took the persistence of this state of affairs as evidence of a widespread network of clandestine groups aimed at subverting legitimate authority, and associated this network with the *mafia*, this shows how powerfully the myth, and the images it contained, worked on the imagination of the police. The simple existence of all manner of alliances, explicit or implicit, between political revolutionaries and malcontents and criminals does not prove that the police were right to see this as all part of the *mafia*, unless, as was often the case, one assumed from the start that this was what the *mafia* was.

Within the rhetorical myth of Sicilian independence, the idea of the *mafia* played a double causal role: it represented this struggle as both spontaneous and conspiratorial. The conspiratorial theme also served to link the activities of the ruling elite to those of the struggling masses below. In terms of Sicilian realities, this image possesses a high degree of cogency. It was a reflection of real events. It was an image which expressed, moreover, what many Sicilians felt; that is, it corresponded to a Sicilian idea of their past history while representing many of their contemporary problems. It was thus an image closely enough keyed to reality in Sicily to enable the police to elaborate the myth into a description of the network of connections that linked crime and politics in Sicily. Yet, for all that it represented reality and expressed a social experience, the *mafia* was still an image; it was not a reality. It was a central image in a myth that dramatized Sicilian history and politics, giving it meaning; yet the image itself was not real.

The police, of course, were not the only group in Sicily that accepted the myth of the *mafia* at its face value. Nor, significantly, were they the only group who tried to act in such a way as to validate that myth. There is evidence that criminal groups, such as extortion rings, did indeed, occasionally, assume the form of a revolutionary Masonic lodge. In these cases, however, the correspondence between myth and reality occurred after the myth was formed, not beforehand. Thus, the relations are inverted. The myth is no longer providing a rhetorical commentary and causal interpretation on past events, but a social perspective in the present. The myth of national identity is providing a code of behaviour. Nature is imitating art.

Antonino Cutrera, whom we cited earlier, wrote that the scope of the *mafia* was, 'robbery, extortion, burglary, malicious vandalism, bloody vendetta, and mutual aid' (Cutrera 1900: 121). By 'mutual aid', Cutrera meant what, in Britain, were called 'Friendly Societies' – popular clubs, in which a member, in return for the payment of monthly dues, was entitled to certain forms of legal or financial assistance. The inclusion of Friendly Societies in this list of criminal activities may strike an incongruous note; none the less, its presence indicates the political aspect in organized criminal operations in Sicily. The *Società di mutuo soccorso* which sprang up in towns all over late nineteenth-century Sicily, wrote Cutrera, were populist, left-wing political clubs. They were, he continued, 'fomentors of perennial disharmony in our towns – so much so that even the *mafiosi* began to organize themselves into mutual-aid societies'.

The example that Cutrera gives is that of the Stoppagglieri of the village of Monreale during the late 1870s. He charges them with a series of vendetta killings, and of terrorizing Monreale, forcing local men to join their society and contribute money to it. Cutrera also describes the Stoppagglieri as a secret republican brotherhood. He writes that local people whom the society wished to intimidate were taken into the countryside, and there 'forcibly administered the Stoppagglieri oath' (Cutrera 1900: 131). The more recent Sicilian writer, Michele Pantaleone, adds two more details to this description. The Stoppagglieri, he writes, were a group of 'stopping' workers, or bottle-stoppers. What is more, the 'oath' of the Stoppagglieri, as well as their hierarchical organization, was derived from the prison *mafia* in Palermo (Pantaleone 1970: 20–1).

In truth, virtually none of this emerges from contemporary police and trial records – though these are very incomplete – or from the scattered references in contemporary newspapers. There was a series of murders (for which part of the trial records survive), and occasional references to and reports on 'the mysterious sect of the Stoppagglieri' in the press, but nothing concerning its organizational form or initiation rituals.[6]

Pantaleone's contention that the Stoppagglieri were a group of 'stopping' workers is usually accepted. If the *mafia* organized itself into working-class clubs, why not a society of stopping workers? Yet the argument seems unlikely. Working with 'stopping' is not a recognized trade in Sicily, much less an organized one. In any case, it emerges from the trial records that almost all the Stoppagglieri were agricultural workers. Pantaleone's interpretation seems nothing more than a false etymology. None the less, it is a significant mistake. In Sicily, as in the United States, there have often been connections between organized

---

[6] The trial records are in ASP, Tribunale civile e penale di Palermo, Fascicoli di procedimenti di assize, anno 1875, b. 143, fasc. 1, 8, 9, 10. The other fascicoli are missing, and the records of appeal are absent.

crime and organized labour, although in Sicily these connections do not begin before the 1890s. From the perspective of Pantaleone, writing in the 1950s, it was natural to associate the Stoppagglieri with some trade. He may indeed have been basing himself on oral memory in Monreale. If so, this would be a typical case of anachronism in social memory.

Perhaps a more likely explanation for the name comes from the dialect phrase *'dari stuppa'*, the meaning of which is more or less paralleled by the English idiom, 'feed someone a line' (Traina 1868, *voce 'stuppa'*). If this slang meaning of the term is the basis of the name, we might, instead of a trade group, consider the Stoppagglieri to be a 'Society of Wise Guys'.

The police considered the Stoppagglieri to be a criminal gang involved in a number of vendetta slayings. There is no mention of the Stoppagglieri as associated with any trade. Yet the police were clearly convinced that some sort of Stoppagliere association did exist. The following scene, preserved in one of the surviving trial depositions, gives a better picture of the Stoppagglieri in the eyes of the police. In August 1872, two men, Giuseppe Sinatra and Giovanni Gudetta, arrived for a drink in a tavern in Monreale. Someone offered them a bottle of wine, shouting to the tavern-keeper, 'Don't take it by the stopper!' (*stuppagghiu*). Sinatra, insulted, replied, 'Don't you know that I'm one of the Stoppagglieri' (*'io sono dei stuppagghiara'*). The two men angrily left the tavern, and were found, shot in the back, two hours later.

Pantaleone's other contention, that the Stoppagglieri took their organizational form and initiation oath from Palermo's central prison, is no less interesting. It would support the collective memory that Palermo's central prison was (and is) the headquarters of the *mafia*. Cutrera, however, gives a different origin – although one that is not entirely incompatible. According to him, the Stoppagglieri took their 'phraseology, along with some of the analogous mimicry' from a popular puppet play, *Vita e Prodezze del Bandito Pasquale Bruno* (Cutrera 1900: 124). If this is the case, it was a very appropriate choice. Pasquale Bruno was an eighteenth-century bandit from eastern Sicily, the legend of whose *geste* had been incorporated into the commemorative myth of Sicily's struggle for independence. According to his legend, Bruno, shortly before his execution, did form some sort of patriotic sect among his fellow prisoners. Curiously, our main source of evidence about this seems to be the story upon which the puppet play was based – *Pascal Bruno*, written by no less an author than Alexandre Dumas *père*. It is not clear where Dumas *père* got the story. Perhaps he was drawing on a local Sicilian legend, or, alternatively, he may have adapted a *camorra* legend from Naples. But, in whatever case, the image of a noble brigand composing a stirring oath on the eve of his execution at the hands of an unjust tyrant could not have been more calculated to stir the imaginations of young Sicilians, already inclined to believe that the *mafia* was a sect of avengers struggling for the independence of Sicily.

The idea that a criminal group might draw its statutes, oaths, and organizational form from pulp literature may seem far-fetched. It suggests that, at a certain level, the Stoppagglieri were neither a band of hardened criminals, nor a group of local political bullies, but were instead a gang of adolescents behaving like Tom Sawyer consulting his collection of adventure stories before embarking on a game of robbers. In fact, there is nothing strange in this suggestion. The Stoppagglieri were a youth gang. Most of their members seem to have been young labourers. There is no reason to suppose that they were any less prone to romantic behaviour than any other adolescent group.

As we have said, the Stoppagglieri probably encountered the story of Pasquale Bruno in a puppet-theatre adaptation. Puppet theatres were a common form of popular entertainment, and companies toured the island. The usual fare had long been chivalric romance. Pitrè remarks that the entire city of Palermo seemed to go into mourning every time the puppet theatre represented the death of Roland (Pitrè 1913). During the early nineteenth century, however, 'patriotic' literature began to be adapted for the puppet theatre. In this way, Amari's version of the 1282 Vespers could, in dramatized form, be brought even to mountain villages. *Li Mafiusi di la Vicaria* was naturally adapted as well – it is still sometimes presented today. In this way, the members of the Stoppagglieri gang would have known both the legend of *mafia* participation in the 1860 uprising as well as the legend of Pasquale Bruno with its prison scene. It is thus easy to imagine why the Stoppagglieri believed that their initiation ritual was the genuine article.

The nineteenth-century socialist leader from Trapani, Cammareri Scurti, called the *mafia* a '*bassa cavalleria*', or chivalry of the lower orders, citing the predilection of young *mafiosi* for the heroic knights in the puppet theatre. He adds the significant detail that these provincial *mafiosi* learned proper *mafia* talk from the puppet theatre as well. Many of the puppet theatres were based in Palermo, and thus many of the puppeteers spoke Palermitan dialect. Puppet theatre shows were largely improvisations, and when these Palermo companies represented *Li Mafiusi di la Vicaria*, the puppeteers made the *mafiosi* speak in argot – Palermo's underworld jargon. This proved immensely popular, and gradually the use of argot spread to other tough-guy characters represented by the puppeteer. Cammareri Scurti thus uncovers another strand in the diffusion of the myth of the *mafia*. Not only did the puppet theatre spread the myth of the national struggle in precisely the form in which the connection of the *mafia* with that struggle was most explicitly stated, but it also diffused a way of talking and acting that supposedly characterized this sect of social avengers (cf. Costanza 1964).

Of course, the Stoppagglieri were not merely engaged in a game of make-believe. It is likely that they were at the bottom of a gang war in Monreale that claimed a number of victims. Yet the difference between playing at *mafia* and being *mafia* may only be one of circumstance. Monreale was politically unsettled during the late 1860s and '70s. What is more, political tensions were exacerbated by a number of blood feuds between property-owning families. Members of the Stoppagglieri seem to have been employed by some of these families, and this may well have been the mechanism through which the Stoppagglieri were dragged into a chain of killings.

Whatever their origins, and whatever their true nature may have been, the Stoppagglieri themselves soon passed into social memory as the 'mysterious sect' par excellence. The first Sicilian immigrant community in the United States was formed during the mid-nineteenth century in New Orleans. At the start of the 1880s, gang warfare broke out there. By the 1890s, in typical Sicilian fashion, both of the gangs involved were telling the police that the other gang was part of *'La Mafia'*. More than this, one gang added that their enemies belonged to a specific *mafia* sect called 'The Stoppagglieri Society' (Nelli 1976: 43; cf. the reference in Scalici 1980: 53).

The Stoppagglieri may have been the first criminal gang in Sicily to use, in Cutrera's words, the 'phraseology and analogous mimicry' of a secret society, but they were by no means the last. Other criminal groups carried the analogy much further. Like the revolutionary sects earlier in the century, the Fratellanza of Favara, in the province of Agrigento, in the 1880s, possessed a set of passwords – such as 'Death to Tyrants', 'Universal Republic', and 'Brotherhood'. Much of the Fratellanza's set of slogans, oaths, and passwords bears a remarkable resemblance to the oath of the Fratelli Pugnalatori, a revolutionary sect created by Giambattista Falcone in 1857 (in Caso 1908: 9–10). Somehow, the oaths of these revolutionary brotherhoods had been preserved and transmitted, though we do not know whether the Fratellanza acquired their oath from the left-wing sects that were active in the Favara area throughout the 1860s, or whether they, like the Stoppagglieri, were drawing on popular fiction. (On the Fratellanza, see Lestingi 1884; Colacino 1885; De Luca 1897.)

The Fratellanza saw themselves as part of a network of revolutionary sects. According to their 'statute', if any 'brother' was sent by the '*capo*-in-chief' to another town, he was to present himself to the '*capo*' of that town and submit himself to a set of questions. He would be asked his name, where he came from, where he was 'made' (i.e., made a member), and the date of his initiation. The date was always 25 March. When asked who was at his initiation, he had to reply '*bona gente*' (good people). When asked who these 'good people' were, he was to make a circle with his hand, and say 'the honourable Fratellanza', whose membership was from 'three people to ninety million'.

The idea of 'the universal republic' and '*bona gente*' figures in much of the ritual of the Fratellanza. So does the date, 25 March. This is the festival of the Annunciation, and was used by the Fratellanza as the date of the commencement of the universal republic. In the initiation ritual, the candidate's finger was pricked, and a few drops of blood sprinkled upon a printed image of Santa Maria Annunziata. The image was then placed in the candidate's cupped hands and set alight. As it burnt, he repeated the following oath:

> I swear on my honour to be faithful to the Fratellanza just as the Fratellanza is faithful to me. And just as this saint and these few drops of blood burn, so will I pour out all of my blood for the Fratellanza. And just as these ashes cannot return to their original state, and this blood to its original state, so I can never leave the Fratellanza. (Colacino 1885: 178–9)

This initiation ceremony is striking for two reasons. First of all, the membership of the Fratellanza was estimated at around 500 (De Luca 1897). Even if we allow that a large proportion of these were probably coerced – local men who joined or contributed money under threat – the number is still far too large for a strictly criminal organization. Furthermore, the Fratellanza was linked to left-wing political factions in neighbouring towns (prefectural reports mention republican Masonic lodges in many of the surrounding towns). In this context, it is hard to maintain that the revolutionary political ideology and the initiation ceremony were nothing more than a cover for criminal activities. In the minds of many of its members at least, the Fratellanza was genuinely fighting for the republic of '*bona gente*'. The killings for which it was probably responsible fall into this pattern as well. The leaders of the Fratellanza wished to establish their control over the entire Favara area. This led to conflict with other political groups and working men's associations. The series of slayings were not connected to extortion, but were the result of vendettas with rival mutual-aid societies who were trying to extend their control over the same territory (Lestingi 1884: 455).

The second striking thing about the initiation ritual is that it is very similar to those used by Siculo-American gangsters in the twentieth century. In 1930, Joe Valachi was initiated into the Cosa Nostra by means of this ritual. In 1947, Jimmy Frattiano was initiated into Joe Dragna's family in Los Angeles by the same ritual (Maas 1969: 88; Demaris 1981: 1–3).

At the end of the 1920s, the leaders of various Siculo-American 'families' in the New York City area were brought together by the curious figure of 'Mr' Maranzano. An ex-seminarian and amateur historian from Castellamare in the province of Palermo, Maranzano tried to unite these families in a single organization. Although his organizational model was the Roman legion, a model which had also been used in Sicilian sects, he was well aware of the Sicilian dimension of the organization. The form of his association, and the ceremony of initiation all derived from Sicily's sectarian past. The name he chose to call it was well adapted: La Cosa Nostra – our, i.e., our 'Sicilian', thing (Maas 1969; Nelli 1976).

Under the leadership of Maranzano, and his more famous successor, Lucky Luciano, the American *mafia* continued to retain many of the trappings of a nineteenth-century secret society. Although the bosses of the Sicilian underworld in the United States were never the pasteboard villains of 'B' movies and television serials, by no stretch of the imagination could they be seen as political idealists or misguided adolescents. They were professional criminals. Why did they organize themselves in such seemingly inappropriate forms?

Personal vanity no doubt played a role. It is surely no coincidence that Joe Bonanno, who specifies that the 'Tradition' had its origins in a group of nobles in the Middle Ages, includes a picture of the Bonanno 'family crest' in his autobiography, together with a discussion of the Bonanno family's noble origins in the Middle Ages. Yet vanity is not the only possible reason. Another reason is that in living up to their imagined tradition, the American *mafia* was also trying to adhere (or seem to adhere) to a criminal 'code of honour'. This lent to their activities an air of legitimacy. But legitimate in the eyes of whom? The initiation ritual, as well as the passwords, were all secret. For whose benefit was the charade? Here it is perhaps not so much a case of the *mafia* posing as 'men of honour' before their community, as one of criminals playing at being '*mafia*'.

The various explanations all converge at a single point: the American *mafia* tried to behave in a way that they imagined to be consistent with their origins and traditions. They were doing more than retaining forms derived from the 'old country'; they were consciously commemorating themselves. We have seen that social memory is often anachronistic.

The past is remembered in the present, where the present provides the external context through which the past is interpreted. Yet the opposite is no less true: a society's view of the present can be anachronistic as well. Social memory is fixed in internal contexts – in images and stories. These images and stories stabilize social memory, allowing it to be transmitted. At the same time, the images, habits, and causal motifs that structure social memory provide a grid through which the present can be understood in terms of the remembered past. In preserving old forms, the *mafia* showed how the perception of the present can still be dominated by perspectives from the past.

Why should the *mafia* act out its own myth? By acting in a 'traditional way', groups often seek to validate their particular idea of the past. It is as if the past might be 'proved true' if commemorated assiduously enough. The strict commemoration of beliefs about the past seems to prove that these beliefs themselves are well founded. The past provides society with standards of what is good and what is real. Societies try to prove that these standards are true by living up to them. In so doing, they validate their beliefs. In this respect it does not matter whether the beliefs themselves are true or not. As in the motif of sexual honour restored, what matters is the meaning. The idealistic secret brotherhood of social avengers and Sicilian patriots is a myth; yet it is still a myth that, in one form or another, Sicilian society has continually sought to make true.

The 1943 Allied invasion came as a surprise to the Sicilian population. It had no precedent in recent Sicilian history, and this made it doubly difficult for Sicilians to understand. Sicilians were forced back onto their myths. Although the United States and Commonwealth troops came as liberators, they came from Africa and seemed to bring the '*Marocchini*' with them. The '*Marocchini*' tried to commit outrages, but they were stopped by the eternal defenders of Sicilian family honour, the *mafia*.

Sicilians later discovered that the United States government had contacted the Siculo-American gang leader Lucky Luciano in a New York state prison. This was another parallel. Had not the revolutionary forces sought the help of the leader of the underworld on other occasions? Had not the meeting taken place in a prison cell? Had it not been there that the uprising in Palermo had been planned? (cf. Gaja 1974, ch. 6).

All of these parallels were specious. The Allies had not used Moroccan troops in Sicily. The United States government had contacted Lucky Luciano about security on the New York docks, not about the invasion of Sicily. In any case, there was no uprising in Palermo in

Conclusion

through spiral upon spiral of the shell of memory that yet connects us
H.D.,
'The Flowering of the Rod'

In their effort to present memory as an object worthy of study, oral historians are sometimes led to heroic assumptions. The British oral historian, Ewart Evans has recently written that the life of the crofters in western Ireland is 'little different from the lives their ancestors lived in neolithic times', and that they are a 'people linked inextricably with the dawn of history' (1987: 2). This is the familiar image of a traditional community, cut off from the mainstream of time; a community where, as Ewart Evans himself puts it, 'their way of life and their thinking ... [are] only minimally affected by the town-based civilization.' Such communities seem to be the repository of a timeless folk wisdom, which is carefully preserved and faithfully transmitted across countless generations.

In reality, these images of unbroken continuity are usually illusions. The transmission of social memory is a process of evolution and change. These changes may be hidden from the community itself, however; for, to them, their stock of memories – their techniques, their stories, and their collective identities – seem to be things that have always remained the same. Yet this is only an appearance, a result of the continuous blotting out of memory as it changes. The process of change in a traditional, agrarian community may be slow; none the less, these communities are not outside history.

If memory cannot be taken either as the faithful bearer of knowledge,

1943. The parallels were not only specious, but also positively misleading in the real situation. The Allies and the Sicilians often could not
understand each other's intentions. The intention of the Allies was not
the conquest of Sicily; they arrived to fight the Axis powers. The
Sicilian understanding of the events of 1943 was anachronistic. In
an unprecedented and, often, incomprehensible external context, the
Sicilians experienced the present through the images of collective
memory.

One parallel was less specious, however. Separatism had been an issue
underlying nineteenth-century Sicilian politics. It was an issue associated with the *mafia* as well. In 1943, this issue reasserted itself. As had
often occurred before, in the vacuum created by a political collapse,
there grew up a movement that demanded the independence of Sicily.
Sicilian separatism was an issue that was also linked with the *mafia*, for
the myth of national identity portrayed the *mafiusu* as a Sicilian freedom
fighter. Thus, the organizers of the separatist movement, invoking the
legend of 1860 as a precedent, recruited the bandit Salvatore Giuliano
into their movement (Carcaci 1977: 167–70, 184–6, 219–25; Barbagallo
1974: 67–71).

The support that the Allies seemed, at first, to give to the separatists,
and the fact that the United States Navy had contacted Lucky Luciano,
were taken as proof of conspiracy. In reality, most of these parallels were
imaginary. The Sicilian independence movement was never controlled
by either the Sicilian or the American *mafia*. None the less, in the minds
of most Sicilians it was. By 1946, the leader of the separatists, Andrea
Finocchiaro-Aprile, had to accept the *mafia* label. Outside social
memory, he discovered, Sicilian history and Sicilian politics were not
comprehensible to Sicilians themselves. If the *mafia* did not exist, he
observed, it would be necessary to invent it.

or even as the record of past experience, can it be of any further interest to the historian? The answer is very simple: behind the display of knowledge and the representation of experience, behind the facts, emotions, and images with which memory seems to be filled, there is only we ourselves. It is we who are remembering, and it is to us that the knowledge, emotions, and images ultimately refer. What is concealed in models of memory as a surface whereupon knowledge or experience is transcribed is our own presence in the background. Whatever memory may be as a purely neurological or purely epistemological object in itself, we can neither know nor experience our memories unless we can first 'think' them; and the moment we 'think' our memories, recalling and articulating them, they are no longer objects; they become part of us. At that moment, we find ourselves indissolubly in their centre.

Only by making memories part of us, first, can we share them with others. Historians are thus right to display little interest in purely theoretical accounts of memory in itself. Memory becomes vital to them only when it is in context; for it is at this point that their story begins. The only sort of theoretical account likely to be of use to historians is, therefore, one that describes what happens when memory comes to the surface, and what happens when we think, articulate, and transmit our memories. This book has therefore concentrated on describing what memory does. Memory has an immense social role. It tells us who we are, embedding our present selves in our pasts, and thus underpinning every aspect of what historians often now call *mentalités*. For many groups, this means putting the puzzle back together: inventing the past to fit the present, or, equally, the present to fit the past. We preserve the past at the cost of decontextualizing it, and partially blotting it out.

We saw that the resequencing, decontextualizing, and suppressing of social memory in order to give it new meaning is itself a social process, and one, moreover, whose history is sometimes recoverable. Luc de Heusch makes an interesting comment: 'The Congolese myths,' he writes, 'are exchanged like merchandise. But they have, properly speaking, no value. They are not the products of labor, and they defy all attempts at appropriation, whether private or collective.... They even elude the ideological function that kings invariably try to force on them' (1982: 247). The transmission and diffusion of the images and stories of social memory is a no less unlikely form of commerce. These images are untouched by the hand of any painter; these stories cannot bear a copyright. The trade is, in fact, nothing more than the exchange of ideas. Yet, for all that these ideas are intangible, their transmission and diffusion is still a real process. Social memory seems indeed to be subject to the law of supply and demand. Memories must be supplied;

they must emerge at specific points. Yet, to survive beyond the immediate present, and, especially, to survive in transmission and exchange, they must also meet a demand. A tradition survives in an oikotypical version because, to the group that remembers it, only this version seems to fit. Behind this sense of 'fit' can be sociological, cultural, ideological, or historical factors. One task that oral historians could set themselves is to explain how and why certain traditions fit the memories of certain groups.

The history of social memory is also the history of its transmission. We saw in French social memory that the image of Roland passed through the Wars of Religion, the Revolution, and even the Resistance. There is nothing surprising in this. As long as the story of Roland itself survived, his image would always be remembered as personifying heroic courage and valour in the face of desperate odds. Roland voyaged with the conquistadores and the settlers to the New World as well. Here, he served as part of the raw material from which innumerable local legends were forged. A society needs its heroes; and Roland is one of the many that Western culture has invented to meet this demand. A society needs its villains, too – if only to keep the heroes busy. Thus, in North America, the heroic Roland might meet the treacherous Ganelon in the Hollywood version of the Italo-American gangster. From the puppet theatre to the big screen, from the fervid freedom fighter on the barricades of Palermo to 'Little Caesar', dying as he gasps, 'Is this the end of ... Rico?', the image of the *mafioso* has also travelled far. The changes that it has suffered in this trajectory are partly sociocultural and partly technological. The myth has turned into cinema. Here may be another story worth the telling for the light it sheds on North America's historical experience in the first half of the twentieth century.

Memories die, but only to be replaced by other memories. In attempting to explain what the images and stories in social memory really mean, we saw a tendency to slide from one topos to another, or else merely to rationalize the images and stories by recontextualizing them into other forms. We may sometimes, it seems, only be deluding ourselves when we think we are 'debunking' social memory by separating myth from fact: all we may get is another story. This does not mean that we must accept social memory passively and uncritically. We can enter into dialogue with it, examining its arguments, and testing its factual claims. But this interrogation cannot uncover the whole truth. It is a mistake to imagine that, having squeezed it for its facts, examined its arguments, and reconstructed its experiences, – that is to say, having turned it into 'history' – we are through with memory.

References

Abraham, D.P., 1964. 'Ethno-history of the empire of Mutapa'. In Vansina et al. 1964: 104–26.

Abrahams, R.D., 1968. 'Introductory remarks to a rhetorical theory of folklore', *Journal of American Folklore*, vol. LXXXI, 143–58.

Actes 1981. *Actes de la recherche en sciences sociales* 1981. Vol. XL.

Ajello, A., 1868. *Angelo Pugliese: ovvero don Peppino il Lombardo*. Palermo.

Alatri, P., 1954. *Lotte politiche in Sicilia sotto il governo della Destra*. Turin.

Alessio, G.C. (ed.), 1982. *Cronaca di Novalesa*. Turin.

Alexander, M., 1966. *The Earliest English Poems*. London.

Allport, F.H., 1955. *Theories of Perception and the Concept of Structure*. New York.

Alongi, G., 1886. *La Maffia*. Turin, reprinted Palermo, 1977.

Amari, M., 1882. *Racconto popolare del Vespro Siciliano*. Palermo, reprinted Palermo, 1982.

Amico, G.G., 1972. *Codice segreto della Mafia*. Milan.

Andersson, T.M., 1964. *The Problem of Icelandic Saga Origins*. New Haven, CT.

Andersson, T.M. and Miller, W.I., 1989. *Law and Literature in Medieval Iceland*. Stanford, CA.

Anido, N., 1980. '*Pajadas* et *desafíos* dans le Rio Grande do Sul: le défi effronté d'une littérature orale partie à la conquête de l'immortalité', *Cahiers de littérature orale*, vol. V, 142–71.

Anthropologie criminelle 1901. *Ve Congrès international d'anthropologie criminelle*. Amsterdam.

Ardener, S. (ed.), 1975. *Perceiving Women*. London.

Aron-Schnapper, I.D. and Hanet, D., 1980. 'D'Hérodote au magnétophone: sources orales et archives orales', *Annales ESC*, vol. XXXV, 183–99.

Armstrong, R.G., 1964. 'The use of linguistic and ethnographic data in the study of Idoma and Yoruba history'. In Vansina et al. 1964: 127–44.

Aschieri, L., 1985. *Le Passé recomposé*. Marseille.

Asor-Rosa, A., 1966. *Scrittori e popolo*. Rome.

Attanasio, S., 1976. *Sicilia senza Italia: luglio-agosto 1943*. Milan.

204   REFERENCES

Auerbach, E., 1953. *Mimesis*. Princeton, NJ.

Austin, J.L., 1946. 'Other minds', *Proceedings of the Aristotelian Society*, supp. XX: 148–87.

Autrand, F., 1977. 'Les dates, la mémoire et les juges'. In B. Guenée (ed.), *Le Métier d'historien au moyen âge*, Paris, pp. 157–82.

Azevedo, J.L.d', 1947. *A evolução do Sebastianismo*. 2nd edn, Lisbon.

Baczko, B., 1984. *Les Imaginaires sociaux*. Paris.

Baddeley, A.D., 1976. *The Psychology of Memory*. New York.

—— 1990. 'The psychology of remembering and forgetting'. In T. Butler (ed.), *Memory*, Oxford, pp. 33–60.

Barbagallo, S., 1974. *Una rivoluzione mancata*. Catania.

Barthes, R., 1966. 'L'introduction à l'analyse structurelle des récits', *Communications*, vol. VIII, 1–27.

—— 1970. 'L'ancienne rhétorique, aide-mémoire', *Communications*, vol. XVI, 172–229.

Bartlett, F.C., 1932. *Remembering*. Cambridge.

Bathily, A., 1975. 'A discussion of the traditions of Wagadu with some reference to ancient Ghana', *Bulletin de l'Institut fondamental d'Afrique noire*, sér. B, vol. XXXVII, part 1, 1–94.

Bauml, F.H., 1980. 'Varieties and consequences of medieval literacy and illiteracy', *Speculum*, vol. LV, 237–65.

Baxandall, M., 1971. *Giotto and the Orators*. Oxford.

Bazin, J., 1979. 'La production d'un récit historique', *Cahiers d'études africaines*, vol. XIX (73–6), 435–83.

Beidelman, T.O., 1970. 'Myth, legend and oral history', *Anthropos*, vol. LXV, 74–97.

Beidelman, T.O. and Finnegan, R., 1972. 'Approaches to the study of African oral literature', *Africa*, vol. XLII, 140–7.

Bell, D.H., 1986. *Sesto San Giovanni*. New Brunswick.

Belmont, N., 1984. 'Mythologie des métiers: à propos de "Légendes et curiosités des métiers" de Paul Sebillot', *Ethnologie française*, vol. XIV, 45–56.

Benediktsson, J., 1986. *Íslendingabók. Landnámabók*. Reykjavík.

Bennison, G., 1968. 'Repetition in oral literature', *Journal of American Folklore*, vol. LXXXI, 289–303.

Bercé, Y.-M., 1974. *Histoire des Croquants*. Geneva.

—— 1987. *Revolt and Revolution in Early Modern Europe*. Manchester.

Berktay, H., 1990. 'The rise and current impasse of Turkish nationalist historiography', *Periplus*.

Berlin, I., 1960. 'History and theory. The concept of scientific history', *History and Theory*, vol. I, 1–31.

Bernardi, B., Poni, C. and Triulzi, A. (eds), 1978. *Fonti orali – oral sources – sources orales*. Milan.

Bertaux, D. and Bertaux-Wiame I., 1980. 'Autobiographische Erinnerung und kollektives Gedächtnis'. In L. Niethammer (ed.), *Lebenserfahrung und kollektives Gedächtnis*, Frankfurt, pp. 108–22.

Bertaux-Wiame, I., 1982. 'The life history approach to the study of internal migration'. In P. Thompson (ed.), *Our Common History*, London, pp. 186–200.

—— 1985. 'Jours paisibles à Sèvres', *Life Stories/Récits de vie*, vol. I, 16–28.

Bertolotti, M., 1979. 'Le ossa e la pelle dei buoi. Un mito popolare fra agiografia e stregoneria', *Quaderni storici*, vol. XLI, 470–99.

Bethmann, L. and Waitz, G. (eds), 1878. *Scriptores rerum langobardicarum et italicarum saec. VI–IX*. Hannover.

Beumann, H., 1951. 'Topos und Gedankengefüge bei Einhard', *Archiv für Kulturgeschichte*, vol. XXXIII, 337–50.

Bishop, P. and Mallie, E., 1987. *The Provisional IRA*. London.

Black-Michaud, J., 1975. *Cohesive Force*. Oxford.

Bloch, M., 1961. *Feudal Society*. London.

Bohannan, L., 1952. 'A genealogical charter', *Africa*, vol. XXII, 301–15.

Bonanno, J., 1983. *A Man of Honor*. New York.

Bonheur, G., 1963. *Qui a cassé le vase de Soissons?* Paris.

Bonnain, R. and Elegoët, F., 1978. 'Les archives orales: pour quoi faire?', *Ethnologie française* vol. VIII, 348–55.

Bonnain-Moerdyk, R. and Moerdyk, D., 1977. 'A propos du chiavari; discours bourgeois et coutumes populaires', *Annales ESC*, vol. XXXII, 381–98.

Bonte, P. and Echard, N., 1976. 'Histoire et histoires. Conception du passé chez les Hausa et les Twareg Kel Gress de l'Ader (République du Niger)', *Cahiers d'études africaines*, vol. XVI (61–4), 237–96.

Bordone, R., 1988. 'Memoria del tempo negli abitanti dei comuni italiani all 'età di Barbarossa'. In *Il tempo vissuto*, Bologna, pp. 47–62.

Borges, J.L., 1956. *Ficciones*. Buenos Aires.

Bosi, E., 1979. *Memória e sociedade. Lembranças de velhos*. São Paulo.

Bosio, G., 1981. *Il trattore ad Acquanegra*. Bari.

Bottéro, J., 1974. 'Symptômes, signes, écritures en Mésopotamie ancienne'. In J. Vernant et al., *Divination et rationalité*, Paris, pp. 70–197.

—— 1987. *Mésopotamie: L'écriture, la raison et les dieux*. Paris.

Bourdieu, P., 1977. *Outline of a Theory of Practice*. Cambridge.

Bouvier, J.C., 1980. *La mémoire partagée. Lus-la-Croix-Haute (Drôme)*. Valence.

Bouvier, J.C., Bremondy, H.P. and Joutard, P., 1980. *Tradition orale et identité culturelle. Problèmes et méthodes*. Paris.

Bozon, M. and Thiesse, A.-M., 1986. 'The collapse of memory: the case of farm workers (French Vexin, pays de France)', *History and Anthropology*, vol. II, part 2, 237–59.

Brancato, F., 1953. 'Origini e carattere della rivolta palermitana del settembre 1866', *Archivio storico siciliano*, 3 ser., vol. V, part 1, 139–205.

—— 1956. *La storia della Sicilia post-unificazione*. Vol. I, *Il primo ventennio*. Palermo.

—— 1958. 'Mafia e brigantaggio', *Quaderni del Meridione* vol. I, part 3, 326–8; part 4, 415–20.

—— 1964. 'Genesi e psicologia della mafia', *Nuovi quaderni del Meridione*, vol. II, part 5, 5–27.

——1972. 'La mafia nell'opinione pubblica e nelle inchieste dall'Unità al Fascismo'. In *Commissione parlamentare d'inchiesta sul fenomeno della mafia in Sicilia*, doc XXIII, 2 septies, Rome.

Brault, G.J., 1978. *The Song of Roland. An Analytical Edition*. Vol. I. London.

Bravo, A., 1982a. 'Italian peasant women and the First World War'. In P. Thompson (ed.), *Our Common History*, London, pp. 157–70.

——1982b. 'Solidarity and loneliness: Piedmontese peasant women at the turn of the century', *International Journal of Oral History*, vol. III, part 2, 76–91.

Bravo, A. and Scaraffia, L., 1979. 'Ruolo femminile e identità nelle contadine delle Langhe', *Rivista di storia contemporanea*, vol. VIII, 21–55.

Bravo, A., Passerini, L. and Piccone Stella, S., 1982. 'Modi di raccontarsi e forme di identità nelle storie di vita', *Memoria*, vol. VIII, part 2, 101–13.

Bremond, C., 1977. 'The clandestine ox: transformations of an African tale', *New Literary History*, vol. VIII, 393–410.

——1979. 'Morphologie d'un conte africain', *Cahiers d'études africaines*, vol. XIX (73–6), 485–99.

Brooke, C.N.L., 1976. 'Geoffrey of Monmouth as a historian'. In idem et al. (eds), *Church and Government in the Middle Ages*, Cambridge, pp. 77–91.

Brown, P.R.L., 1977. *Relics and Social Status in the Age of Gregory of Tours*. Reading.

——1981. *The Cult of the Saints*. London.

Bulletin 1982. *Bulletin de l'Institut d'histoire du temps présent*, supp. III.

Burke, P., 1978. *Popular Culture in Early Modern Europe*. Aldershot.

Butterfield, H., 1931. *The Whig Interpretation of History*. London.

Buttitta, A. (ed.), 1968. *Il convegno di studi per il 52° anniversario della morte di Giuseppe Pitrè*. Palermo.

Bynum, C.W., 1984. 'Women's stories, women's symbols'. In R.L. Moore and F.E. Reynolds (eds), *Anthropology and the Study of Religion*, Chicago, pp. 105–25.

——1987. *Holy Feast and Holy Fast*. Berkeley, CA.

Byock, J.L., 1982. *Feud in the Icelandic Saga*. Berkeley, CA.

——1986. 'The age of the Sturlungs', in E. Vestergaard (ed.), *Continuity and Change*, Odense, pp. 27–42.

——1988. *Medieval Iceland*. Berkeley, CA.

Cabré, M., 1990. *El monacat femení a la Barcelona de l'Alta edat mitjana: Sant Pere de les Puel.les*. Barcelona.

Cadorna, G.R., 1988. 'Il sapere dello scriba'. In Rossi 1988b: 3–28.

Caggiano, G., 1950. *Mala vita*. Milan.

Cammarata, F., 1969. *Pupi e mafia*. Palermo.

Campbell, J., 1986. *Winston Churchill's Afternoon Nap*. New York.

Cantel, R., 1980. 'De Roland à Lampião ou la littérature populaire du Nordeste brésilien', *Cahiers de littérature orale*, vol. V, 27–63.

Capuana, L., 1892. *La Sicilia e il brigantaggio*. Rome.

Carcaci (Francesco Paternò Castello, duca di Carcaci), 1977. *Il movimento per l'indipendenza della Sicilia*. Palermo.

Casey, E.S., 1987. *Remembering*. Bloomington, IN.

Caso, G., 1908. *Giambattista Falcone e la setta dei Fratelli Pugnalatori*. Foggia.

Cavallo, G., 1988. 'Cultura scritta e conservazione del sapere: dalla Grecia antica all'Occidente medievale'. In Rossi 1988b: 29–67.

Chadwick, H.M., 1912. *The Heroic Age*. Cambridge.

Chandler, B.J., 1978. *The Bandit King. Lampião of Brazil*. College Station, TX.

Chavanon, J. (ed.), 1897. Adémar de Chabannes, *Chronique*. Paris.

Cingolani, S., 1991. '"Pur remenbrer des ancessurs"'. In G. Severino and F. Simoni (eds), *Storiografia e poesia nella cultura medioevale*.

Cirese, A.M., 1968. 'Giuseppe Pitrè; storia locale e antropologia'. In Buttitta 1988: 19–51.

Ciuni, R., 1979. 'Un secolo di Mafia'. In *Storia di Sicilia*, vol. IX, Naples.

Clanchy, M.T., 1970. 'Remembering the past and the good old law', *History*, vol. LV, 165–76.

—— 1979. *From Memory to Written Record*. London.

Cohen, D.W., 1989. 'The undefining of oral tradition', *Ethnohistory*, vol. XXXVI, 9–18.

Cohen, G., 1976. 'Visual imagery in thought', *New Literary History*, vol. VII, 513–23.

Colacino, T.V., 1885. 'La Fratellanza: associazione di malafattori', *Rivista di discipline carcerarie*, pp. 177–89.

Colajanni, N., 1885. *La delinquenzia della Sicilia, e le sue cause*. Palermo.

—— 1900. *Nel regno della Mafia*. Palermo, reprinted Palermo 1971.

Collard, A., 1989. 'Investigating "social memory" in a Greek context'. In E. Tonkin et al. (eds), *History and Ethnicity*, London, pp. 89–103.

Collins, R.J.H., 1983. 'Theodebert I, "rex magnus Francorum"'. In C.P. Wormald (ed.), *Ideal and Reality in Frankish and Anglo-Saxon Society*, Oxford, pp. 7–33.

Collomb, G., 1982. 'Le discours de la légende et le discours de l'histoire', *Le monde alpin et rhodanien*, vol. X, 89–99.

Commager, H.S., 1967. *The Search for a Usable Past*. New York.

Connerton, P., 1989. *How Societies Remember*. Cambridge.

Conrad, D.C., 1985. 'Islam in the oral traditions of Mali: Bilali and Surakata', *Journal of African History*, vol. XXVI, 33–49.

Cook, R.F., 1987. *The Sense of the 'Song of Roland'*. Ithaca, NY.

Costanza, S., 1964. 'Una inchiesta poco nota sulla mafia', *Nuovi quaderni del Meridione*, vol. II, part 5, 52–8.

Courtès, J., 1972. 'De la description à la spécificité du conte populaire merveilleux français', *Ethnologie française*, vol. II, 9–42.

Crépeau, P., 1978. 'The invading guest: some aspects of oral transmission', *Yearbook of Symbolic Anthropology*, vol. I, 11–29.

Crespi, P., 1979. *Capitale operaia*. Milan.

Cressy, D., 1989. *Bonfires and Bells*. London.

Croce, B., 1970. *History of the Kingdom of Naples*. Eng. trans., Chicago.

Crowley, D.J., 1969. 'The uses of African verbal art', *Journal of the Folklore Institute*, vol. VI, 118–32.

Cunnison, I., 1951. *History on the Luapula*. Rhodes-Livingstone Papers XXI. Oxford.

Curtin, P.D., 1969. 'Oral tradition and African history', *Journal of the Folklore Institute*, vol. VI, 137–55.

—— 1975. 'The uses of oral tradition in Senegambia: Maalik Sii and the foundation of Bundu', *Cahiers d'études africaines*, vol. XV (57–60), 189–202.

Curtius, E.R., 1967. *European Literature and the Latin Middle Ages*. Eng. trans., Princeton, NJ.

Cutrera, A., 1896. *I Ricottari*. Palermo, reprinted Palermo 1979.

—— 1900. *La Mafia e i mafiosi*. Palermo.

Dahl, N.A., 1948. 'Anamnesis. Mémoire et commémoration dans le christianisme primitif', *Studia Theologica*, vol. I, part 4, 69–95.

Dakhlia, J., 1987. 'Des prophètes à la nation: la mémoire des temps anté-islamiques au Maghreb', *Cahiers d'études africaines*, vol. XXVII (105–8), 241–67.

—— 1990. *L'Oubli de la cité*. Paris.

Darnton, R., 1984. *The Great Cat Massacre*. London.

D'Asdia, A., 1980. Introduction to Scalici 1980.

Davis, J., 1974. 'How they hid the red flag in Pisticci in 1923, and how it was betrayed'. In idem (ed.), *Choice and Change*, London, pp. 44–67.

Davis, N.Z., 1975. *Society and Culture in Early Modern France*. Stanford, CA.

Debouzy, M., 1986. 'In search of working-class memory: some questions and a tentative assessment', *History and Anthropology*, vol. II, part 2, 261–82.

De Certeau, M., Julia, D. and Revel, J., 1970. 'La beauté du mort: le concept de "culture populaire"', *Politique aujourd'hui* (dec 1970), pp. 3–23.

de Heusch, L., 1977. 'Mythologie et littérature', *L'Homme*, vol. XVII, parts 2–3, 101–9.

—— 1982. *The Drunken King; or, The Origin of the State*. Eng. trans., Bloomington, IN.

Delano Smith, C., 1987. 'Cartography in the prehistoric period in the Old World: Europe, the Middle East and North Africa'. In Harley and Woodward 1987: 54–101.

Delehaye, H., 1961. *The Legends of the Saints*. Notre Dame, IN.

De Luca, F., 1897. 'Favara', *Scuola positiva*, vol. VII, part 4, 434–45.

Demaris, O., 1981. *The Last Mafioso: The Treacherous World of Jimmy Fratianno*. New York.

Dennett, D.C., 1979. *Brainstorms*. Hassocks.

Dennis, A., Foote, P. and Perkins, R. (trans.), 1980. *Laws of Early Iceland: Grágás*, vol. I. Winnipeg.

Detienne, M., 1981. *L'Invention de la mythologie*. Paris.

Di Matteo, A., 1967. *Cronache di un quinquennio: anni roventi, la Sicilia dal 1943 al 1947*. Palermo.

Dolci, D., 1963. *Waste*. Trans. R. Munroe, London.

Donald, D., 1961. *Lincoln Reconsidered*. New York.

Doria, G., 1935. *Storia di un capitale*. Naples.

Dorson, R.M., 1971. 'Sources for the traditional history of the Scottish Highlands and Western Islands', *Journal of the Folklore Institute*, vol. VIII, 147–84.

Douglas, D., 1960. 'The "Song of Roland" and the Norman conquest of England', *French Studies*, vol. XIV, 99–116.

Douglass, D., 1981. '"Worms of the earth": the miners' own story'. In R. Samuel (ed.), *People's History and Socialist Theory*, London, pp. 61–7.

Dournes, J., 1976. *Le Parler des Jörai et le style oral de leur expression*. Paris.

Dronke, P., 1984. *Women Writers of the Middle Ages*. Cambridge.

Dronke, U., 1981. '*Sem jarlar forðum*. The influence of *Rígsþula* on two saga-episodes'. In idem et al. (ed.), *Speculum Norroenum*, Odense, pp. 56–73.

Dubar, C., Gayot, G. and Hédoux, J., 1982. 'Sociabilité minière et changement social à Sallaumines et à Noyelles-sous-Lens (1900–1980)', *Revue du Nord*, vol. LXIV, 365–463.

Du Boulay, F.R.H., 1981. 'The German town chronicles'. In R.H.C. Davis and J. M. Wallace-Hadrill (eds), *The Writing of History in the Middle Ages*, Oxford, pp. 445–69.

Duby, G., 1973. *Hommes et structures du Moyen Age*. Paris.

—— 1988. *Mâle Moyen Age*. Paris.

Dumézil, G., 1987. *Du mythe au roman*. 3rd edn, Paris.

Dunbabin, J., 1991. 'Aristocratic families and their perception of the past in twelfth-century France'. In P. Magdalino (ed.), *The Perception of the Past in Twelfth-century Europe*.

Dundes, A., 1971. 'Folk ideas as units of world-view', *Journal of American Folklore*, vol. LXXXIV, 93–104.

—— (ed.) 1982. *Cinderella: A Folklore Casebook*. New York.

Durkheim, E. and Mauss, M., 1963. *Primitive Classification*. Trans. R. Needham, Chicago.

Duverdier, G., 1971. 'La pénétration du livre dans une société de culture orale: le cas de Tahiti', *Revue française d'histoire du livre*, N.S., vol. I, 27–53.

Eco, U. and Sebeok, T.A. (eds), 1983. *The Sign of Three*. Bloomington, IN.

Eickelmann, D.F., 1978. 'The art of memory: Islamic education and its social reproduction', *Comparative Studies in Society and History*, vol. XX, 485–516.

Ellis, J.M., 1983. *One Fairy Story Too Many*. Chicago.

Engels, F., 1891/1968. *The Origin of the Family, Private Property and the State*. In K. Marx and F. Engels, *Selected Works*, London, pp. 455–593.

Evans-Pritchard, E.E., 1937. *Witchcraft, Oracles and Magic among the Azande*. Oxford.

—— 1965. *Theories of Primitive Religion*. Oxford.

Ewart Evans, G., 1987. *Spoken History*. London.

Faith, R., 1981. 'The class struggle in fourteenth-century England'. In R. Samuel (ed.), *People's History and Socialist Theory*, London, pp. 50–60.

—— 1984. 'The "Great Rumour" of 1377 and peasant ideology'. In R.H. Hilton and T.H. Aston (eds), *The English Rising of 1381*, Cambridge, pp. 43–73.

Falassi, A., 1980. *Folklore by the Fireside*. Austin, TX.

Falcionelli, A., 1936. *Les Sociétés secrètes italiennes*. Paris.

Falzone, G., 1975. *Storia della Mafia*. Milan.

Farinelli, G. and Paccagnini E., 1989. *Processo per stregoneria a Caterina de Medici 1616–1617*. Milan.

Fasoli, G., 1967. 'Carlo Magno nelle tradizioni storico-leggendarie italiane'. In W. Braunfels and P.E. Schramm (eds), *Karl der Grosse*, vol. IV, Düsseldorf, pp. 348–63.

Faulkes, A.R. (trans.), 1987. Snorri Sturluson, *Edda*. London.

Febvre, L., and Martin, H.-J., 1958. *L'Apparition du livre*. Paris.

Ferretti, R., 1989. *L'immaginario collettivo sui monti di Castiglione: il ciclo folklorico di S. Guglielmo*. Castiglione della Pescaia.

Filippini Cappelletto, N., 1983. *Noi, quelle dei campi*. Turin.

Finnegan, R., 1977. *Oral Poetry*. Cambridge.

—— 1988. *Literacy and Orality*. Oxford.

Fischer, R., 1979. 'Mémoire et prédiction: pour une psycho-biologie de la divination', *Diogene*, vol. CVIII, 22–46.

Flint, V.I.J., 1979. 'The *Historia regum Britanniae* of Geoffrey of Monmouth: parody and its purpose', *Speculum*, vol. LIV, 447–68.

Foisil, M., 1970. *La Révolte des Nu-Pieds*. Paris.

Folz, R., 1950. *Le Souvenir et la légende de Charlemagne dans l'empire germanique médiéval*. Paris.

Forty, A., 1986. *Objects of Desire*. London.

Fourcaut, A., 1987. 'Mémoires de la "banlieue rouge". Occultation du mythe et inversion des images'. Unpublished paper read to the Sixth International Oral History Conference, Oxford, 11–13 Sept. 1987.

Francis, H., 1985. 'The law, oral tradition and the mining community', *Journal of Law and Society*, vol. XII, 267–71.

Frank, R., 1978. *Old Norse Court Poetry. Islandica*, vol. XLII. Ithaca, NY.

Frisch, M., 1972. 'Oral history and Hard Times', *Red Buffalo*, vols II–III, 217–31.

—— 1990. *A Shared Authority*. Albany, NY.

Fussell, P., 1975. *The Great War and Modern Memory*. Oxford.

Gagnon, N., 1981. 'On the analysis of life accounts'. In D. Bertaux (ed.), *Biography and Society*, Beverly Hills, CA, 47–60.

Gaja, F., 1974. *L'esercito della lupara*. Milan.

Ganci, S.M., 1968. *L'Italia anti-moderata*. Parma.

Ganshof, F.L., 1971. *The Carolingians and the Frankish Monarchy*. London.

Gardner, H., 1985. *The Mind's New Science*. New York.

Gentili, B., 1983. 'Oralità e scrittura in Grecia'. In Vegetti 1983: 30–53.

Gérard, A., 1970. *La Révolution française, mythes et interprétations (1789–1970)*. Paris.

Giarrizzo, G., 1970. 'Sicilia politica 1943–1945', *Archivio storico per la Sicilia orientale*, vol. LXVI, parts 1–2, 9–279.

Gibson, J.J., 1950. *The Perception of the Visual World*. Boston, MA.

Gilson, E., 1932. 'Michel Menot et la technique du sermon médiéval'. In idem, *Les Idées et les lettres*, Paris, pp. 93–154.

Ginzburg, C., 1980. *The Cheese and the Worms*. London.

—— 1988. *Storia notturna: una decifrazione del sabba*. Turin.

Giornale di Sicilia, 1878. *Profili e fotografie per collezione*. Palermo.

Goffart, W., 1988. *The Narrators of Barbarian History (AD 550–800)*. Princeton, NJ.

Gombrich, E.H., 1980. *Art and Illusion. A Study in the Psychology of Pictorial Representation*. Revised edn, Oxford.

Goody, J. (ed.), 1968. *Literacy in Traditional Societies*. Cambridge.

—— 1977. *The Domestication of the Savage Mind*. Cambridge.

—— 1978. 'Oral tradition and the reconstruction of the past in Northern Ghana'. In Bernardi et al. 1978: 285–95.

—— 1986. *The Logic of Writing and the Organization of Society*. Cambridge.

—— 1987. *The Interface between the Written and the Oral*. Cambridge.

Goubert, P. and Denis, M., 1964. *1789. Les Français ont la parole* .... Paris.

Gough, R., 1981. *The History of Myddle*, ed. D. Hey. London.

Gramsci, A., 1971. *Selections from the Prison Notebooks*. Trans. Q. Hoare and G. Nowell Smith. London.

—— 1991. *Letteratura e vita nazionale*. Rome.

Gregory, R.L., 1984. *Mind in Science*. London.

Greimas, A., 1966. *Sémantique structurale*. Paris.

Greimas, A. and Courtès, J., 1976. 'The cognitive dimension of narrative discourse', *New Literary History*, vol. VII, 433–47.

Grele, R.J., 1985. *Envelopes of Sound. The Art of Oral History*. 2nd edn, Chicago.

Gribaudi, M., 1987. *Mondo operaio e mito operaio*. Turin.

Guenée, B., 1978. 'Les généalogies entre l'histoire et la politique: la fierté d'être Capetien, en France, au Moyen Age', *Annales ESC.*, vol. XXXIII, 450–77.

—— 1980. *Histoire et culture historique dans l'occident médiéval*. Paris.

Gurevič, A.J., 1986. *Contadini e santi: problemi della cultura popolare nel Medioevo*. Ital. trans., Turin.

Häfele, H.F. (ed.), 1962. Notker der Stammler, *Taten Karls des Grossen*. Berlin.

Halbwachs, M., 1925. *Les Cadres sociaux de la mémoire*. Paris.

—— 1941. *La Topographie légendaire des Evangiles en Terre Sainte*. Paris.

—— 1950. *La Mémoire collective*. Paris.

—— 1980. *The Collective Memory*. New York. Trans. of Halbwachs 1950.

Halphen, L. and Poupardin R. (eds), 1913. *Croniques des comtes d'Anjou et des seigneurs d'Amboise*. Paris.

Hanning, R.W., 1966. *The Vision of History in Early Britain*. New York.

Harley, J.B. and Woodward, D. (eds), 1987. *The History of Cartography*, I. *Cartography in Prehistoric, Ancient and Medieval Europe and the Mediterranean*. Chicago.

Hastrup, K., 1984. 'Defining a society: the Icelandic free state between two worlds', *Scandinavian Studies*, vol. LVI, 235–55.

—— 1990. *Island of Anthropology*. Odense.

Havelock, E.A., 1963. *Preface to Plato*. Oxford.

—— 1978. *The Greek Concept of Justice*. Cambridge, MA.

—— 1982. *The Literate Revolution in Greece and its Cultural Consequences*. Princeton, NJ.

Henige, D.P., 1974. *The Chronology of Oral Tradition. Quest for a Chimera*. Oxford.

—— 1982. *Oral Historiography*. London.

Hermannsson, H., 1930. *The Book of the Icelanders (Íslendingabók) by Ari Thorgilsson. Islandica*, vol. XX, Ithaca, NY.

Herzfeld, M., 1982. *Ours Once More*. Austin, TX.

Hess, H., 1973. *Mafia and Mafiosi: The Structure of Power*. Eng. trans., London.

Hey, D.G., 1974. *An English Rural Community. Myddle under the Tudors and Stuarts*. Leicester.

Heyd, U., 1954. *Language Reform in Modern Turkey*. Jerusalem.

Hill, C., 1958. *Puritanism and Revolution*. London.

Hilton, R.H., 1985. *Class Conflict and the Crisis of Feudalism*. London.

Hobsbawm, E.J., 1959. *Primitive Rebels*. Manchester.

—— 1972a. *Bandits*. 2nd edn, London.

—— 1972b. 'The social function of the past: some questions', *Past and Present*, vol. LV (1972), 3–17.

—— 1983. 'Mass-producing traditions: Europe, 1870–1914'. In Hobsbawm and Ranger 1983: 263–307.

Hobsbawm, E.J. and Ranger, T. (eds), 1983. *The Invention of Tradition*. Cambridge.

Hofstadter, D.R. and Dennett, D.C. (eds), 1982. *The Mind's I*. London.

Holder-Egger, O. (ed.), 1911. *Einhardi Vita Karoli Magni*. Hannover.

Horn, K., 1974. 'L'Arbre secourable dans le conte populaire allemande', *Ethnologie française*, vol. IV, 333–48.

Horton, R., 1967. 'African traditional thought and Western science', *Africa*, vol. XXXVII, 50–71, 155–87.

—— 1971. 'Stateless societies in the history of West Africa'. In J.F.A. Ajayi and M. Crowder (eds), *History of West Africa*, vol. I, London, pp. 72–113.

Hume, D., 1739. *Treatise of Human Nature*. Standard edns.

Ifeka-Moller, C., 1975. 'Female militancy and colonial revolt'. In Ardener 1975: 127–57.

Illich, I. and Sanders, B., 1989. *A.B.C.: The Alphabetization of the Popular Mind*. London.

Ivey, W. 1970. '"The 1913 disaster": Michigan local legend', *Folklore Forum*, vol. III, 100–14.

Jackson, K.H., 1964. *The Oldest Irish Tradition*. Cambridge.

Jakobson, R. and Bogatyrev P., 1973. 'Le folklore, forme spécifique de la création'. In R. Jakobson, *Questions de poétique*, Paris, pp. 59–72.

James, E., 1988. *The Franks*. Oxford.

Jameson, R.D., 1982. 'Cinderella in China'. In Dundes 1982: 71–97.

Jewsiewicki, B., 1986. 'Collective memory and the stakes of power: a reading of popular Zarian historical sources', *History in Africa*, vol. XIII, 195–223.

Jewsiewicki, B. and Moniot, H., 1987. 'Presentation', *Cahiers d'études africaines*, vol. XVII (105–8), 235–40.

Johnson, R. with Dawson, G., 1982. 'Popular memory: theory, politics, method'. In Centre for Contemporary Cultural Studies, *Making Histories*, London, pp. 205–52.

Johnston, G. and Foote P., 1963. *The Saga of Gisli*. London.

Jones, P.M., 1988. *The Peasantry in the French Revolution*. Cambridge.

Jonin, P., 1979. *Le Chanson de Roland*. Paris.

Joutard, P., Estèbe, J., Labrousse, E. and Lecuir, J., 1976. *La Saint-Barthélemy, ou les résonances d'un massacre*. Neuchâtel.

Joutard, P., 1977a. *La Légende des Camisards*. Paris.

—— 1977b. 'Protestantisme populaire et univers magique: le cas cévenol', *Le Monde alpin et rhodanien*, vol. V, 145–71.

—— (ed.) 1979. *Les Cévennes: de la montagne à l'homme*. Toulouse.

—— 1982. 'La distinction entre le légendaire historique d'origine savante et celui d'origine populaire est-elle toujours pertinente?' *Le Monde alpin et rhodanien*, vol. X, 179–92.

—— 1983. *Ces voix qui nous viennent du passé*. Paris.

Kedward, H.R., 1978. *Resistance in Vichy France*. Oxford.

Keesing, R.M., 1985. 'Kwaio women speak: the micropolitics of autobiography in a Solomon Island society', *Man*, vol. LXXXVII, 27–39.

Kessler, H.L., 1985. 'Pictorial narrative and church mission in sixth-century Gaul', *Studies in the History of Art*, vol. XVI, 75–91.

Kirk, G.S., 1970. *Myth*. Cambridge.

Kogan, N., 1956. *Italy and the Allies*. Cambridge, MA.

Kosslyn, S.M., 1980. *Image and Mind*. Cambridge, MA.

Kristjánsson, J., 1988. *Eddas and Sagas*. Reykjavík.

Krusch, B. and Levison, W. (eds), 1951. *Gregorii episcopi Turonensis Libri Historiarum*. 2nd edn, Berlin.

Lang, A., 1893a. 'Introduction' to M.R. Cox, *Cinderella*, London, pp. vii – xxiii.

—— 1893b. 'Cinderella and the diffusion of tales', *Folklore*, vol. IV, 413–33.

Langlois, E. (ed.), 1920. *Couronnement de Louis*. Paris.

Law, R. 1982. 'Making sense of a traditional narrative: political disintegration in the Kingdom of Oyo', *Cahiers d'études africaines*, vol. XXII (85–8), 387–401.

Leach, E.R., 1961. *Rethinking Anthropology*. London.

—— 1964. *Political Systems of Highland Burma*. 2nd edn, London.

—— 1969. *Genesis as Myth and other Essays*. London.

—— 1976. *Culture and Communication: The Logic by which Symbols are Connected. An Introduction to the Use of Structuralist Analysis in Social Anthropology.* Cambridge.

Lefebvre, G., 1973. *The Great Fear of 1789*. London.

Le Goff, J., 1985. 'Aspects savants et populaires des voyages dans l'au-delà au Moyen Age'. In idem, *L'Imaginaire médiéval*, Paris, pp. 103–19.

—— 1988. *Historie et mémoire*. Paris.

Lequin, Y. and Métral, J., 1980. 'A la recherche d'une mémoire collective: les métallurgistes retraités de Givors', *Annales ESC*, vol. XXXV, 149–66.

Leroi-Gourhan, A., 1965. *Le Geste et la parole II: La Mémoire et les rythmes*. Paris.

Le Roy Ladurie, E., 1975. *Montaillou, village occitan de 1294 à 1324*. Paris.

—— 1987. *The French Peasantry 1450–1660*. Aldershot.

Lessa, O., 1973. *Getúlio Vargas na literatura de cordel*. Rio de Janeiro.

Lestingi, F., 1884. 'L'associazione della Fratellanza nella Provincia di Girgenti', *Archivio di psichiatria, scienze penali e antropologia criminale*, pp. 452–63.

Levi, C., 1948. *Christ Stopped at Eboli*. Trans. F. Frenaye. London.

Levi, G., Passerini, L. and Scaraffia, L., 1977. 'Vita quotidiana in un quartiere operaio di Torino fra le due guerre: l'apporto della storia orale', *Quaderni storici*, vol. XXXV, 433–49.

Lévi-Strauss, C., 1976. 'Structure and form: reflections on a work by Vladimir Propp'. In idem, *Structural Anthropology*, vol. II, pp. 115–45.

Lewin, L., 1979. 'The oligarchical limitations of social banditry in Brazil', *Past and Present*, vol. LXXXII, 116–46.

Lewis, G., 1985. 'A *Cévenol* community in crisis: the mystery of "l'homme à moustache"', *Past and Present*, vol. CIX, 144–75.

Lewis, G.M., 1987. 'The origins of cartography'. In Harley and Woodward 1987: 50–3.

Lewis, N., 1964. *The Honoured Society*. Glasgow.

Leyser, K., 1979. *Rule and Conflict in an Early Medieval Society*. London.

Linares, V., 1980. *I racconti popolari*, ed. E. Giunta. Palermo. (Originally published c.1840.)

Lindow, J., 1982. 'Narrative and the nature of Skaldic poetry', *Arkiv för nordisk filologi*, vol. XCVII, 94–121.

Liverani, M., 1978. 'Le tradizioni orali delle fonti scritte nell'antico oriente'. In Bernardi et al. 1978: 395–406.

Lord, A.B., 1960. *The Singer of Tales*. Cambridge, MA.

Loschiavo, G.G., 1962. *100 anni di Mafia*. Rome.

Löwe, H., 1970. 'Das Karlsbuch Notkers von St. Gallen und sein zeitgeschichtlicher Hinterland', *Schweizerische Zeitschrift für Geschichte*, vol. XX, 269–302.

Luria, A.R., 1975. *The Mind of a Mnemonist*. London.

—— 1976. *Cognitive Development*. Cambridge, MA.

Maas, P., 1969. *The Valacchi Papers*. New York.

MacGaffey, W., 1961. 'Comparative analysis of central African religions', *Africa*, vol. XXXI, 21–31.

—— 1970. *Custom and Government in the Lower Congo*. Berkeley, CA.

—— 1974. 'Oral tradition in central Africa', *International Journal of African Historical Studies*, vol. VII, part 3, 417–26.

Mack Smith, D., 1950. 'The peasants' revolt of Sicily in 1860'. In *Studi in onore di Gino Luzzatto*, vol. III, Milan, pp. 201–40.

—— 1968. *A History of Sicily*. 2 vols, London.

Magoun, F.P., 1953. 'Oral-formulaic character of Anglo-Saxon narrative poetry', *Speculum*, vol. XXVIII, 446–67.

Mandrou, R., 1964. *De la culture populaire aux XVIIe et XVIIIe siècles*. Paris.

Marino, G.C., 1976. *Partiti e lotta di classe in Sicilia*. Bari.

—— 1986. *L'opposizione mafiosa*. 2nd edn, Palermo.

Marino, L., 1988. 'I luoghi della memoria collettiva'. In Rossi 1988b: 275–313.

Marotti, G., 1978. *Canudos. Storia di una guerra*. Rome.

Marr, D., 1982. *Vision: A Computational Investigation into the Human Representation and Processing of Visual Information*. San Francisco, CA.

Martin, J.-C., 1984. 'La Vendée, région-mémoire'. In Nora 1984: 595–617.

Martino, E. de, 1975. *Morte e pianto rituale*. Turin.

Marx, K., 1852/1973. *The Eighteenth Brumaire of Louis Bonaparte*. Trans. B. Fowkes. In K. Marx, *Surveys from Exile*, London, pp. 143–249.

—— 1867/1976. *Capital. A Critique of Political Economy*. Vol. I. Trans. B. Fowkes. London.

—— 1973. *Grundrisse*. Trans. M. Nicholaus. London.

Mazzamuto, P., 1970. *La Mafia nella letteratura*. Palermo.

McEwen, J.M., 1971. 'Tonypandy: Churchill's albatross', *Queen's Quarterly*, vol. LXXVIII, 83–94.

McGinn, C., 1982. *The Character of Mind*. Oxford.

Meredith-Jones, C., 1936. *Historia Karoli Magni et Rotholandi, ou Chronique du pseudo-Turpin*. Paris.

Meyer, J., 1974. *La Cristiada*, vol. III. *Los cristeros*. México.

Meyer, P. and Longnon, A. (eds), 1882. *Raoul de Cambrai*. Paris.

Meyers, G.E., 1968. *William James: His Life and Thought*. New Haven, CT.

Michel, H., 1962. *Les Courants de pensée de la Résistance*. Paris.

Miller, J.C., 1978. 'The dynamics of oral tradition in Africa'. In Bernardi et al. 1978: 75–101.

—— 1980a. *The African Past Speaks*. Folkestone.

—— 1980b. 'Listening for the African past'. In Miller 1980a: 1–59.

Miller, W.I., 1983a. 'Choosing the avenger', *Law and History Review*, vol. I, 159–204.

—— 1983b. 'Justifying Skarpheðinn', *Scandinavian Studies*, vol. LV, 316–44.

Mishkin, M. and Appenzeller, T., 1987. 'The anatomy of memory', *Scientific American*, vol. CCLVI, part 6, 80–9.

Moniot, H., 1986. 'The uses of memory in African studies', *History and Anthropology*, vol. II, part 2, 379–88.

Monnier, M., 1863. *La Cammorra: mystères de Naples*. Paris.

Montaigne, M. de, *Essais*. Standard edns.

Morgan, P., 1981. *The Eighteenth-Century Renaissance*. Llandybïe.

—— 1983. 'From a death to a view: the hunt for the Welsh past in the Romantic period'. In Hobsbawm and Ranger 1983: 43–100.

Mosca, G., 1980. *Uomini e cose di Sicilia*. Palermo (originally appearing as articles in *Corriere della Sera* in 1901–8).

Moti, 1981. *I moti di Palermo del 1866*. Archivio di stato, Rome.

Munn, N.D., 1973. 'The spatial presentation of cosmic order in Wallbiri iconography'. In A. Forge (ed.), *Primitive Art and Society*, Oxford, pp. 193–220.

Namer, G., 1983. *La commémoration en France 1944–82*. Paris.

Natoli, L., 1982. *Storia e leggende di Sicilia*, Palermo.

Needham, R., 1972. *Belief, Language and Experience*. Oxford.

—— 1981. 'Inner states as universals: sceptical reflections on human nature'. In P. Heelas and A. Lock (eds), *Indigenous Psychologies: The Anthropology of the Self*, London and New York, pp. 65–78.

Neisser, U., 1981. 'John Dean's memory: a case study', *Cognition*, vol. IX, 1–22.

Nelli, H.S., 1976. *The Business of Crime: Italians and Syndicated Crime in the U.S.* New York.

Nicastro, N., 1978. *Teatro e società in Sicilia (1860–1918)*. Rome.

Nora, P. (ed.), 1984. *Les Lieux de la mémoire*. Vol. I. *La République*. Paris.

Notopoulos, J.A., 1938. 'Mnemosyne in oral literature', *Transactions and Proceedings of the American Philological Association*, vol. LXIX, 465–93.

Okpewho, I., 1983. *Myth in Africa*. Cambridge.

Ong, W., 1982. *Orality and Literacy*. London.

Opie, I. and Opie, P., 1988. *The Singing Game*. Oxford.

Oppenheim, A.L., 1964. *Ancient Mesopotamia: Portrait of a Dead Civilisation*. London.

Oré, M.T. and Rochabrun, G., 1986. 'De la leyenda indígena a la conciencia popular: la evolución de la memoria colectiva en un valle peruano'. In M. Vilanova (ed.), *El poder en la sociedad*, Barcelona, pp. 205–15.

Ory, P., 1984. 'Le centenaire de la Révolution Française'. In Nora 1984: 523–60.

Ozouf, M., 1984. 'Le Panthéon'. In Nora 1984: 139–66.

Pagano, G., 1867. *Avvenimenti del 1866: sette giorni di insurrezione*. Palermo.

Page Arnot, R., 1967. *South Wales Miners. Glowyr De Cymru*. London.

Pálsson, H. and Edwards, P., 1972. *The Book of Settlements. Landnámabók*. Manitoba.

Panofsky, E., 1970. *Meaning in the Visual Arts*. London.

Pantaleone, M., 1970. *Mafia e politica, 1943–1962*. Turin.

Paris, G., 1865. *Histoire poétique de Charlemagne*. Paris.

Parry, A. (ed.), 1971. *The Making of Homeric Verse: The Collected Papers of Milman Parry*. Oxford.

Passerini, L., 1979. 'Work ideology and consensus under Italian Fascism', *History Workshop*, vol. VIII, 82–108.

—— 1987. *Fascism in Popular Memory*. Cambridge.

—— 1988. *Storia e soggettività. Le fonti orali, la memoria*. Florence.

Paynter, W., 1972. *My Generation*. London.

Peel, J.D.Y., 1983. *Ijeshas and Nigerians: The Incorporation of a Yoruba Kingdom: 1890s–1970s*. Cambridge.

Pelen, J.-N., 1982. 'Le légendaire de l'identité communautaire en Cévennes, du XVIIIe au XXe siècle', *Le monde alpin et rhodanien*, vol. X, 127–41.

—— 1983. *Le Temps cévenol*, vol. III, Part 2. Nîmes.

Peloso, S., 1984. *Medioevo nel sertão*. Naples.

Pender-Cudlip, P., 1972. 'Oral traditions and anthropological analysis: some contemporary myths', *Azania*, vol. VII, 3–24.

Penrose, R., 1989. *The Emperor's New Mind*. Oxford.

Pereira de Queiroz, M.I., 1977. *O messianismo no Brasil e no mundo*. 2nd edn, São Paulo.

Perrot, C.H. and Terray, E., 1977. 'Tradition et chronologie', *Annales ESC*, vol. XXXII, 326–31.

Person, Y., 1962. 'Tradition orale et chronologie', *Cahiers d'études africaines*, vol. II (5–8), 461–76.

—— 1976. 'La chimère se défend' (review of Henige 1974), *Cahiers d'études africaines*, vol. XVI (61–4), 405–8.

Peukert, D., 1980. 'Ruhr miners under Nazi repression, 1933–45', *International Journal of Oral History*, vol. I, 111–27.

Piaget, J., and Inhelder, B., 1956. *The Child's Conception of Space*. Eng. trans., London.

Pi de Cabanyes, O., 1979. *La Renaixença*. Barcelona.

Pietri, L., 1983. *La Ville de Tours du IVe au VIe siècle*. Rome.

Pitrè, G., 1870. *Canti popolari siciliani*, vol. I. Palermo.

—— 1882. *Il Vespro siciliano nelle tradizioni popolari della Sicilia*. Palermo (republished Palermo 1979)

—— 1887–8. *Usi e costumi, credenze e pregiudizi del popolo siciliano*. 4 vols, Palermo.

—— 1913. *La famiglia, la casa, la vita del popolo siciliano*. Palermo (republished Palermo 1978).

Pitzalis Acciaro, M., 1978. *In nome della madre*. Milan.

Plato, *Phaedrus*. Standard edns.

Polk, W.R., 1974. Labid ibn Rabiah, *The Golden Ode*. Chicago.

Poly, J.-P. and Bournazel, E., 1980. *La Mutation féodale, X^e–XIIe siècles*. Paris.

Portelli, A., 1981a. 'The peculiarities of oral history', *History Workshop*, vol. XII, 96–107.

—— 1981b. 'The time of my life: functions of time in oral history', *International Journal of Oral History*, vol. II, 162–80.

—— 1985. *Biografia di una città. Storia e racconto: Terni 1830–1985*. Turin.

Poujol, R., 1981. *Histoire d'un village cévenol: Vébron*. La Calade.

Price, R., 1983. *First-time. The Historical Vision of an Afro-American People*. Baltimore, MD.

Propp, V., 1968. *Morphology of the Folktale*. 2nd edn, Austin, TX.

—— 1975. 'L'albero magico sulla tomba. A proposito dell'origine della fiaba de magia'. In idem, *Edipo alla luce del folclore*, Turin, pp. 3–39.

Rabelais, F., *Gargantua et Pantagruel*. Standard edns.

Rafnsson, S., 1974. *Studier i Landnámabók*. Lund.

Raphaël, F., 1980. 'Le travail de la mémoire et les limites de l'histoire orale', *Annales ESC*, vol. XXXV, 127–45.

Ray, R.D., 1974. 'Medieval historiography through the twelfth century: problems and progress of research', *Viator*, vol. V, 33–59.

Ree, J., 1987. *Philosophical Tales*. London.

Reid, E., 1952. *Mafia*. New York.

Renza, L.A., 1977–8. 'The veto of the imagination: a theory of autobiography', *New Literary History*, vol. IX, 1–26.

Revelli, N., 1977. *Il mondo dei vinti*. Turin.

—— 1985. *L'anello forte*. Turin.

Reverchon, C. and Gaudin, P., 1986. 'Le sens du tragique dans la mémoire historique', *Le Monde alpin et rhodanien*, vol. XIV, 97–113.

Riess Jones, M., 1980–1. 'Only time can tell: on the topography of mental space and time', *Critical Inquiry*, vol. VII, 557–76.

Rigoli, A., 1978. 'Lo sbarco degli Alleati in Sicilia 1943, tra prospettiva storiografica "egemone" e prospettiva "subalterna"'. In Bernardi et al. 1978: 173–208.

Rizzotto, G., 1962. *I Mafiusi de la Vicaria di Palermo*, reprinted in Loschiavo 1962: 211–359.

Robertson, H.S., 1972. *The Song of Roland. La Chanson de Roland*. London.

Rogerson, J.W., 1978. *Anthropology and the Old Testament*. Oxford.

Rohe, K., 1987. 'The constitutional development of Germany and Great Britain in the nineteenth and twentieth centuries in German and English history textbooks. A study of comparative political culture'. In V.R. Berghahn and H. Schissler (eds), *Perceptions of History*, Oxford, pp. 51–70.

Rorty, R., 1980. *Philosophy and the Mirror of Nature*. Oxford.

Rosaldo, R., 1980. *Ilongot Headhunting, 1883–1974*. Stanford, CA.

Paolo Rossi, 1988a. 'La memoria, le immagini, l'enciclopedia'. In Pietro Rossi 1988b: 211–37.

— 1989. *La scienza e la filosofia dei moderni*. Turin.

Pietro Rossi (ed.), 1988b. *La memoria del sapere*. Bari.

Rychner, J., 1955. *La Chanson de geste. Essai sur l'art épique des jongleurs*. Geneva.

Sacks, O.W., 1989. *Seeing Voices*. Berkeley, CA.

Sahlins, M., 1985. *Islands of History*. Chicago.

Saki Olal N'Diaye, 1971. 'The story of Malik Sy', *Cahiers d'études africaines*, vol. XI (41–4), 467–87.

Salmon, P. 1986. *Introduction à l'histoire de l'Afrique*. Brussels.

Samuel, R. (ed.), 1989. *Patriotism: The Making and Unmaking of British National Identity*. 3 vols, London.

Samuel, R. and Thompson, P. (eds), 1990. *The Myths We Live By*. London.

Scalici, E. (ed.), 1980. *La mafia siciliana*. Palermo.

Sceusa, F., 1877. *Mafia ufficiale*. Naples.

Schmandt-Besserat, D., 1978. 'The earliest precursor of writing', *Scientific American*, vol. CCXXXVIII, part 6, 38–47.

Schmitt, J.-C., 1979. 'La parola addomesticata', *Quaderni storici*, vol. XLI, 416–39.

— 1981. 'Les traditions folkloriques dans la culture médiévale: quelques reflections de méthode', *Archives des sciences sociaux des religions*, vol. LII, pp. 5–20.

Schneidmüller, B., 1979. *Karolingische Tradition und frühes französisches Königtum*. Wiesbaden.

Schofield, M., 1978. 'Aristotle on the imagination'. In G.E.R. Lloyd and G.E.L. Owen (eds), *Aristotle on the Mind and the Senses*, Cambridge, pp. 99–140.

Scholes, R., 1980–1. 'Language, narrative, and anti-narrative', *Critical Inquiry*, vol. VII, 204–12.

Schonen, S. de, 1974. *La Mémoire: connaissance active du passé*. Paris.

Scichilone, G., 1952. *Documenti sulle condizioni della Sicilia dal 1860 al 1870*. Rome.

Searle, J., 1987. 'Minds and brains without programs'. In C. Blakemore and S. Greenfield (eds), *Mindwaves*, Oxford, pp. 209–33.

Sebeok, T.A. and Umiker-Sebeok, J., 1983. '"You know my method": A juxtaposition of Chas S. Peirce and Sherlock Holmes'. In U. Eco and T.A. Sebeok (eds), *The Sign of Three*, Bloomington, IN, pp. 11–54.

Segal, L., 1973. *The Juniper Tree, and Other Tales from Grimm*. New York.

Seward, D., 1984. *Naples*. London.

Seznec, J., 1972. *The Survival of the Pagan Gods*. Princeton, NJ.

Shorter, A., 1969. 'Religious values in Kimbu historical charters', *Africa*, vol. XXXIX, 227–37.

Sitton, T., Mehaffy, G.L. and Davis, O.L., Jr., 1983. *Oral History: A Guide for Teachers (and Others)*. Austin, TX.

Smith, B.H., 1980. 'Narrative versions, narrative theories', *Critical Inquiry*, vol. VIII, 213–36.

Smith, D., 1983. 'Tonypandy 1910: definitions of community', *Past and Present*, vol. LXXXVII, 158–84.

—— 1984. *Wales! Wales?* London.

Smith, J.D., 1977. 'The singer or the song? A reassessment of Lord's oral theory', *Man*, N.S., vol. XII, 141–53.

Smith, P. (ed.), 1975. *Le Récit populaire au Rwanda*. Paris.

Smith, R.S., 1988. *Kingdoms of the Yoruba*. 3rd edn, London.

Sondern, F., Jr., 1959. *The Brotherhood of Evil: The Mafia*. London.

Sorabji, R., 1972. *Aristotle on Memory*. London.

Soriano, M., 1977. *Les Contes de Perrault*. 2nd edn, Paris.

Spence, J.D., 1984. *The Memory Palace of Matteo Ricci*. London.

Spiegel, G.M., 1971. 'The *Reditus regni ad stirpem Karoli Magni*: a new look', *French Historical Studies*, vol. VII, 145–74.

—— 1986. 'Pseudo-Turpin, the crisis of the aristocracy, and the beginnings of vernacular historiography in France', *Journal of Medieval History*, vol. XII, 207–23.

Sportiello, A., 1981. *Les Pêcheurs du Vieux-Port*. Marseille.

Stinger, C.L., 1985. *The Renaissance in Rome*. Bloomington, IN.

Stock, B., 1983. *The Implications of Literacy*. Princeton, NJ.

Straw, P. and Elliott B., 1986. 'Hidden rhythms: hidden powers? Women and time in working-class culture', *Life Stories/Récits de vie*, vol. II, 34–47.

Süskind, P., 1986. *Perfume*. London.

Sveinsson, E.Ó., 1953. *The Age of the Sturlungs. Islandica*, vol. XXXVI. Ithaca, NY.

Tannen, D., 1990. *You Just Don't Understand*. New York.

Tatar, M., 1987. *The Hard Facts of the Grimms' Fairy Tales*. Princeton, NJ.

Terkel, S., 1970. *Hard Times*. New York.

—— 1974. *Working*. New York.

Tey, J., 1951. *The Daughter of Time*. London.

Thomas, K., 1983. *The Perception of the Past in Early Modern England*. London.

Thomas, L.V., 1964. 'De quelques attitudes africaines en matière d'histoire locale'. In Vansina et al. 1964: 358–75.

Thomas, R., 1989. *Oral Tradition and Written Record in Classical Athens*. Cambridge.

Thompson, P., 1988. *The Voice of the Past. Oral History*. 2nd edn, London.

Thompson, S., 1955–8. *Motif-Index of Folk-Literature*. 2nd edn, 6 vols, Copenhagen.

Thorpe, L. (trans.), 1969. *Einhard and Notker the Stammerer, Two Lives of Charlemagne*. London.

—— (trans.) 1974. Gregory of Tours, *The History of the Franks*. London.

Tonkin, E., 1982. 'The boundaries of history in oral performance', *History in Africa*, vol. IX, 273–84.

—— 1991. *Narrating our Pasts: The Social Construction of Oral History*. Cambridge.

Traina, A., 1868. *Nuovo vocabulario siciliano-italiano*. Palermo.

Tulving, E., 1983. *Elements of Episodic Memory*. Oxford.

Turville-Petre, G., 1976. *Scaldic Poetry*. Oxford.

Uccello, A., 1974. *Carcere e Mafia nei canti popolari siciliani*. Bari.

Umiltà, A., 1878. *Camorra e Mafia*. Neuchâtel.

Vance, E., 1970. *Reading the Song of Roland*. Englewood Cliffs, NJ.

Van Dam, R., 1985. *Leadership and Community in Late Antique Gaul*. Berkeley, CA.

Vansina, J., 1955. 'Initiation rituals of the Bushong', *Africa*, vol. XXV, 138–53.

—— R. Mauny, and L.V. Thomas (eds) 1964. *The Historian in Tropical Africa: Studies Presented and Discussed at the Fourth International Seminar, at the University of Dakar, Senegal, 1961*. Oxford.

—— 1964. 'The use of process-models in African history'. In Vansina et al. 1964: 375–89.

—— 1966. *Kingdoms of the Savanna*. Madison, WI.

—— 1977. 'Une recension imparfaite: un cas de parti pris', *Cahiers d'études africaines*, vol. XVIII (65–8), 369–73.

—— 1983. 'Is elegance proof? Structuralism and African history', *History in Africa*, vol. X, 307–48.

—— 1985. *Oral Tradition as History*. London.

Vegetti, M. (ed.), 1983. *Oralità, scrittura, spettacolo*. Turin.

Verdier, Y., 1978. 'Grandes-mères, si vous saviez ... le Petit Chaperon Rouge dans la tradition orale', *Cahiers de littérature orale*, vol. IV, 17–56.

Vernant, J.-P., 1974. 'Parole et signes muets'. In idem et al., *Divination et rationalité*, Paris, pp. 9–25.

—— 1988. *Mythe et pensée chez les Grecs*. 2nd edn, Paris.

Veyne, P., 1988. *Did the Greeks Believe in Their Myths?* Chicago.

Viano, C.A., 1988. 'La biblioteca e l'oblio'. In Rossi 1988b: 239–73.

Vickers, A., 1990. 'The historiography of Balinese texts', *History and Theory*, vol. XXIX, 158–79.

Victorio, J. (ed.), 1988. *L'Epopée. Typologie des sources du Moyen Age occidental*, vol. XLIX. Turnhout.

Vidal, C., 1971. 'Enquête sur le Rwanda traditionnel: conscience historique et traditions orales', *Cahiers d'études africaines*, vol. XI (41–4), 526–37.

—— 1976. 'L'ethnologie à la imparfait: un cas d'ethno-histoire', *Cahiers d'études africaines*, vol. XVI (61–4), 397–404.

Wachtel, N., 1977. *The Vision of the Vanquished*. Hassocks.

—— 1986. 'Memory and history: introduction', *History and Anthropology*, vol. II, part 2, 207–24.

Wallace-Hadrill, J.M., 1962. *The Long-haired Kings*. London.

Warnock, M., 1987. *Memory*. London.

Webber, S., 1985. 'Women's folk narratives and social change'. In E.W. Fernea (ed.), *Women in the Family in the Middle East*, Austin, TX, pp. 310–16.

White, H., 1973. *Metahistory. The Historical Imagination in Nineteenth-Century Europe*. Baltimore, MD.

—— 1980–1. 'The value of narrativity in the representation of reality', *Critical Inquiry*, vol. VII, 5–27, 793–8.

—— 1982. 'The politics of historical interpretation', *Critical Inquiry*, vol. IX, 113–37.

Whitehead, F. (ed.), 1946. *La Chanson de Roland*. 2nd edn, Oxford.

Wickham, C.J., 1985. 'Lawyers' time: history and memory in tenth- and eleventh-century Italy'. In H. Mayr-Harting and R.I. Moore (eds), *Studies in Medieval History Presented to R.H.C. Davis*, London, pp. 53–71.

—— 1991. 'The sense of the past in Italian communal narratives'. In P. Magdalino (ed.), *The Perception of the Past in Twelfth-century Europe*, London.

Wilks, I., 1975. *Asante in the Nineteenth Century*. Cambridge.

Williams, G., 1974. 'Prophecy, poetry and politics in Medieval and Tudor Wales'. In H. Hearden and H.R. Loyn (eds), *British Government and Administration*, Cardiff, pp. 104–16.

Williams, G.A., 1979. *Madoc. The Making of a Myth*. London.

Willis, R.G., 1964. 'Traditional history and social structure in Ufipa', *Africa*, vol. XXXIV, 340–52.

—— 1980. 'The literalist fallacy and the problem of oral history', *Social Analysis*, vol. IV, 28–37.

Wilsdorf, C., 1962. 'La Chanson de Roland, l'épopée française et l'épopée chrétienne', *Le Moyen Age*, vol. LXVIII, 405–17.

Wilson, S., 1988. *Feuding, Conflict and Banditry in Nineteenth-Century Corsica*. Cambridge.

Wolf, E.R., 1966. *Peasants*. Englewood Cliffs, NJ.

Wollheim, R., 1980. 'On persons and their lives'. In A.O. Rorty (ed.), *Explaining Emotions*, Berkeley, CA, pp. 299–321.

Wood, I.N., 1983. 'The ecclesiastical politics of Merovingian Clermont'. In C.P. Wormald (ed.), *Ideal and Reality in Frankish and Anglo-Saxon Society*, Oxford, pp. 34–57.

—— 1988. 'Clermont and Burgundy: 511–34', *Nottingham Medieval Studies*, vol. XXXII, 119–25.

Woolf, D.R., 1988. 'The "common voice": history, folklore and oral tradition in early modern England', *Past and Present*, vol. CXX, 26–52.

Yates, F.A., 1964. *Giordano Bruno and the Hermetic Tradition*. Chicago.

—— 1978. *The Art of Memory*. London.

Young, M.W., 1983. '"Our name is women: we are bought with limesticks and limepots"', *Man*, N.S., vol. XVIII, 478–501.

Zonabend, F., 1984. *The Enduring Memory*. Manchester.

Zumthor, P., 1980. 'L'Ecriture et la voix (d'une littérature populaire brésilienne)', *Critique*, vol. CCCXCIV, 228–39.

Guide to Further Reading

A book that sets off in as many directions as this one risks having a guide to reading as long as its bibliography, or longer. The books that follow are merely indicative; in many cases they contain their own bibliographical guides. Those already in the bibliography will be cited by the Harvard system, as elsewhere in the book.

Some of the philosophical underpinning of the development of modern memory theory can be found in Warnock 1987; see further Connerton 1989; Sorabji 1972. For memory training, the basic texts are Yates 1978; Rossi 1988b; Luria 1975, for a modern mnemonist; and, for the medieval period, the remarkable M.J. Carruthers, *The Book of Memory* (Cambridge, 1990), which unfortunately appeared too late for us to use. The classic texts on social memory are Halbwachs 1925; Halbwachs 1980.

On oral tradition, see, as guides, Vansina 1985; Henige 1974; Henige 1982 (with a large bibliography); Tonkin 1991, which is also interested in genre; and, pursuing the issue of genre into modern oral literature, Finnegan 1977; Finnegan 1988; and K. Barber, *I Could Speak Until Tomorrow* (Edinburgh, 1991). On oral history, the basic introductions are Thompson 1988; Joutard 1983; and Passerini 1988, which has some particularly valuable methodological critiques; see also Johnson et al. 1982. Empirical oral-historical analyses which we have found particularly stimulating include Joutard 1977a; Passerini 1987; the articles in Samuel and Thompson 1990; and, among anthropological discussions, MacGaffey 1970, Rosaldo 1980, and J. Rappaport, *The Politics of Memory* (Cambridge, 1990), which focuses on the Colombian Andes. On the use of social memory for national self-creation, see Hobsbawm and Ranger 1983; and, among many interesting recent studies on the general issue of nationalism, E. Gellner, *Nations and Nationalism* (Oxford, 1983); and E.J. Hobsbawm, *Nations and Nationalism since 1780* (Cambridge, 1990). On social memory in the medieval period, Folz 1950 is the classic; Clanchy 1979 and Stock 1983 take the general cultural issues further, as does Carruthers, above. The special case of Jewish memory has its own, huge, bibliography; a starting-point is Y.H. Yerushalmi, *Zakhor: Jewish History and Jewish Memory* (London, 1982).

Index